PEOPLE IN GLASS HOUSES

PEOPLE IN GLASS HOUSES

AN INSIDER'S STORY OF A LIFE IN & OUT OF *Hillsong*

TANYA LEVIN

Published by Black Inc.,
an imprint of Schwartz Publishing Pty Ltd
Level 5, 289 Flinders Lane
Melbourne Victoria 3000 Australia
email: enquiries@blackincbooks.com
http://www.blackincbooks.com

The National Library of Australia Cataloguing-in-Publication entry:

Levin, Tanya, 1971- .
People in glass houses : an insider's story of a life in and out of Hillsong.

ISBN 9781863954143 (pbk.).

1. Levin, Tanya, 1971- . 2. Pentecostal churches - Australia.
3. Big churches - Australia. I. Title.

289.940994

Book design by Thomas Deverall
Printed by McPherson's Printing Group

CONTENTS

This book is dedicated to

My father and mother, because it's the only commandment that comes with a promise, and because they are the two finest human beings I have ever met

&

My sun, Sam: may freedom of thought be the revival of your generation

You don't want the truth, because deep down, in places you don't talk about at parties, you *want* me on that wall. You *need* me on that wall.

We use words like honour, code, loyalty ... we use these words as the backbone of a life spent defending something. You use them as a punchline.

I have neither the time nor the inclination to explain myself to a man who rises and sleeps under the blanket of the very freedom that I provide and then questions the manner in which I provide it. I would rather you just said thank you and went on your way. Otherwise, I suggest you pick up a weapon and stand a post. Either way, I don't give a damn what you think you are entitled to.

—*A Few Good Men*

SOMEONE TO WATCH OVER ME

> Perhaps it would be as well, first of all, to try to make out what one means by the word *Christian*. It is used these days in a very loose sense by a great many people. Some people mean no more by it than a person who attempts to live a good life. In that sense I suppose there would be Christians in all sects and creeds. The word does not have quite such a full-blooded meaning now as it had in the times of St. Augustine and St. Thomas Aquinas. In those days, if a man said that he was a Christian it was known what he meant.
>
> —Bertrand Russell, *Why I Am Not a Christian* (1927)

A number of terms are used to describe people who attend churches like Hillsong. In some situations they can be used interchangeably, but to do so in others will result in partial or total inaccuracy. In this book I have used definitions that are to the best of my theological understanding of the fraction of Christian climates I have studied. They are broad characterisations, intended simply as an overview of religious beliefs held by millions of people worldwide.

Being a Christian means—what? The problem with nailing a definition is that there are too many contending authorities. The 'Christian church' has an infinite number of fragments and offshoots, in a body that requires itself to have unity. 'Christianity' evolves continually, and with it the doctrines that underpin it.

Being a *born-again Christian* narrows it down a little. Born-again Christians believe 'Jesus' when he allegedly said that no one can see the kingdom of God unless he is born again. This involves repentance of your sins and acceptance of Jesus Christ as your personal Lord and Saviour. *Liberal born-again Christians* think very differently to fundamentalists, who are generally quite conservative.

Fundamentalist Christians believe that every single mark on the pages of 'the bible' is there as 'God' breathed it, and that every word should be taken literally. If it says it rained for forty days and nights, then that's what happened. Thus, since Jesus said it, all fundamentalist Christians know they must be born again.

An *evangelical Christian* believes that you must be born again and that it is each born-again Christian's responsibility to convince others of the same. This is in direct response to The Great Commission Jesus gave the eleven men closest to him, instructing them to go and make disciples of all nations. Not all evangelicals are fundamentalists, but all fundamentalists are evangelical.

Southern Baptists are strict fundamentalists, particularly when it comes to matters of sexuality and women's rights. They are born-again evangelicals who often aim to share their puritanical morality with everyday citizens by gaining political power. Southern Baptists are not often Pentecostal, although they are fond of demon exorcisms.

Only *Pentecostals* have the lot. Taking born-again, evangelical, fundamentalist Christianity literally, Pentecostals seize upon the verses in Acts 2:1–5:

When the day of Pentecost came, they were all together in one place. Suddenly a sound like the blowing of a violent wind came from heaven and filled the whole house where they were sitting. They saw what seemed to be tongues of fire that separated and came to rest on each of them. All of them were filled with the Holy Spirit and began to speak in other tongues as the Spirit enabled them. When they heard this sound, a crowd came together in bewilderment, because each one heard them speaking in his own language.

If it was good enough for the disciples, then the Pentecostals decided it was good enough for them. They are distinguishable by the 'signs and wonders' that accompany them.

Founded in 1914 in Hot Springs, Arkansas, the Assemblies of God was an organisational exercise designed to ensure representation on the Pentecostal council for white ministers not faring well in a majority African-American church. This Pentecostal offshoot had minor theological differences with its forerunners, but grew to sizeable proportions through both world wars.

The structure of the Assemblies of God has remained much the same for generations. While each church was, and technically still is, autonomous, things have changed significantly since the rise of churches such as Hillsong.

Brian Houston is the Senior Pastor of Hillsong, the largest Pentecostal church in Australia. He is also the President (formerly known as General Superintendent) of the Assemblies of God National Executive. The National Executive exists as a board of leaders who provide direction and integrity to the organisation. When problems arise in individual churches, a member of the National or State Executive may intervene to resolve complex issues appropriately. However, should any concerns arise regarding Hillsong, or its pastors, it is impossible to seek independent assistance from the AoG national body. You can't call the authorities on Brian. He is all of the authorities.

One notable characteristic of the AoG is the deep conviction that we are living during the end times or 'last days', when Jesus is due back. This is sometimes called the Latter Rain movement, and infuses Pentecostal doctrine with a great sense of urgency.

The Word of Faith movement is also at the core of the mainstream Pentecostal church. Its premise is that the Protestant bible (out of a choice of the simpler translations) is the Truth. Scripture is God-breathed, therefore every word in the bible, even the laws on cleansing from mildew, is holy. The Word of Faith proponents also believe that every word, every phrase is relevant to the reader. This started out sweetly in the beginning. There are 21 promises in Romans 8, I was taught as a child. The promises often come with conditions, which must be kept. Any promise can be generalised to anyone. In Joshua 1:9, when "the Lord said to Joshua, son of Nun, Moses's assistant ... Do not be terrified; do not be discouraged, for the Lord your God will be with you wherever you go," the Word of Faith believers claim this assurance as applicable to them (and you if you want it!).

Prosperity theology would be nothing without the Word of Faith movement. Bible verses about money can be selected, emphasised, with context removed, and made to fit any situation, generally to show that a previously unjustifiable level of wealth is part of Christian doctrine. With the Word of Faith doctrine, anything is possible, if you can find it in the Word.

Blessed with an AoG Pentecostal born-again evangelical Jewish Australian upbringing, and plagued by a Gen-X post-modern mind and a middle-class education, I can only offer one opinion.

By the way, a lot of people don't like my identifying as Jewish, considering I've been a born-again Christian. As if I could undo a bloodline like this that easily. From what I can deduce, they think I'm being greedy. And yes, I am. My mother always taught me I was entitled to double blessings, as the bible says, first for the Jew and then for the Gentile. I'm not giving that up for anyone.

A note on the bible

As there are so many interpretations of the same Word of God, I have chosen the New International Version purely for sentimental reasons and for argument's sake. I have used my own multicolour highlighted New International Version bible that I bought in 1987. The pastors always said, 'God is not a man that he should lie, nor son of man that he should change his mind.' If it was true then, and Jesus Christ is the same yesterday, today and forever, then it's true now.

Prologue

THANK YOU FOR THE MUSIC

JOANNA: If I am wrong, I'm insane ... but if I'm right, it's even worse than if I was wrong ...

—*The Stepford Wives* (1975)

This book could never have been written without Hillsong. They are, in fact, the very people who gave me the strength and the determination to make sure it got done. They were the Hills Christian Life Centre when I was around, but the message was almost the same.

The eighties were my formative years, and while other teenagers were gyrating to rock'n'roll, we were praying for revival. We were taking communion, not cocaine. We treated virginity like a wedding present, not a cold sore.

And why wouldn't we? We were told we could be, we already were, anything we wanted to be. We could overcome anything, and to him who overcomes is given the authority over the nations.

We were armed and dangerous. Armed with the power of God and dangerous in the eyes of Satan. For, after all, we were wrestling not with flesh and blood but with principalities and powers. It was a spiritual battle we were fighting. And Jesus had already won the war.

If God was for us, who could be against us? No weapon formed against me shall prosper. We were sold out for Jesus, on fire for God. Why would we fear man, or sickness, or death, or ridicule? We were in the world, but not of the world. We had faith way bigger than mustard seeds. And we were bound to move mountains.

As it turned out, many of us did. The generation that, with me, spent their youth being raised up as warriors for God has succeeded and supported one another in the pursuit of excellence.

It's not hard to see why. When you have no fear but the fear of God, nothing really matters. We were saved, born again, sanctified, washed, cleansed, made righteous, justified, just-as-if-we'd-never-sinned. We were living only to spread the Word that Jesus was the Answer. To everything. To anything. Whatever you need to know, it's all in the Book. What else is there? What else could there possibly be?

So we walked on adolescent water, unfazed by being left out of high school drinking games and groping sessions, hoping for an opportunity to minister, to share the Good News. We formed our own rebellion, and were proud to be renegades against mainstream society.

We didn't need passion pop to give us passion. We had a simple goal of taking over the world. And there was no reason why we couldn't. Except now, it looks like they weren't kidding when they said they wanted Australia for Jesus. And then the world. I never thought they'd get the numbers. Boy, was I wrong.

I have to sincerely thank Hillsong and the crew backstage for propelling me into becoming the person that I am. For giving me a confidence that in a psychiatrist's office would have been called delusional. For telling me that the only person I have to keep happy is my creator. That I should rejoice when persecuted. Expect to be called crazy. Delight in being driven out of town. As long as it is in the name of Truth. That God has no favourites. That the strangest people are used in the strangest ways. And that God is powerful enough to save me from the fire, but that even if he does not, I still will not serve your gods or worship the image of gold you have set up.

Without these things being drummed into my head, week after week after year after year, I would never have had the guts to write all this down. Even the bible agreed with me.

'Command those who are rich in this present world not to be

arrogant nor to put their hope in wealth, which is so uncertain, but to put their hope in God, who richly provides us with everything for our enjoyment', it says in 1 Timothy. 'Command them to do good, to be rich in good deeds, and to be generous and willing to share.'

Can you say Amen to that?

WITH OR WITHOUT YOU

Chapter 1

TWO TRIBES

> 'I have heard what the prophets say who prophesy lies in my name. They say, "I had a dream! I had a dream!" How long will this continue in the hearts of these lying prophets who prophesy the delusions of their own minds …
>
> 'Therefore,' declares the Lord, 'I am against the prophets who steal from one another words supposedly from me. Yes,' declares the Lord, 'I am against the prophets who wag their own tongues and yet declare, "The Lord declares." Indeed I am against those who prophesy false dreams,' declares the Lord. 'They tell them and lead my people astray with their reckless lies, yet I did not send them or appoint them. They do not benefit these people in the least,' declares the Lord.
>
> —Jeremiah 23:25–26, 30–32

Dr Andrew Evans thought he was the one. If anyone was going to be running the Assemblies of God, if anyone was going to be overseeing the great revival promised to the land considered the uttermost ends of the earth, Andrew Evans knew it was going to be him. He was born for the job. In 1977, Dr Evans had nothing to fear.

New Guinea hadn't worked out. Missionary work was not for Andrew and his wife, Lorraine. He might have been a missionary's kid, but he was no missionary. Anyway, Lorraine hadn't been the same after a nasty experience in a meeting, with snakes and spiders and all kinds of things coming for her. It really had been time to come home back to paradise in South Australia, where Andrew's father, Tommy, pastored the Klemzig Assemblies of God church. Andrew renamed it Paradise after the church moved to a new building in a neighbouring suburb.

Pastor Tommy Evans had been a holy man of God, a man of visions and prophecy, hellfire and brimstone. He had predicted repeatedly that Jesus would take him alive before death got him. Blind at 95, he did not go willingly. His wife, Stella, had herself gone to be with her Maker, kicking and screaming that God was going to pay them for what they'd done.

Some say Stella told an eight-year-old Andrew that he was this generation's Elijah, a prophet of a new land. In families such as these, it is a divine appointment of kings. In heaven and on earth, Andrew was destined for the role.

Tommy and Stella passed the mantle on. All the saints were gathered as the power of the Lord came down on Andrew, seated onstage alongside Lorraine on chairs that would be thrones. Tommy took his coat off and put it on Andrew's shoulders. The congregation swooned and handed up monies of support. It was an exciting Adelaide night. The future was in God's hands.

Where this left the other family members was neither clear nor relevant. Andrew's older sister had married out of the AoG and had no interest in such visions. It surely wasn't going to be his younger brother Freddie, no matter how charming or persuasive he was. It had been Freddie who had dated Lorraine first but, after bible college, it was Andrew who had married her. And it wasn't going to be Evie. Little sister Evelyn was delighted, for the most part, to play the role of many sisters in the Assemblies of God. They learn as a pastor's daughter, they support as a pastor's sister and, having married a youth pastor, produce sons to compete in vain with the sons of their brothers.

Andrew had campaigned hard for the role of General Superintendent, leader of the National Executive, the AoG ruling body. Before he took the role, it was an unpaid position that involved a lot of travelling. Once the job was his, Dr Evans eliminated both. He made it clear that he was a man of change.

Andrew Evans was only forty in 1977 when a 55-year-old Frank Houston made his pilgrimage from New Zealand to Sydney. What Andrew knew about Frank Houston is uncertain, but it's doubtful he saw him as any threat. The evangelical movement is a young man's game. While Frank's reputation for revival and the gifts of the Spirit was known throughout New Zealand, Dr Evans would surely not have been concerned about this old ex-Salvo and his five grown children, three of them girls. His city of Adelaide was the City of Churches; it was where the Spirit was moving. Sure, there were a couple of shows in Melbourne, and Clark Taylor had Brisbane covered with his Christian Outreach Centre, but no one was doing Sydney. When it came to the power of God in the late seventies, Adelaide was the undisputed victor. Sydney was some kind of poor relative. In those days, you couldn't give Sydney away.

Frank had told everyone about his vision to move to Australia, of course, something the Evanses were well steeped in. Prophets have visions. It happened regularly in the Evans family and, according to recent exclamations from Andrew's sons, still does. Perhaps if Frank's vision had involved Adelaide, there might have been some conflict. But it didn't, so there wasn't. The Lord called Frank and Hazel Houston to Sydney.

Frank had taken control of the New Zealand AoG National Executive years before, and was renowned for his determined kindness and rousing messages. He was made of faith and fire, his reputation would precede. He was also well known for his deep desire to see miracles and healings, and the gifts of the Spirit. He moved in Words of Knowledge, and tangible experiences with God. Some even knew Frank could raise men from the dead. Andrew Evans would surely have wanted more of that. He would probably do some good for the reputation of the AoG.

Theologically, Andrew Evans and Frank Houston weren't too different. Rebelling against Tommy, Andrew had run away to the Salvation Army after school, impressing many a young cadet with his charismatic ways. Not long after that, he returned to work for his dad.

Frank's father was a staunch Protestant, whose spirituality consisted of hating Roman Catholics. When in 1941 a swearing, smoking 18-year-old Frank gave his life to the Lord following a close friend's tragic death, he joined the Salvation Army. There he met Hazel who relinquished her resolution not to marry in the Army and was courted and won by the charmingly sincere officer, despite his constant battles with illnesses that often times put him out of the good race.

The Houstons spent their first years in the Army with Frank in a social work role at the Temuka boys' home, where he learnt first-hand to care for needy young men. For the rest of their twelve years of service, the Captains Houston committed to where Frank knew he belonged: in a preaching role, moving town with each Army appointment. Deep down, though, Frank longed for the miraculous, an area that the Salvation Army was not concerned with, charity and gospel being priorities.

A most unmiraculous event occurred when an audit of Captain Houston's books by Colonel Bethe showed serious financial inconsistencies. When this was discovered, Frank suffered what doctors called a bout of hysterical amnesia where he was brought home delirious. The couple regretfully resigned. Frank suffered a deep depression accompanied by vivid hallucinations, including ones that he was preaching in front of a huge congregation, as detailed in Hazel's biography of her husband, *Being Frank*.

'Hazel,' he'd say. 'Here are all these people waiting for the meeting to begin and we have no pianist. Will you get one?' I humoured him by saying I would. These were the only bright spots in the day.[1]

It's unlikely that Frank or his beloved Hazel would have mentioned to Dr Evans or the Australian AoG the struggles Frank had with psychotic illnesses, physical sickness and psychosomatic combinations of the two. Poor Hazel. Five kids. An angry, sick husband. If Frank wasn't recovering from a bout of a disabling disease, he was convalescing in homes, and in the old days a nervous breakdown or a case of hysterical amnesia meant he could be in hospital for months. There were episodes, too, where a longstanding headache could turn into depression, and then another breakdown.

'Feel this lump in my neck,' he would say to me. I could never feel a lump but he would get angry when I told him so. Fearing another nervous breakdown, I talked to our doctor. He listened to my story but he didn't seem to realise the seriousness of it. If only Frank had come with me, but he wouldn't. He would be very angry if he knew I was there.[2]

When he was well, though, he was on fire. After the Army, Frank was able to concentrate his passion for the spiritual by investing more time in the pursuit of the supernatural. Shortly after some disillusionment with Christianity he received the baptism in the Holy Spirit, as evidenced by speaking in tongues, at an AoG rally. Then a sceptical Hazel joined him. From that time on, the couple knew that the stories about the Pentecostal experience were true.

Over the following years, Frank's reputation as a preacher and as a man of God in the charismatic movement grew. He was General Superintendent of the AoG in New Zealand, but when he came to Australia he saw no need for the formality of the Assemblies of God hierarchy. He was no competition for Andrew's position, nor were his sons any competition for Ashley and Russell Evans. Graeme was a fireman and while Brian had been attending his dad's bible college in New Zealand, he was nothing to write home about. The Evanses were Aussie and three generations strong.

And it is completely unlikely that Frank had mentioned the sexual offences he had committed against teenage boys. Some news of these had travelled through the ministerial networks in New Zealand, but the one pastor who confronted him had received a clear denial, one that Frank maintained for over twenty years before, cornered by his son, he confessed.

It's also probably unlikely that Frank knew where his visions had come from. To say that the whole of Hillsong is based on a deliberate lie told by a man running from his own demons would be unfair. It seems much more accurate, if not also a little comforting, that Frank himself believed he had a vision from God no matter what his medical and psychiatric history showed.

Chapter 2

C'MON AUSSIE, C'MON, C'MON

> Train a child in the way he should go, and when he is old he will not turn from it.
>
> —Proverbs 22:6; my mother

All of this had nothing to do with me. My family immigrated in January of 1977 so when the Houstons arrived, we had only been in the country a few months and I was but six years old.

My father, Fred, is one of those Englishmen who was born forty years old in a suit, and has been in banking since time began. Following his commercial instincts, of which I inherited none, he traded in his position at Barclays in London for the sights, sounds and banking opportunities of South Africa, a perfectly reasonable employment choice in 1964. Throw in the added rugby and cricket loyalties of the South Africans, and my dad was where life must have made sense: banking, sport, and someone else to mow the lawn so he shouldn't suffer the hayfever the English develop in the tropics.

South Africa had already missed out on the sixties. It was far too conservative and far too isolated to be affected by the lunacy going on in the rest of the Western world. The government was stiflingly repressive, with everyone censored heavily. In the country that banned Pink Floyd's 'Another Brick in the Wall', TV was only permitted from 1976, having been denounced as the 'evil black box'.

Still, liberated by overseas anonymity, Fred made one last conscious bid for freedom from the world of economics and got a job as a rep for a packaging company. It was not to be and he returned after a few months to a lifetime of banking. He decided to take his chances in Durban, by the sea.

Elaine, my mother-to-be, had had her hair set as usual on that fateful Friday afternoon. When a friend called to offer her an evening with a handsome young Englishman, she felt it would be a shame to waste a hair set and dinner at the Oyster Box, the hotspot of Umhlanga Rocks. Durban always had a thriving nightlife. It's a city where everyone is in bed by 9.30 on the big weekends. My mother speaks fondly of those nights when people drank Coca-Cola and let the caffeine have its wicked way.

Apparently things worked out for Fred and Elaine, because they were married within a year. The heart-warming story goes something like this: Fred got the flu. His devoted Jewish girlfriend made him some soup, and tended to him at his bedside. If we were married, she told him, I could look after you like this all the time.

The wedding was attended by all the family including Elaine's son, Paul, from her first marriage. He was seven and ready for someone to play rugby and cricket with apart from his cousins. Then, some three years later, on the same birthdate as Elvis Costello, Claudia Schiffer and Sean Connery, a screaming, crying, fireheaded girl-child burst into these good folks' previously peaceful existence.

Give my mother any passing opportunity and she will tell you about the crying. It started with the first three colicky months when screaming is still considered reasonable. Apparently another two years of walking around crying, grizzling, dummy in mouth, blanket in hand is not. I don't know what it was all about, though it does remind me of how I felt after George W. Bush got back in and how some people think my attitude is generally, all these years later. I maintain there's a lot to grizzle about.

Somewhere in there, Fred and Elaine got saved. Fred had been to a Cliff Richard concert where he had met Jesus for the first time, despite his Church of England altar boy upbringing. Elaine was and always will be a harder nut to crack. She tells the tale of being one of three Jewish girls in primary school and of a whole class of girls lining up and marching across the playground towards them shouting: 'The Jews killed Jesus, the Jews killed Jesus!' Maybe some Jews convert out of guilt. Maybe they can relate to the suffering of Jesus, having suffered so much themselves. Whatever happened, my mother was born again, her family ignored it, and I arrived into a Christian household.

At age three, I cried all the way to nursery school and all the way home. My mother would sing catchy songs from church crèche with me (*I have decided to follow Jesus, I have decided to follow Jesus, I have decided to follow Jesus, no turning back, no turning back*) until I realised we were there, and then I would spend my days at nursery school, I'm told, crying for my mother. No turning back.

I do remember pressing my little forefingers together in the sign of the cross, after sticking my little thumb over my shoulder (*the world behind me, the cross before me, the world behind me, the cross before me, the world behind me, the cross before me, no turning back, no turning back*) and wondering about this world that at three or four I had already left behind.

I don't remember the crying, though. I thought three was fun. I was in Red Group at nursery school and my best friend was Linda Jane. Four was good as well. I had graduated to the more sophisticated Yellow Group and Linda Jane's mother was my teacher. Blue Group, however, was becoming daunting. It was taught by a huge woman who was not impressed that I could already read and, having all the gentleness of an Afrikaner, was causing my relatively simple life to complicate.

I was saved in the end by the 1976 Soweto uprising. Elaine had never wanted to set foot outside of Durban, and with double-features at the bioscope on Saturdays, who could blame her? She had been to Joburg and it was cold. Fred, however, who was not from Durban, had noted that tension and violence were rising around the African state. In 1976, he attended an international banking summer school, as only people like my dad can, and was offered a job in Australia by a bona fide Australian bank.

It was hard even in those days for a South African to get out. And to get in somewhere else was even scarier. For a year my parents waited for the visa to be approved, even though they had employment sponsorship. Then the Soweto riots happened. Hundreds of people were killed in demonstrations against education in the Afrikaans language. Among them were Africans and Europeans, adults and children, all made equal by the open fire of police. Even Elaine knew it was time to leave.

At the same time, the minister from our Presbyterian church had been given the chance to go to America. He and Fred often talked till late into the night after they realised their families had to move. The minister and his family sailed to America and we got on our boat's last voyage. Two weeks later, I climbed out from the *Galileo Galilei* cabin's bunk and onto the shores of Sydney Harbour. We got the Datsun off the back and started all over again. Years later, the minister's family would be called by God away from the steel town that had been their oasis and to a beach location in California. The *Galileo* returned to Europe and was used as a floating restaurant.

Fred and Elaine had sold their jewellery and left with the minuscule 10,000 rand they were allowed to take out of the country. We stayed at the bank's apartment at seaside Manly while shopping for houses.

There have only been two destinations for Jewish South Africans in Sydney: the eastern suburbs, such as Bondi, and the north shore, particularly St Ives. My parents could afford neither, it turned out. They shopped further and further out and settled on Baulkham Hills, a suburb bordering on what would become Sydney's sprawling west. It was a newish area—the trees had not yet grown to shield us from the belting western Sydney heat—and barren, littered only with houses. The highways weren't built, so there was no getting anywhere. But Baulkham Hills was a nice enough family suburb, which was just as well because there was no leaving it.

None of this mattered to me. I liked school and had none of the real estate compulsions I have now. It wasn't just because I was a kid, though; no one had any idea what the area would turn into. Least of all me, and least of all Brian Houston, who was then youth pastor at his dad Frank's church in the city.

It was hot in those summer days, and it wasn't a wealthy area then. No one had a pool. We rode our bikes in the street, went to the shop for lollies and waited for the cricket to end on TV. It was boring. It was suburbia.

My parents had become members of the local Presbyterian church and we went there, Sunday in and Sunday out, for a couple of years. An hour or so of some hymns in the morning and a nice Christian message. No controversy. Out by midday.

Over time, I heard some conversation at home about wanting to take things further, wanting to know more. Kids didn't sit in on decision-making the way they do now and in any case, what would I have known? All I remember is that we started going to a Pentecostal church in the western suburbs. I didn't know what Pentecostal meant any more than I had known what Presbyterian meant; I just knew the drive was longer. There weren't very many of us, maybe thirty or forty people. One pastor was a handsome young suit-wearing man while the other was 95 years old in the shade, and looked every bit the wise and faithful evangelist from the goldrush era.

This place didn't have any fancy stained glass like our old church, because the congregation was so new that the services were held in a school hall. They clapped while they sang their songs, which was okay with me as a kid. Hymns had previously been way out of any singing range for me, or anyone apart from my dad and the 90-year-old Presbyterian ladies. I did notice, though, that people tended to yell out long nonsensical sentences quite randomly, and that others did this more quietly as well. I was not to wonder about it for long.

My mother had developed a love for information after we came to Australia. For years she sent off to the Christian Gospel Cassette Lending Library and, about once a month, a brown-paper package would arrive with twenty or so tapes. Elaine would listen to all of them, wrap them up and return them with a new order. (I asked about a library system for the poorer people at Hillsong not long ago so that we could all access the wisdom, regardless of yearly income. The assistant looked at me like I spoke Swahili, and said that no one had ever asked that question.)

I tried to listen to my mother's tapes with her, but there was always a eunuch who started the tape with a monotoned: 'This is the Christian Gospel Cassette Lending Library tape number two-zero-three-eight ... of the series "Faith and God", 17.' I was eight and well into ABBA by then. I had my own tapes and was too busy practising 'Take a Chance on Me' to sit still and listen. My grandmother, who had come out from South Africa some months before, had taken me to see *Dot and the Kangaroo*, but we ended up accidentally in a showing of *ABBA: The Movie* instead, an event that was probably the closest thing I had to a conversion experience for years. A seven-year-old went in to see a cartoon and came out a yearning, burning disco queen.

One day my mother picked me up from the bus stop at the end of the street. As we walked home, she described the tape she had been listening to that day. She said that even though we knew Jesus, there was more for us all. She told me that God was our Father and that Jesus was our Saviour, but that a lot of Christians didn't know about the baptism of the Holy Spirit.

The man on the tape had explained all this. My mother sat with me after we got home and told me that this is what God wanted for all Christians, and that we would know if the baptism worked by whether you could speak in tongues. I asked her to show me and she did. We prayed for me and I tried to do tongues but I don't think it worked. It didn't matter to my mother. She had only wanted to tell me what she had learnt.

Which was just as well. The new Pentecostal church was full of these things called tongues, people were doing it all over the place. Without being warned, an outburst of tongues can be scary to anyone, let alone a little kid, so I was glad that I was finally in the know.

The next step was to be baptised. Pentecostals believe in full water immersion baptism, like Jesus did with John the Baptist. Just like the church itself, there were no icons attached; no holy water or special baptismal font. People were often baptised at a moment's notice in the ocean, not long after they got saved.

Who knows if I was saved or baptised in the Holy Spirit? All I remember is that one Sunday lunchtime after church, we went to the handsome pastor's house and I stood in his suburban backyard pool in a pair of shorts and a t-shirt while I was lowered into the water and brought back up again. They say that when I came out I was praising God and speaking in tongues. I can't recall. I know that lunch that day was extra special and that the pastors seemed like nice people.

I also became an Australian when I was eight. It took three years for immigrants to gain citizenship and, like all good South Africans, we arrived punctually to throw our useless passports away and pledge allegiance to the Queen all over again, something as a budding republican I had no say in either.

Settlers we weren't. Fred and Elaine had started from scratch as New Australians, and Fred's banking forte had paid off. He was offered the position of senior vice-president for the New York branch of the bank, and he accepted. When they told me it was for three years, I was shocked. That equalled a third of my life. Yet at nine years of age, I could feel the pull towards America myself. It was 1981, and life was good.

We spent three years living in Westchester County, New York, about forty-five minutes out of Manhattan. My mother was twice as indignant now that she'd had to leave Durban *and* its placebo replacement. She reeled at the number of TV channels that were available in America, and my father worked harder and commuted. My brother, who since leaving school had taken a temporary job in the Sydney bank with my dad, had also become enmeshed in commerce and was relocated to the New York bank, and they commuted together. After hanging around the dealing room a couple of times, his natural talents exploded and he became a foreign exchange dealer from that time on.

We didn't go to church much. No special reason. I seem to remember some boring ones we tried, and none of them felt right. Finding a good church is like finding a good therapist. It's not always easy to feel comfortable and if you don't, chances are you're not going to stay for long. I didn't mind. I liked being home on Sundays, if the truth be known.

In the middle of 1984 we came back to Sydney short one family member (my brother had fallen in love with an American and America and chose to stay), again living in the bank's apartment for a year. Manly was not too far from the Christian City Church in Dee Why. Run by a husky-voiced New Zealander, Phil Pringle, it had a casual surfie feel, but since we weren't staying in the area we didn't commit. Nice church, though, nice people. A little bit loud, but very down-to-earth.

Though the trip to America had been a prosperous one to the best of my knowledge, we still didn't make it to St Ives or Bondi and ended up in a new northern suburb called Cherrybrook, which had all the character and excitement that its name implies. The housing estates had not shot up like bamboo then. It was made up of big brick houses in a slightly fancier version of Baulkham Hills, from what I could make out. I liked the one we picked. It was lovely, and I had a cat and room to play more Bruce Springsteen, my adolescent evolutionary step from ABBA, even if there seemed no reason on God's earth why my parents couldn't pick a place to live that had something to do or somewhere to go.

Fred was ready to settle into a church. We went to a couple before we landed at the Hills Christian Life Centre. It was a relief. I didn't want to spend months going from church to church for no reason, smiling at people I would never see again. It was too much like starting a new school.

The people at Hills seemed as nice as any other. By that time it was important to my parents that I was happy with the church we attended, and I liked it. They had never let me hang out with kids my age at church, since kids that talk during the service are universally known to be plotting with Satan. So, it didn't really matter where we went, in some ways; I was going to be stuck sitting next to them. The Hills place seemed as good as any. And so, in September of 1985, my diary reads: 'Went to a church called Hills Christian Life Centre. Liked it, will probably go back.'

Chapter 3

THE JUSTICE LEAGUE

> The church was very exciting. It took a long time for me to disengage myself from this excitement, and on the blindest, most visceral level, I never really have, and never will. There is no music like that music, no drama like the drama of the saints rejoicing, the sinners moaning, the tambourines racing, and all those voices coming together and crying holy unto the Lord. There is still, for me, no pathos quite like the pathos of those multi-colored, worn, somehow triumphant and transfigured faces, speaking from the depths of a visible, tangible, continuing despair of the goodness of the Lord. I have never seen anything to equal the fire and excitement that sometimes, without warning, fill a church, causing the church to 'rock'.
>
> —James Baldwin, *The Fire Next Time* (1963)

Even today, when I hear Brian Houston's voice, I feel better. I still like it, even if it's just on TV, when the singing is over and Brian comes on stage, gives his approval to the choir, greets the congregation and takes command of the auditorium. There is something to him—his history, his heritage—that instils security, ultimate trust. Daddy's home. Finally, we can relax: Brian's here.

There is no feeling like the feeling of Brian looking down upon us early on a Sunday morning, beaming, and telling us how great we look, how great it is to be in the Lord's house this fine day, and to know he is pleased with us—Brian, that is, like a father, pleased with his children. And there is nothing like the feeling on a hot summer's night in church, Brian pleased with the numbers who have turned out in support of the celebration of God. And we are pleased, pleased we did turn the TV off and make it to the church that a man like Brian leads. You know you are in the right place at the right time in history.

Brian's history had indeed begun. His father, Frank Houston, launched Christian Life Centre Sydney in March of 1977, hiring Sherbrook Hall in Sydney's Double Bay. As it grew, it moved into the Koala Motor Inn in Darlinghurst, then into Dainford House in Goulburn Street.

In February of 1978, 24-year-old Brian and his wife of one year, Bobbie, made the pilgrimage to Australia from New Zealand. Brian became associate pastor to his father and was in charge of home fellowships, known before that as home bible study and these days as cell groups.

In 1983, Brian and Bobbie rented a school hall in an industrial area northwest of Sydney's centre. With a headcount of forty-five, the stage was set. In the beginning, there were six pastors at Hills: Brian was senior pastor, Michael Smith was 2IC, Geoff Bullock was in charge of music, Pat Mesiti and Donna Quinn were associates, and Mike Murphy was on the team too. But it was Brian's show. It never crossed anyone's mind that it could be different.

When I was a teenager and people asked me what religion I was, I said I was a Christian. For those who enquired as to the denomination, I would say that I went to a Pentecostal church, but that it wasn't really a denomination. I was just a regular Christian. I was grateful that only a small percentage of people asked the third question—'What is Pentecostal?'—because it seemed to take some hours to explain. We were all just Christians, I would say, if I could get away with it.

At Hills, we had no idea that there was anything special about this church or this denomination that wasn't really one, since we all just loved Jesus together. My impressions in September of 1985 were of a bunch of nice people. Having changed schools all those times, I was always scared of a new set of kids and had to get some bearings first. I almost didn't see the young people for a while because there was too much going on. It wasn't important in the beginning. I had all the kids at school to deal with; I couldn't take on another community of teenagers, no matter how much they loved God. And at fourteen, I didn't need any extra rejection. So I started off just going to church. And watching.

There can be no simpler way to run a church than the warehouse Hills Christian Life Centre had moved into and that's exactly how it appeared. What seemed so generic had not, however, fallen off the back of an Acme truck.

Frank Houston's Christian Life Centre in Sydney was started in the same vein as the Haight-Ashbury Jesus People Movement in San Francisco. The Jesus People had rejected their formal, generally Methodist upbringings and, while not wanting to leave Jesus, had mounted a rebellion. They rejected a church that was high on rhetoric and low on substance and that insisted leaders adhere to strict codes and go through years of seminary training.

The Haight-Ashbury idea was to have a level playing field. This new church was going to be free of the cumbersome overcoats of formality. It was going to be a meeting of Christians. At Hills, the pastors were just regular guys with jobs, except for Brian the senior pastor, who was like a full-time hall monitor who helped out in church on the weekends. They were people like us. Some of them had been to bible college and some hadn't. Who needed credentials to pastor? It's not brain surgery, it's tending the flock. We knew God took care of the rest.

Up until I remember, or had any right to know, many of the pastors at Hills were still struggling to make ends meet. They were working full-time elsewhere, had several children, wives who didn't work, and huge commitments on the weekends that exploded as the church grew. Every new family that joined the church came with a new set of problems. They all needed pastoring and they didn't always keep reasonable hours. Pastors were battlers like everyone else and the stress they were under was apparent. They managed, but it was easy to feel sorry for their sacrifices, and admiration for their hard-won convictions.

The leadership were regular folk and, apart from the odd rich one, generally the congregation was a working-class, family-oriented group of a few hundred people. The rich stood out in those days, a time when having a politician attend sincerely was an honour, not a badge of honour.

And what would a member of parliament be doing in these humble premises? Truly, they were humble. At the back of suburbia in Baulkham Hills, the houses stopped and the farming began along with factories, some office areas and warehouses. Hills Christian Life Centre rented a warehouse. When I began going, there were about 300 people. It was still a small space, until they knocked down a wall, rented next door and expanded to accommodate the growing children's church.

This was the new church; it had none of the symbols of old. No stained-glass windows. No hard wooden pews. Plastic chairs were set up, the sort you sit on in conferences. Comfy. Informal.

A photocopied church newsletter, occasionally printed on coloured paper, was handed out at the entrance. There were no hymnbooks. All the words to songs were displayed on a screen with an overhead projector. It was usually a youth's job to keep the piece of plastic straight, and move it along in time for the chorus. Sometimes the words were handwritten and had been smudged. The typed ones were easy to see, but it didn't really matter. It was only for new people. We already knew all the words.

The 'altar' in a tangible form did not exist in my childhood. Anything representing formality of any kind was gone. The pulpit had been eliminated and replaced by a lectern. This was a church to learn in, not a place to atone in humble silence. It was a place to find out more about Jesus than just the idea that you were saved. Being with God was a happy time, not an uncomfortable, painful time. We were celebrating, weren't we?

There were no deacons or overseers. There were volunteers who helped people find a place to sit. The new ushers tuned stereos instead of fluffing cushions on pews. The organ had been replaced by a piano which competed with guitars.

Along with the new culture came a new language. This New-Speak was devoid of thous and thines. Completely. No ministers, just pastors, and no hierarchy, none needed. There weren't formal sermons, only conversational 'messages' a leader had received from God during the week that he wanted to share with the others. The only reason the guy speaking was standing higher up than anyone else was in order to be seen. Microphones later allowed preachers to roam around and still be heard, getting down to the people's level.

Brian often used to talk to people in the congregation. He'd make them stand up and show their baby, or wave for whatever good reason there was to share. He might wander around and chat with people for five minutes, have a laugh, make everyone feel comfortable.

People in the congregation often used to talk to Brian, too, or whoever was preaching. If a preacher became passionate, or if he said something people agreed with, someone might yell out an 'Amen' or a 'Hallelujah'. Every so often a cheeky young man might chuck in a wisecrack from the front rows and we all had a laugh.

Sunday mornings were traditionally the more formal services.

We still started with the fast songs, the clapping songs. I liked them. Their 4/4 beat made me who I am today. With the introduction of the simple chorus in church, everybody could sing along and feel comfortable since the PA system covered a multitude of bad singers. It was equality all around.

Communion was taken in the warehouse days, after passing around an oval silver platter with shreds of white bread in the centre and a multitude of tiny plastic goblets filled with grape juice. We took the time, some moments of silence—which in the Pentecostal church is always a feat—and examined our hearts, albeit briefly, then we ate and drank. Not a tangibly profitable exercise, but still peculiarly Christian. Communion is no longer taken at Hillsong.

Following this, there was the awkward 'go and greet the people around you' instruction. I didn't want to greet the people around me. I didn't know what I was supposed to say to them. Mostly I pretended to be engrossed in the newsletter.

Then the faithful reassembled for church news and the giving of tithes and offerings. Church news was not about building projects but who had got engaged or had a baby. The cash, cheque or envelope could be placed into the milkshake cups that were at the end of each row, passed down and the ushers took them away. No more was generally said about money, not then.

Morning church would always go for at least two hours. Singing, fast songs then slow songs, went for a good forty-five minutes all up, if you include the excruciatingly long ten minutes of free singing, where you could sing your own song, particularly in tongues if you felt led by the Spirit. I never knew what to do with that time either, and if a day is like a thousand years with the Lord and a thousand years is like a day, I was sure that bit was never going to end. Singing is not my strong point, and making up my own song to Jesus proved very hard for me, since Jesus and I rarely sang to each other when we were alone. I didn't know if God wanted me to try to be as spiritual-looking as the other people lost in song with their Creator, or to once again appear difficult by not conforming. Usually I found a happy medium by closing my eyes and swaying, occasionally thrusting out a palm heavenward, which I still find these days helps to keep people away.

With a bit of luck, or if one of the lead singers didn't end it with an ad-lib gospel solo, many of these eternally long sessions would be rounded off with an outburst of tongues or a prophecy. The only thing is, bible rules say that if someone yells out in tongues through some sudden movement of the Spirit, it's a prophecy that must be interpreted. People's eyes would snap open and I would know that we could sit down soon and stop being so publicly exposed.

So, after the minute or so of commands in this unknown language, the room would wait. I am yet to hear an interpretation that I couldn't have read in Athena Starwoman. But someone had to do something. If someone didn't, the leader might have to. The standard revelation went a little like this: 'Yea, though you are travelling through a difficult time, you will emerge. The Lord would say that he is here today and that he will never leave you or forsake you. For I am the Lord.' Did anybody else wonder how it was that the tongues might go for a long while but the interpretation was short? I thought it would run a bit like a foreign movie, a little out of sync but still roughly syllable for syllable. If someone's going to pour out tongues for two minutes straight, it's a hefty statement. Sounded like God was really saying something and I would've thought the interpretation needed to last for more than thirty seconds. It was brave, too, because only nerds had that gift. I never saw one leggy blonde yell out in tongues right before the sermon.

Tongues is spooky and I think it's supposed to be. My personal preference was for a straight prophecy in English which would run more like this: 'The Lord would say that he is here today in this place amongst you and he knows the troubles of your heart and he has promised that you ALREADY have the victory! You have had it for 2000 years. He will never leave you or forsake you because he is the Lord.' The straight prophecy eliminates the uncomfortable waiting following tongues, and also provides a lovely drumroll effect for the main act. The congregation can then give heavenly applause after the prophecy out of thankfulness to God. I was just as thankful that the unstructured part was over and lunch might come soon. I was always starving after church. Like swimming, it seemed to really take it out of me.

So the speaker of the day gets to walk on after a fairly intense build-up and agrees with the crowd that there's no doubt that God is here with us *now*. There are some pretty amazing things going on, are there not? God is in the House, all right. You can feel him, and he's giving us miracles. And all the believers said:

Amen.

You call that an Amen? ALL THE BELIEVERS SAID?

AMEN!

And SHOUTED?

Hallelujah!

Please be seated.

At Hills, church was reliable. Most Sunday mornings, at both services, one of the other pastors spoke. We'd have sung our hearts out, put in our offerings, taken communion and were ready to listen. Brian would have spoken over communion or the offering, and would also be seated to listen to Pat or one of the Michaels, or even Donna later on down the track. People took turns in those days, singing, preaching or sharing an experience. Even regular folk occasionally stood up and gave a report of a miracle in their life.

As mornings were deemed more formal, revival, signs, wonders, healings and miracles were anticipated as night-time events. Mornings were the time for teaching and, from the bible, verse by verse, as it related to our lives, we were taught by one of the familiar faces on the team.

Sometimes Brian preached in the morning, but evangelism nights were his real domain. He was our senior pastor, and he was juggling this with his travelling commitments. He was there most Sundays, but when he wasn't we knew he was out on the battlefield. Which made us love him all the more.

Brian was goofy and Brian was fun. He was clumsy and with a self-deprecating humour in his jokes we all could relate to. Everyone had families and bills and embarrassing run-ins with people on the street. Brian was never a teacher. He was a preacher. When I would complain to my father that every Sunday night I was hearing the same old thing—get saved, celebrate, stay strong, move mountains—he would remind me that Brian's gift was evangelism. The church knew that Brian was doing all he could for us, and for the gospel.

Brian Houston's charisma is universally known. He speaks internationally, lectures at bible colleges, and fills stadiums wherever he goes. I still can't figure out what the precise appeal is, but there it is en masse.

Brian's raspy voice sounded different again when he spoke about his father's 'serious moral failure'. I heard it rise to emphasise, and drop for finality. I heard it swoop people up with waves of hope, carry them along the great battle upstream, and dump on the shores of Brian's reality. I heard the voice whitewash as smoothly, unebbing, as it had preached. That raspy voice, with its New Zealand twang, was just another tool of the trade. You can listen to it any time on the squillions of CDs, but it won't have the same effect on you, not the first time, anyway. After a couple of hundred times, though, after he's built you up with hope and promise and destiny, like a race caller calling the closest race you've ever heard, when the Hand of God is on your life and you can feel that God is right here today, and you know that your future is in his hands and THEN! when you hear Brian's voice drop, and he says something slowly, your heart may also drop with it as swiftly as it learns to rise. Brian laughs. You laugh.

When I see him now, I can't help but stare. What is it like to be Brian? What does he see when he looks around him? His brother, Graeme, is a fireman, a much more practical superhero, one might think. He doesn't go to church. Then there's the three sisters. One rebel went back to New Zealand with her husband. She's not in attendance. Maureen became pregnant out of wedlock and was banished but got a last-minute reprieve from her parents and was allowed to keep the baby. She doesn't go to Hillsong. Then there's Judith. She goes to Hillsong and she stares at Brian adoringly.

Is Brian looking at his sons and watching history repeat as they take up their roles as youth pastors and musicians? Joel travels internationally as a singer, songwriter and performer. Ben married Lucille, who looks strikingly like his mother. The two of them are youth pastors, and Bobbie says Lucille's 'chocolate'. The youngest, Laura, is now working full-time for Hillsong.

Is Brian aware yet of the impact his work has on people's lives? Does he see what happens after the lights go down? I have to stop staring. It's rude.

Despite all this, I still miss it. It's a strange attachment, I concede. I was never close to Brian, never spent much time with him at all, if ever.

Yet I have some instinctual loyalty forever reserved for him in my psyche. After long years of feeling otherwise and knowing otherwise, I still wish I could sit in row five and hear Brian say that his church looks fantastic, and know that he means me too.

He instilled that loyalty in every one of the men and one woman who started Hills Christian Life Centre. They were in their late twenties at the time, just some people who ran a church on weekends, each supporting Brian in his vision to see people saved.

PASTOR PAT MESITI

Saturday, 16 July 1988: Tonight at youth, Pat Mesiti came up and laid his hand on my forehead and prophesied over me. I cannot remember exactly what he said, but his words were to this effect: that God will use me to change the hard and cynical hearts of people and friends, that I will speak with boldness, love and authority. 'I am the Lord and I will FASHION you.' Later, when he began to prophesy over others, one girl was crying and he called me and Lucinda to pray for her. That made me feel so special. More special than anything in the natural because this man who was in charge of us all called me, and made me feel like the chosen one. I love him very much. But I really love God and want to be the best for him. You know, I really want so many things but they seem so silly in the light of Jesus Christ. I am confused and yet I won't let it trip me up. I am going to give God so much.

An evangelical Danny DeVito, that's how we all knew Pat. That's how Brian talked about Pat, and how Pat talked about himself. Short, feisty, Italian, unsexy. Pat Mesiti and Danny DeVito.

He was twenty-eight when I first met him. Pat was the chief youth pastor as well as a youth evangelist. He was out there working with young people in schools and all over the place, saving them from their terrible heathen fates. Kids were converting, he would tell us, at incredible rates where he preached, throwing their drugs and rock music away for God.

Pat could preach it. Thank God for that. When you knew Pat was due to speak, you knew it was going to be good. He was funny and entertaining. He could catch you offguard and make you laugh. A second-generation Italian Australian from Sydney's multicultural working-class Bankstown, Pasquale Mesiti would tell his story to home and away crowds: his alcoholic parents, his praying grandmother, his delinquent adolescence, his surrender to Jesus, his life committed to helping young people.

It was a compelling tale. A lonely boy, who would have ended up just like his father before him but for the faith of the little old woman, his grandmother, who demanded her son let Pat go to bible college. We bought it, line, tackle and reel. We hurt with Pat when he recounted stories of that horrible household, filled with drunken rage and fear. We laughed with Pat when he imitated his nonna and celebrated her determination in her old age. We cheered when we realised he had made it through bible college and was living out the dream he had fought so hard for.

He was inspirational and endearing. He'd married Liz, the girl he'd dated since he was thirteen years old, and they had two little girls. She was as short as he, and seemed to match him. He was good fun, our Pat, and he had launched youth organisations all over New South Wales. We sat there, year after year, drinking in the drama that Pat was pouring out. It was an emotional roller-coaster and he ran the ride by ripping open his heart.

I didn't spend much time with Pat, him being a grown-up and all. Still, he always greeted me and asked how I was going, always friendly. The strange thing was, every time he saw me he asked after my father. 'Hi, Tanya, how's your dad?' was his standard line. I loved my dad, and was happy that the pastors did too.

Everybody loved Pat, and why wouldn't they? He was a solid family man and he was scoring big numbers in heaven. His youth rallies had a deep impact on their audiences. Young people poured down to the altar call to get saved. Pat could tally up more salvations at one concert than Hills could in a month of Sundays. That was Pat, able to get people to believe anything, as if it were the first time you had heard the story. Sometimes it was good to hear the retelling just to enjoy the character and the jokes all over again. We knew in Pat we had the genuine article.

PASTOR DONNA QUINN

Donna, the junior youth pastor, was twenty-four when I first met her. She had come from a hippie horseriding background and the Jesus Movement was one she could relate to. She was a passionate believer and genuinely seemed to care about us, and she was the only woman we had. Bobbie Houston was almost unheard of in those days. She was merely the pastor's wife.

It was Donna in her t-shirts and jeans who took on the energetic youth in this alternative church. She was the one who preached at youth group, and explained to us when hard things happened that God was still very much around. It was great having a female youth leader. She was strong and not aggressive, determined and committed, and always spoke with a soft emotive voice. She was a rarity in that boys' world. It was amazing to have her.

Not that we were best friends or anything. It's not like we used to hang out. We did talk at church, though. She would ask and know about us all, and in any case she preached from what God had put on her heart.

Donna was single and, refreshingly, never mentioned not having a boyfriend. Mainly this was because Brian did it all for her. Week after week, Brian would make comments from the pulpit. He was trying to find a husband for Donna. At any opportunity, Brian would make a joke at Donna's expense about her mid-twenties spinsterhood. He would laughingly allude to a romantic opportunity for her if a visiting pastor was a bachelor. This got uncomfortable after a while. It was repetitive and I didn't appreciate feeling forced to laugh at someone, not with them.

By 1992, Donna found a husband. I attended the wedding with the rest of the youth group and hoped Brian was happy now. Our single female role model was officially gone. Donna had never planned on getting married. It was a lovely wedding, but I was just sorry things *had* to be that way.

Donna doesn't remember it that way at all. She tells her story very differently from the pulpit. She says that it was her own private unmarried angst that drove her to Brian's office.

'I asked him, "What's wrong with me?"' she recalls. '"Why aren't I married? I'm nearly 30."'

'Nothing wrong with you,' Brian looked up to say. 'You're great, mate.' No wonder she finds he and Bobbie so supportive. She told me they were awesome.

Donna recently celebrated twenty years in ministry. Her family were treated with a trip to Disneyland, courtesy of Hillsong. She preaches with the team and travels a lot, with her husband and three kids, the youngest of whom is called Mercedes—Mercy for short, by far my favourite Hillsong name. It manages to combine prosperity theology, a New Testament attribute and an ad for Mercy Ministries, the Hillsong-sponsored women's rehab centre.

PASTOR MICHAEL SMITH

I can't really say much about Michael Smith. I remember him only as another pastor on the team. He had a moustache and walked like Charlie Chaplin. The one thing I do remember is that he seemed to be the most devoted to biblical teaching. If Michael Smith spoke on a Sunday morning, you knew you might learn something. And even though I blame him for my hungriest Sundays because he always went over time, it was because I'd been learning something. I can't remember what. It's just that when all you've been fed is 'Jesus saves' over and over and over, anyone who wants to talk about the bible in church can make a refreshing change. He left in 1991 to start a new church.

PASTOR MICHAEL MURPHY

With Irish eyes that smiled with kindness, Pastor Mike was easily the most handsome of the crew, or at least he got lucky by having both height and a jawline on his side. He would have made a lovely parish priest. Mike Murphy was warm and genuine. Born and raised a good Catholic, he had turned many a head before he settled down to take Valery's hand in marriage. She was an ex-flight attendant and the relationship was a little controversial as she was some years older than he, unlike the traditional Hills marriage where the bride got her braces removed for her hen's night. They had three sweet children, whom I babysat to give Mike and Val a few hours off and me an excuse not to study. Babysitting for pastors had to be God's will over Modern History.

Pastor Mike was the type of guy who made you feel cared for before you'd been introduced, one of those people who you believed when you shook his hand that he had a heart for people. Everybody loved Michael Murphy.

1.15 am, 28 July 1989: Something has happened. I went to talk to Michael Murphy about my upset life last Thursday and he was very kind. Michael Murphy said school is not my problem, but God wants to deal with past hurts and rejections now and that is why I have been suffering. Well, I cried for about an hour with fear, pain, hatred for myself and it's like now it's over.

I am in control of me. I am detached. My only fear is that God has used this time to test me and I think I failed.

I'm in love with Jesus again. I'm ready to die for him, I really mean that, I don't value my life. I just want God to be pleased with me. And I hope I don't have to be tested again because this was a hard test.

My mother and I both like people with nice faces and we agreed that I should be sent to Michael Murphy (who is known by two names, like Buddy Holly, whereas Brian is always Brian, like Elvis) when I refused to leave my new boyfriend. This time kind didn't cut it. I went for counselling and tried to explain that I didn't mean to worry my parents, but I was not going to budge. All the confidence, sympathy and prayer in Michael Murphy's office couldn't shift the questions in my head or the way my boyfriend looked at me. That in itself made me even more depressed. Kindness, compassion and purity dropped way down on the list when the man who had represented them couldn't use them to help me.

In 1995, Mike and Val took over the Christian Growth Centre, a small AoG congregation. He was accused by some longer-term members of that church of ruthlessly instituting the rules, culture and employees of Brian Houston's Assemblies of God the moment he took control. To meet Mike Murphy, or to see his Shire Christian Centre now, you could never dream it possible. He is such a nice man.

Did being nice get him a place in 2005 on the AoG National Executive? Now in charge of 'church planting' and 'missions' all over the globe, Michael Murphy is on Brian's Dream Team again, playing with the big boys. He must have done something right.

PASTOR GEOFF BULLOCK

> *Cartman:* Inspiration. Wait a minute! That's it! Inspiration, you guys. Don't you see?
> *Stan:* See what?
> *Cartman:* Our band should play *Christian* rock!
> *Kyle: Christian* rock?!!
> *Cartman:* Think about it. It's the easiest, crappiest music in the world, right? If we just play songs about how much we LOVE Jesus, all the Christians will buy our crap.
> *Kyle:* That's a retarded idea, Cartman.
> *Cartman:* It worked for Creed.
> *Stan:* I don't want to be in a stupid Christian rock band.
> *Cartman:* You just start that way, Stan, and then you cross over. It's genius.
>
> —'Christian Rock Hard', *South Park*, episode 709

Christian music to me has always been the same as Christian fashion, Christian schools, Christian counselling: the product would have been fine were it not for the word 'Christian'. That word takes all the fizz out of the soda. I never disagreed with those people who said that good music belongs to the sweet devil, I only wondered whether we could borrow it for a while, if the words weren't sinful and we promised not to get pregnant while playing it.

When I was a youngster, Christian music belonged in a Christian context, that is, in church. The further it got away from church, the more its artists tried to engage in secular fashion, and in being cool. There is nothing more cringe-worthy than Christians trying to be superstars. People get into rock'n'roll for a reason, and it's not for the Diet Coke. Pretending you can be the same only different is always a mistake. I was convinced that the music side of things at Hills CLC would never go far.

At the time, I didn't understand why we needed a music pastor. Surely we could just sing some songs and get on with learning about Jesus. Why we needed a full-time person to be in charge of songs and to write more of them was beyond me.

At Hills we had Geoff Bullock. Married to Janine since forever with five children, two more than Brian, Geoff was our Piano Man. Short and stocky, with blue eyes that pierced you like laser beams, Geoff wrote most of the songs and music that we sang, and ran the choir. I liked the clapping songs. They were fun. He wrote good songs, good music, played well and enjoyed his part of church. Still, to me he was just the organ lady.

My friend Jewels went to a performing arts high school. She was interested in dance and drama and performing in the musical 'items' that became more common in the early church's services. These were also beyond me. In the bible there had been sermons, healings, exorcisms, and although people did all kinds of odd things to Jesus, breaking perfume bottles and grabbing his robe, at no point did pubescent girls in bad costumes perform 'items'. I gave it little thought, placing it between nail-polish colours and wanting babies on the growing list of things I didn't understand about being a normal girl.

Eventually doing music, dance, drama and creative arts for Jesus was so popular that people wanted to spend a week at it. By 1987, Geoff created a music conference he called Hillsong which, just quietly, made me hope they'd all gather together and get it out of their arty systems, so that we could get on with the business of changing the world. Much to my annoyance, the annual

Hillsong conference did very well, which gained them more attention. By 1999, the church was known worldwide by the music conference so it was decided to call the city and Hills churches Hillsong.

Stubbornly, I ignored the growing number of attendees at the conferences. I hoped there were just more arty people than we knew what to do with, and that they would meet and dance their Christian dances in private. I also paid no attention to the growing number of music pastors who joined Geoff in his work. Neither, it seems, did Geoff, until his monster grew a life of its own.

THE WAY WE WERE

I am standing in a cemetery in the hills as the coffin of my friend's mother is lowered into the ground. I have never met her but she is known to be a good woman. As a tireless nurse, she led many a patient to salvation, until her battle with cancer forced her to stop work.

They are pillars of the church community, this family. They have been believing that God will raise their mother from the dead. They have been praying for three days since she died. They left her coffin open during the funeral, in case.

Frank Houston is widely known to have raised people from the dead. Theirs is not an unreasonable expectation.

Her coffin is being lowered into the ground. I'm guessing she's staying dead. I would never have asked for such a thing in case it didn't happen. I marvel at their faith. I still do. They talk about having recovered from their mother's death. Somewhere, I haven't.

*

I am sitting with my friend in the car park while she cries, blows her nose, cries, and turns Mariah Carey up and down on her stereo. 'You don't understand, Tanya,' she says, 'I've given him EVERYTHING, I gave him everything.' I don't know what you're supposed to say to make it better after a breakup, but I am thinking, you can always give someone else everything, can't you?

She couldn't have been talking about sex. Her boyfriend was an elder in the church. It just couldn't have been sex, that was outside of the realms of possibility for us. But the impossible had happened.

She loved him with all the intensity of the first adult relationship. By the time the relationship began to disintegrate, the routine was set. He would meet up with her on Friday and despite their best efforts at restraint, they would have sex on the weekend. Directly afterwards, he would insist that they both pray on their knees for forgiveness, which they would do. By the end of Sunday night's church service, he would be overwhelmed by his guilt and would break up with her. Until Friday.

This girl took the morning-after pill so many Mondays in a row that it was getting dangerous. Obtaining contraception implies intent. It isn't an option for Christian girls, reality or not. She was not the only person who had given this elder everything. And as time went on, she was not to be the last.

The pastors found out about his sexual behaviour and removed him from leadership for twelve months. Later he married and he and his lovely wife – an elegant blonde – went on to pastor a church of their own, although I understand it was taken away from them. They now attend Hillsong. He was always a strange sort of fellow, though she doesn't seem to mind him. Having had two children of the same sex, he decided a couple of years ago to pray that God would change the sex of their third as-yet-unborn child, after the ultrasound gave an unwanted result. It was a prayer God did not answer.

Chapter 4

FRIENDS FOREVER

Marshall Frady, in his book *Billy Graham*, quotes Billy as saying to him: 'I love Chuck to this very day. He's one of the few men I have ever loved in my life. He and I had been so close. But then, all of a sudden, our paths were parting. He began to be a little cool to me then. I think ...' He pauses and then offers with a faint little smile, 'I think that Chuck felt sorry for me.'

It will sound unforgivably condescending, but I do. He has given up the life of unrestricted thought. I occasionally watch Billy in his televised campaigns. Forty years after our working together he is saying the same things, using the same phrases, following the same pattern. When he gives the invitation to come forward, the sequence, even the words are the same. I turn off the set, and am sometimes overtaken by sadness.

I think Billy is what he has to be. I disagree with him at almost every point in his views on God and Christianity and think that much of what he says in the pulpit is puerile, archaic nonsense. But there is no feigning in Billy Graham: he believes what he believes with an invincible innocence. He is the only mass-evangelist I would trust.

And I miss him.

—Charles Templeton, *Farewell to God* (1996)

Shazza introduced herself to me at the door of the warehouse in Gladstone Road. She was one of the people who handed out the church newsletter and greeted newcomers.

'Hi, I'm Shazza,' she said. I told her my name. She said she was fifteen, like me. Apart from that, she didn't seem anything like me. She had long blonde hair, a babydoll face and movie-star teeth. She was quiet and friendly. Still, she was at least thirty years younger than my parents.

After my initial culture shock and some church growth, I was no longer the new kid on the block, and I was ready to blend in a little with others. If I was going to get involved with this church, it wasn't going to be by sitting next to my mother while she watched to see whether I was looking at boys that I wasn't looking at. Mainly Fred and Elaine just bored me at church and it was uncool to still sit next to your parents.

After nagging long enough, I eventually got to go to youth group. I wanted to get into the experience. There was no way that I was going to be all hand-raising and worshipping with my parents standing next to me. I was happy to sing and go along with the basic set-up, but I wasn't going to reveal any extra vulnerability alongside the people who called the shots in my life. I mean, when the preacher says, 'If there's anyone here with sin they're struggling with right now, put your hand up,' you're hardly going to run down to the altar in front of the people who hand out your pocket money.

So it wasn't till I got to youth group that I started feeling more involved. Saturday night youth group seemed to reinforce what we were learning on Sundays, and vice versa. By the time I was sixteen I was attending youth group every Saturday night and church twice on Sundays. I also went to an afterschool home fellowship group on Tuesdays.

Even then I still wasn't fitting in. I didn't know how to talk to this kind of teenager. But Shazza was there, and it wasn't too long before I met her best friend, Jewels. Jewels was cool. In 1987, she wore a headband around her long brown hair, and stockings under denim shorts. She was a much more rhythmical Pentecostal than me; she knew how to clap, when to close your eyes, when to throw a hand up in the air during the prayers. She was sincere. She just happened to be cool at the same time.

I was desperate for someone who was my age, who was Pentecostal, and who wanted to discuss life. I had no one my age to talk to about the goings-on of the church or God. I found someone in Jewels.

Jewels was being raised by a widow, who had only intended initially for the church to broaden her daughter's horizons. A Pentecostal for twenty years before leaving for reasons unknown, Jewels's mother had become Eastern in her spirituality. She was a nurse and a therapist, and a great fan of Jung.

After the ashrams, as part of her religious education, Jewels's mother took her to a small Pentecostal church down the road from their house in Baulkham Hills. Jewels was saved that night, aged twelve, and has never looked back, despite her mother's indignation. She went to school on Monday and invited Shazza to Hills, and Shazza found Jesus too, having been looking for God at the time.

While my parents were cursing my friends from school for their worldliness, Jewels's mother was wringing her hands at her daughter's devotion to this little group. Bloody born-again Christians, she would say. Jewels and I thought we might have been swapped at birth.

The foundations of our friendship were set on the things we both believed in, and yet those things became the focus of our disagreements. I had questions, questions, questions, questions. She had faith enough to listen to them, and respond with her thoughts. Over the years, and mainly after some trauma or another, I would ask more questions and, patiently, Jewels would listen. She didn't always have answers, and somewhere there I knew none of them would be good enough if she did. I wouldn't accept them, but she never stopped my questioning.

A Jewels is a rare creature. She is a tranquil soul. In twenty years of knowing her, I have never seen her eyes flash with fury, heard a genuinely bitter word drop from her mouth, or seen her come anywhere close to the despair I wake up with every second day. She is constant and consistent. And still we manage to laugh a lot together.

I think she's a bit sheltered and, like her mother, I always wished she had gone to university instead of bible college, or even as well as. But she is one of the people the System has rewarded. She agrees with them so they agree with her. Above all, she was one of the very first members of the Hills Christian Life Centre and they'd better give her a star in their walk of fame.

To this day, I really couldn't tell you why she wanted to be my friend. I know we giggle at the same things, the details in life that we know will amuse each other. I know we are sad at the same things, and curious about the same things. I know that she has always been passionate, determined and committed about whatever she is doing, something I always like in someone even if it's geology that they're passionate about. I know that her consistency and unshakeable belief have made her a soothing force all my life. It's deeply reassuring to believe that someone somewhere hasn't taken their eyes off the prize.

And trust me, I tried to distract her. I've raged and sniggered, and maligned and threatened and disrespected all of her truths in my speeches. She never did the same to me. I've preached and proselytised, I've campaigned and informed, challenged and cursed when all she was doing was a load of washing. She never converted. She just listened. And laughed with me.

There's a chicken and egg riddle that goes around in my brain when it comes to Jewels. Is anybody really this chilled out, this together and this good in heart because of Jesus, or is it because of Jewels? And does she stay committed to me because of Jesus or because of Jewels?

After all, I am told by the godly and godless alike that I am difficult. I am intense, and I never know when it's time to go home. I think too much. For glaze-eyed born-again Christians this can be hard to manage. They don't like talking about stuff for too long or too deeply and where they have to use their own powers of reasoning. Jewels was different. She was never afraid of a theological challenge. Somewhere, somehow she was given a shot of Jesus and she had been immunised against anything else. I must have been away that day.

Her best friend, Shazza, didn't understand the need for the challenge. To her it was redundant and futile. 'When you love someone, Tanya,' she would say, 'these things don't matter.' Jewels eased my mind; Shazza broke my heart. While Jewels spent time trying to work with my understanding, Shazza summed up faith in a simple teenage sentence. Neither of them succeeded. Once again, love was never enough. In the end, any honeymoon I'd had was over, and I wanted better.

The most common story I hear is that when you leave the AoG, nobody goes with you. You go from having a family to being spiritually homeless. There is suddenly no follow-up; the phone doesn't ring and nobody comes to visit. People you've spent years with in deep and intimate fellowship disappear off the radar, even those friends who promised faithfully that your leaving wouldn't make a difference.

That was my experience almost completely. Except for Jewels, the only one who practised what I'd heard preached. I assumed when I considered leaving Hills that it would be hard, that everybody would notice me gone and would try to drag me back. I had justifications ready for such events, events which never came about.

And for over twelve years, while I tried to find me in the midst of the confusion of Jesus vs Hell, Jewels stood by me with the patience of Job and made sure I didn't get lost completely. I always knew I had a home in her heart and that she thought I was worth more than just a wretched backslider. Sometimes I wanted her to love me with the love of God, because I couldn't see it any other way. Sometimes I wanted her to love me from herself, because she was such a great person. Sometimes I hated God for giving her a more equal share of faith. Some girls get upset about girls who eat junk food and don't put on weight. I hate the ones who can listen to a lifetime of Christian propaganda and not get blown up by the letter bomb it comes in.

Girls like Jewels remain unscathed, not maimed or twisted, but rather refined. By being herself, Jewels saved my life a hundred thousand times. Without her, I would have had nowhere to expunge so much of the turmoil and the turbulence. Nowhere to go to find out if God could still love me after all I'd done.

No one else understood in the church or out of it. She understood, disagreed and she loved me anyway. Even though I ended up standing against everything she had fought hard all her life to preserve, she loved me. And that's what we used to call, in the old days, a Christian.

DEAR DIARY

4 January 1987
I can't sleep ... I haven't been able to lately ... I'll be thin if it kills me! Maybe not kills me. I will be the perfect person yet, if it does kill me!

Sun, 4 January 1987
This is the day I was freed from the Spirit of rock'n'roll. I started up a conversation with John O'D who DJs at 2-Day FM and he told me he despises the music. He told me the worst person Satan has anointed is Bruce Springsteen. I told him he was telling the wrong person. He disagreed. We talked. Rock'n'roll is all about fornication, especially 'Dancing in the Dark'. It hit so hard. He told me to pray when I got home. Then he offered to pray for me. He released me from the spirit of RNR and seduction and I cried. He told me God loves me and has so much for me. I came home and for 1 1/2 hours I sat in the dark crying, taking down posters, breaking records, destroying tapes. I am giving rock music up. I can't believe I'm saying this. I will be free but I'm gonna miss my Bruce and I'm dying to hear Thunder Road.

My parents are very proud. I am very scared and Michael Murphy is one of the most beautiful people in the world. He has an incredible joy bursting out. My walls are so empty. I'm very confused. I must talk to John again.

5 January 1987
Yes, it's like someone died. I tried to exercise. I couldn't. I rang up John. He is so good! I feel born again. I am a bit confused about some things he says but he is a great friend and he prayed and called me his young sister. I feel free but I miss Thunder Road. (John was the first person in Melbourne to play it.) He is a good man. Why he stays in radio, I don't know. That is very strange. However my walls are bare of the High Priest of Satan but now

there is definitely only one Lord of my life. I love Jesus heart & soul & always will. I can't let something get in the way of us again. We hung on to a couple of tapes. Billy Joel and stuff. I'll make a couple of copies & give 'em to Mum to keep.

I'm gonna miss this life but I am gonna make it.

John says he spiritually prophesies a life of glory & beauty for me. I love him. He is so powerful but I can't believe him 100%. But I keep thanking God that I was freed from the spirit of rock'n'roll.

Wed, 7 January 1987
It's okay! I'm surviving. I've never felt closer to God! Sometimes I just sit there and feel Him love me. I took communion by myself this morning and instantly I felt warmth and love. Jesus loves me and He loves everyone and I want to tell everyone.

9 January 1987
I know that whatever sadness, regrets, worries, doubts etc. I have, Satan tries to play with my mind (and I won't let him). I would do the same again in a split second never looking back. I love my Lord. All barriers are broken down We are so close. I hang around the house all day restless. I read The Stand and watch Days. I am alive. I am Christian. With so many 'bad' witnesses no wonder there are so many bad people.

Sun, 11 January 1987
It's okay. Lara came over for the last three days. Every day she comes to visit. I really wanted to talk to John O'D but he wasn't in church today.

12 January 1987
Just quickly I read the bible so much now. Today about 1 1/3 yester 1 2/3 hours, that's a lot for me but I need it. I'm going to beat this cancer. The days are running away sprinting, it'll be school soon. I love my Lord Jesus!

21 January 1987
I enrolled in a Christian Foundations course, we sent for Vol I. This morning when I woke up the intense craving for my love was gone. I really wanted to be rid of it! I feel ashamed for wanting it back. I'm very confused guilty unhappy but taking it one day at a time. God will help me. His angels will be of constant assistance and aid—they will make me realise the purpose for which I am here. Believe me, if I can live without it, you can! Although I feel guilty for wanting to compromise my sacrifice! I still feel there MUST be some acceptable music. Tell me, is it out there for me?

I have no right to cry myself to sleep over music from Satan. I can tell you now that I love God with all my heart, mind and soul. When I said goodbye to Bruce a barrier was taken away and I could see clearly. I could touch God and really know he was there. I have only one Lord now. This is what it must be like to be saved. Thank you Jesus.

28 January 1987
I miss Bruce but it's worth it.

P.S. Footnote: When I finally spoke to John O'D on Sun 18 Jan (he had been sick) he spoke well but I felt I was getting a tape-recorded message and at the end he said, 'Tanya, isn't it?' I laughed a little cynical ironic laugh so I am no longer overawed. He doesn't like to listen, only talk. On last Sunday he preached. He just told stories, not any meaning, any point!! I like him but I used to like him much more.

5 February 1987
It's so hard. I just had a huge fight with Mum and I can't listen to Thunder Road and I miss him so much. God, will I ever survive this? I'm so alone. I try to remind myself of all my blessings but it's so hard when you're alone.

12 March 1987
I'm so fat and I have no boyfriend. I can't live without it. It hurts

me so much. It kills me. I almost regret my actions. I'm going crazy and I can't hear anything from God, I miss it so much. I try so hard to be good. Oh God help me, I'm going crazy.

3 July 1987
Tomorrow is independence day and 6 months since I got my freedom. I am fasting from 4 today till tomorrow sometime. With independence comes turmoil, and I've been through turmoil but I thank God (regardless of the doubts that filter thru my dusty mind) for my freedom. I don't have doubts actually—I have ripples and blank feelings that can't be placed. I don't know what God is doing to me but I will see it through.

22 July 1987
You know I look around at everyone getting on with their lives and I stay at home. I am nearly 16 and I'm not living!! God won't talk to me. He's letting Satan attack me like never before with doubts and fears.

Commit your way to the Lord
Trust in Him and He will do this:
He will make your righteousness shine like the dawn
The justice of your cause like the noonday sun
Be still before the Lord and wait patiently for Him.

Sat, 14 November 1987
I thought I'd write so that I can look back and say remember when? Satan has been whispering things to me for a year that cause seeds of doubt to grow. He hurts me and tells me Jesus isn't real and I'm not going to heaven. Well I don't believe him and I won't believe him but it's been hell.

I was talking to Geoff Bullock and I said how I used to love the concerts and he said 'I used to play in the concerts' and I said I'd always stayed away from heavy metal because I was afraid. He said, 'You have more power than the devil.' How true, through Jesus I have more power than the devil.

Sun, 15 November 1987
Thank God for my church. Today we started multiple services in the morning. We went to the 8.30 one. Then at 6 church started and we sang and Brian spoke on meeting Jesus face to face and Satan was upsetting me telling me I wouldn't be there. About 15 or 20 people came forward and Brian said, 'This woman lost 2 sons in an accident 2 weeks ago.' I started to cry a little. Then he said, 'There are some people here who are under condemnation and the devil is telling them that they aren't good enough etc. and it's not true,' so they went forward and he said 'Anyone out there lift up your hands and receive from the Holy Spirit,' and my hands shot up and I started crying and crying. There was so much hurt in me and I feel so much lighter now. I didn't cry loudly then I was talking to Egan and she asked me what was wrong and then I really started and Evelyn came up to hug me and Julia and Jodie even talked nicely to me. R came up and said, do you know the Lord loves you? I don't know if he knew I was crying but they're so nice. He said, 'I think of this one as a daughter.' I love these people so much I can't tell you.

Brian even said, I've seen people still around the church weeping and it's so beautiful so beautiful is this part of the body of Christ that I can't put it down on paper.

17 July 1987
Jodie asked to come to church and Nicole was coming so I prayed and fasted heaps, like huge amounts, they backed out!

Church was perfect for them. Pat preached, Darlene sang. Anyway, they'll come next week. Pat wanted to pray for people and he named those 4 and then he was calling out for people who need to realise God's grace and then people who don't like themselves and I was crying because they would have got saved for sure and Pat sees and says, 'Tanya, I want you out here.' He prayed that God would see me through his eyes or something and that God would grant me the desires of my heart.

John King came up and prayed that the mantle of healing and

the anointing of God would fall on me and held my hands and said to receive healing in my hands and said that God had not created me without a purpose and that healing would not fall short of me and I just worshipped God for ages at the front. Life is incredible. I don't understand some of the things God does but I accept them.

Chapter 5

REASON TO BELIEVE

> It was, for a long time, in spite of—or, not inconceivably, because of—the shabbiness of my motives, my only sustenance, my meat and drink. I rushed home from school, to the church, to the altar, to be alone there, to commune with Jesus, my dearest Friend, who would never fail me, who knew all the secrets of my heart. Perhaps He did, but I didn't, and the bargain that was struck, actually, down there at the foot of the cross, was that He would never let me find out.
>
> He failed His bargain. He was a much better Man than I took Him for.
>
> —James Baldwin, *The Fire Next Time* (1963)

Believing is beautiful. To know that every mountain range, every sunset, every laugh from a child, every moment of peace was created by the God that you know as your personal Saviour is everything beautiful wrapped into one. Daunting, sure, but beautiful. The world is the Lord's and everything in it. Jesus, his only Son, is my best friend.

To know that, regardless of your standard of work, the boss will never sack you is an ultimate relief. That he has cast your sins into the seas of his forgetfulness, as it says in Isaiah. That whatever took place during the day, or during your life, as long as you are repentant, God will forgive you. The best father in the world, and the closest person to your heart.

It's nice to know you're clean in an unclean world. That you are on the side of light and not darkness, heaven and not hell, and you're someone who isn't diseased with their sin, but cleansed and purified, old man dead, brand-new man comes alive. I knew it was gory that Jesus had already sacrificed his blood to get me cleaned up, but I figured it was a one-off event, and he had already been sitting at the right hand of God for around 2000 years, so it wasn't all my fault he got hurt.

It never occurred to me then that I hadn't asked anyone to go through all that for me. I was just relieved that I was on the winning team.

It's comforting to know that every morning when you wake up, God knows what's in store and that he has already worked out his perfect plan for your redeemed life. To know that as long as you do your best, and do it according to how you think he would want you to, you can't fail.

I'd always liked Jesus. He talked in riddles but kept it simple. The challenge of the message to me was the anti-bourgeois paradoxes. Put yourself last, and you get to be first. Pray for your enemy. Repay evil with good. Give when people ask. Imagine if we did these things. What would happen if we all just kept giving to each other and worked diligently never to exploit each other or let another be hurt? I never got over the homeless I had seen sitting on the subway grates on Fifth Avenue when I was ten, and couldn't figure out why we had starving people when we had plenty of planes and food.

Plus, there was all that drama. With the backdrop of lepers, and adulteresses, and demons, and women who wouldn't stop bleeding, it was a compelling way of thinking, speaking and acting. We didn't need soap operas. We had the bible.

And with Pentecostalism, there is so much more drama. You never knew when someone might have an explosive gift of the Spirit, a Word from the Lord, a moment, an insight, a healing. We were drama junkies, and deep down we knew it. The bigger the performance, the more God must be here right now.

For me, the signs and wonders didn't cause or help my faith. The demon expulsions, the tongues, the healings, the great 'coincidences' generally had little impact on my belief in God. Much later, I clung to them for longer than anything else, hoping that nothing would explain them away and I could then prove God's existence by default. They were terrifying, of course, for where the Spirit of the Lord is, there is liberty. Sometimes, a little too much. It is a celebration for the saints when an evil spirit leaves, or when a brother or sister receives the baptism of tongues. To see God move in such ways, if falling and shouting and writhing on the floor was moving, can be horrifying and sobering. Not that which you can relay on Monday morning when people ask about your weekend. Just enough to scare you into believing whatever it was you were doubting.

Believing is beautiful in so many ways. I remember it clearly, so personally, intimately, privately that no one else could ever imagine.

No, none of those miracles or revelations you hear about matter in the end. In the places we don't talk about, for me, it was the moments that me and Jesus created together. It was the secret times that I loved the most. When everything in my world was quiet and I could be alone with God.

It was in solitude that I sought God. When there was no other influence, no distraction, no contamination, then I knew I would find him. Whether or not I indeed found God is nobody's business. Whatever I discovered, the understanding, the deals, the pleas, the questions and the answers in whatever forms they revealed themselves, were as close to *it* as I would ever, and may well ever, get.

Believing is lovely. It is gentle and warm, and strong and fearless, and exciting and hopeful. It is reassuring and healing. It is rhyme and reason. It is family and faith. Loving your neighbour is a fantastic postmodern plan for peace. It was about helping the poor because we can and generally being nice to people and not getting upset if they aren't nice back. It was licence to do good, and if people rip you off, well, you were doing what Jesus would have you do. If they killed you for it, then so be it.

It was a life worth dying for. And one to be grateful for every day.

I loved believing. I wondered, as we all did, how other people lived without God. Imagine having the chance to believe and not believing!

We were proud to belong to Jesus. In any case, you have to be. Jesus said not to be like Peter, who denied his teacher quicker than you can say Mel Gibson. 'If you deny me in front of men,' Jesus said, 'I will deny you in front of the Father.' This is why fundamentalist Christians tell everyone they can, as often as they can, just to be on the safe side.

So I floated around high school, knowing that nothing really mattered. Nothing. Why be afraid of those who kill the body but cannot kill the soul? Rather be afraid of the One who can destroy both soul and body in hell. I was not ashamed of the gospel of his name, and since through Christ all things are possible, let my opinions flow loudly.

You see, as long as you are doing the right thing, as long as you are seeking first the kingdom of God, then all these things will be added unto you. Why would I care whether stupid, unsaved boys liked me—after all, I couldn't be unequally yoked with those unbelievers. For what does light have in common with darkness? It would mean only misery and heartache and immorality, and that would take me further away from Jesus, the one who loved me, died for me, and would have died for me even if I'd been the only person on the planet.

Pagans, pagans everywhere, and some of them really hot, but pagans nonetheless.

So mainly I walked around doctrinally convinced that I was going to heaven whenever this exercise called life was over, which was undoubtedly soon. The nuclear explosion at Chernobyl in 1986 had poisoned thousands of Ukrainians and since, as Brian explained, Chernobyl means wormwood (it actually means black grass or stalks), Revelation 8 was coming true before our eyes. 'A great star, blazing like a torch, fell from the sky on a third of the rivers and on the springs of water. The name of the star is Wormwood. A third of the waters turned bitter and many people died from the waters that had become bitter.' We were in the end times. Jesus was coming back by 2000, if we even had that long.

Testimonies of the old life from new Christians were always fun. The more depraved the story, the sweeter the salvation. It was the only time we got to hear about the big bad world with its sex and drugs and rock'n'roll lifestyle. Demon manifestations always got a good response.

There was a guy who Jewels and I used to call 'Rats in his Eyes' because his testimony was so full of filth and debauchery that we were sure he'd told one part where rats were coming out of his eyes.

While the others turned away from stories of perversity with good middle-class horror, I wanted to know more. Why did I feel so sad for their stories? Why did the recounting of the horror of sin make me empathise and envy all at once?

I was more interested in what led them to the Before, rather than the After. Everyone else was celebrating the happily-ever-after scene, when the prince and the princess get married. I wanted to hear more about what they were doing before they met. But I knew that was wrong so I suppressed the questions. I would help make the world a better place, once and for all. While I was alive, I was going to improve the world for Jesus.

My weekdays were spent undermining the system in whatever small ways I could justify, because I was never able to have any respect for authority. Not unless it was Christian authority and could be backed by the bible. Romans says that all authority has been established by God. So I might obey school rules, but it doesn't mean I respect them. I know the God who put you there in the first place, you unrepentant heathen.

I would pray every morning. In my last two years of high school I did what I had been taught to do, à la the Word of Faith movement. The backbone of Pentecostalism: select a bible verse and make it your own. Name it and claim it. I selected a verse, Proverbs 16:3: 'Commit to the Lord whatever you do, and your plans will succeed.' I had been taught that if you follow the formula, the outcome *has* to follow.

I had the final two years of school to achieve university entrance. I would be diligent, faithful and obedient. Couldn't lose.

So I committed to God every morning—my life, my day and 'whatever I did'—and I knew this, combined with my rigorous study, of course, would cause my 'plans to succeed'. I would be the lawyer I had wanted to be since I was eleven.

I worked hard at school and, because of my parents' focus on my education from an early age along with a relatively peaceful home life and a drive to succeed, it wasn't too painful. I would come home from school and get on with study. I had to keep my part of the formula.

Believing is beautiful, but it can also be painful. I spent hours reading the bible and praying. Sometimes it was good, and sometimes traumatic. I know what it's like to ache for someone's salvation, to beg the Lord to show them the light. There were so many kids in school around me whose problems I didn't understand. How could I? I lived in a sheltered Christian world. But I could see their pain. And when they befriended me, they told me about it. And I had no idea. I had no idea what to say or do.

All I knew was that if they found Jesus they too could forget their worries, be healed and have a hope and a future like I did. I prayed and I prayed and I prayed. And I did what Pastor Brian said and I invited them to church. And I prayed and prayed, I prayed in English and I prayed in tongues, for them, not for me, I had it all, I had the joy of the Lord as my strength, I had salvation, redemption, forgiveness and baptism in the Holy Ghost. The only way I could do anything for the kids around me was to pray for them, talk with them if they asked me and dare them to come to church.

Some of them did. And some of them got saved. Some of them said no, though I'd fasted, I'd prayed in secret, I had asked the

Lord, I had bound the devil, and Jesus said whatever is bound on earth *will be bound in heaven*, and I had asked God to get them to go with me and they had said they would and then sometimes they suddenly said no.

Believing hurts. When Christians cry for their unsaved friends and family, I remember their pain. I remember it, like watching someone dying in front of you; you know that they are going to the flames of hell and there's nothing you can do.

Christians are not condescending, not the genuine ones. They just want you to have what they have, the free gift of salvation. They don't mean to treat most of the world like they're the minority, it's just the way it is, in their Truth. In fact, if it were true that fundamentalist Christianity was the only way to heaven, around eighty per cent of the world is going to hell, as have the majority of people who ever lived. But, as my mother used to say, he's God, he can do what he likes.

Not believing is horrible. They say no one wakes up one morning and decides to be an alcoholic. No Christian chooses to be an unbeliever.

Not believing eats away at you like a long, slow death. A crumbling erosion that starts subtly like a change in the weather and it ends like an avalanche before the mountain falls down as well.

Maybe it's like finding out you're adopted. Only Satan is your birthmother. Maybe it's like waking up to a loveless marriage. I don't know. All I know is that no one, no one, no one was there, when I prayed and I pleaded and I beseeched the Lord to hear my cry and make me feel like I could believe.

It's degenerative and, in Christian terms, it's eternally fatal. But it starts with just a twitch.

One morning in church when I was sixteen, I looked around and saw a young man with his arms outstretched, singing in tongues to the Lord. Before I knew it, I thought, 'He's talking rubbish.' (I had noticed this before. Sometimes tongues consists of 'ba ba ba ba ba ba ba ba ba ba ba ba'.)

'Leave me alone, Satan,' I thought to the devil. Quickly

putting on the helmet of salvation from the full armour of God, I instantly defended my mind. I looked around and saw a room of pretenders. Oh God, help me, he's in, get him out of my head. But he didn't budge.

There I was in a room full of the most beautiful people in the world, my family, my church, the individuals, the groups who loved me, pastored me, watched over me and protected me from Evil, and there I was inviting the devil in with Doubt.

I went home and the agony began.

Not believing is psychotic. To lose Jesus is to lose everything. To think about losing Jesus is terrifying. To have your mind overtaking what your entire world has been about is a fate I thought would be way worse than death. They had warned us about it, and here it was happening to me.

Not believing is like going into your bedroom and looking in your mirror, only it's a funny mirror now. It's warped and you can't see what you're supposed to, what everybody else is still seeing. So you look in other mirrors and they're all the same. No turning back.

There's no telling anyone. What? Tell a church leader you doubt God, but that you didn't ask for any of this? Tell your parents you're worried that it's slipping, slipping, that the room full of funny mirrors is spinning and you can't stop it whatever you do? Not a chance.

I had been a nerd Christian for so long. I was a nerd to the letter of the law, confidently looking forward to an adulthood of nerdy Christianity. So why me? Why now?

I spent hours and nights trying to count down all my sins. Why? Why! Why was Satan attacking me like this? I went to church as much as I could. I went more than ever.

Why couldn't I be like the Christian girls at school? They were Anglicans, most of them. No tongues, no miracles, no hot sweaty nights, no prayers for revival. Just nice quiet girls who were good at English, who didn't know the urgency of evangelism or, if they did, weren't fussed by it. Why didn't Satan plague them?

Was it my rebellious spirit? Why did I want to taste and smell and know?

I prayed. I begged God and I envied the apostle Paul, for Paul was only tormented three times, and then he was taken to the third heaven and given a special message. When would it stop? The thorn in his side went. Mine was twisting and fermenting.

I had faith. I knew that the men of the Old and New Testaments had been put to much worse tests than this—from Abraham nearly sacrificing his son right up to John being exiled to the Greek isle of Patmos where Revelation was written. Crucified upside down, we were told.

I believed that God would stand by his Word. We'd been taught he has to. God is faithful; he will not let you be tempted beyond what you can bear. But when you are tempted, he will also provide a way out so that you can stand up under it. So I waited. I read my bible, prayed, fasted, and I believed in the power of God to get me out of this place. There had to be a way.

I committed everything I did to the Lord. I never went over the speed limit. Any slight lapse in character and I prayed for hours. I gave as much as I could, and devoted myself to study. Getting into uni was the key. Once I was a lawyer, then people would know who Jesus was and I would have proof of him for myself.

And since boys didn't like me at school, or at church, I didn't have all that much temptation to fight off. Which gave me more time to work. I pitied my friends who cried themselves through wasted study nights about boys who did or didn't call. I had a destiny and a future.

Not believing is something I never wanted to do. I had told Jewels to stop me if I ever backslid. I prayed to God to keep me straight. I did everything I could think of, and I was the most sinless, boring (if smart-mouthed and irritating) kid you knew. My life was as close to without sin as I could possibly make it and I was going as close to insane as I had ever feared.

The HSC was, in 1989, largely a case of memory. Going over material was no problem for me. I went over the bible and my textbooks again and again and again. I was going to leave no stone unturned in either of my quests.

I was also a nerd among the kids at Hills with my constant questions. I couldn't explain to them what I was going through. The best the pastors could offer me was to smile, and suggest bible college. The other kids went out places. I found staying home and going to Hills was safest. Going anywhere else took away from study time and in reality would only introduce more opportunity for sin, which I was full of from my plagued head anyway. If I was serious about committing to God, I knew I had to do my part. If you don't, we had been cautioned, God can't do his part. That's how the Word of Faith formula works.

Not believing is something I wouldn't wish on my worst enemy. It was the reason I believed I should never have children. Why would I wish this no-win situation on an innocent being? Living a regular life, but staring at eternity every time you closed your eyes? I was too scared of going straight to hell, so I never made any suicide attempt. But, like Freddie Mercury said, I sometimes wished I'd never been born at all.

Of course, at the time, none of this mental instability or depression seemed important, comparatively. Missionaries suffer constantly, are brutally tortured for their faith and a number die every day, that figure depending on who's preaching. Who was I to question like this? You think men of the bible didn't doubt? Fix yourself up and move on.

Then Madonna arrived in the middle of 1989. I had been nearly three years without buying albums, listening to the radio or having anything to do with secular music. It had been an interesting time with quite a puritanical mindset, and it had been relaxing not to have pop beats going round and round in my head, but I still longed for my Bruce. I had missed 1987's *Tunnel of Love* completely.

Just before final exams, I crumbled. I bought the 'Cherish' single. I listened to it over and over. Even the Anglican girls at school were listening to Madonna. I couldn't hold out any more.

By the time I was sitting for Economics I had nothing else in my brain. It was like after any broken diet—the floodgates crashed in. I had purged all those years. Now it was time to binge. No turning back.

The syrupy lyrics of Madonna had a honeying effect on my brain; that harmless, familiar, reliable beat and those happy lyrics soothed me like my dummy and blanket had when I was two. In 1989, there was no mindless Christian pop. If you wanted repetitive meaningless music, you had to seek it out there in the world.

Thus, armed with two years of godly hard work and commitment, and a joyful return to 4/4 music, exams went swimmingly. Even my insatiable dissatisfaction was exhausted. I had done all I could do, surely, God. Surely my plans would succeed.

Chapter 6

SYMPATHY FOR THE DEVIL

> How you have fallen from heaven, O morning star, son of the dawn! You have been cast down to the earth, you who once laid low the nations! You said in your heart, 'I will ascend to heaven; I will raise my throne above the stars of God; I will sit enthroned on the mount of assembly, on the utmost heights of the sacred mountain. I will ascend above the tops of the clouds; I will make myself like the Most High.' But you are brought down to the grave to the depths of the pit.
>
> —Isaiah 14:12–14

> You believe that there is one God. Good! Even the demons believe that—and shudder.
>
> —James 2:19

I am running away from the school hall. I had gone out to get some air but I find myself running onto the ovals, somewhere, anywhere, away. I am crying but I don't know why. It is too much to encounter, too much to process. I am running away from something that I know will never ever go away and towards nothing but somewhere else.

The problem was that it was the closest example of Pentecostal reality I have ever had. There were no stage bands. No blond people. There was an old preacher, Derek Prince, but he was more of a bible teacher. He was speaking about the realities of demons, and with his simple, quiet English accent he had required the small gathering of a hundred or so people to denounce the devil by speaking a verse from a Psalm. 'I shall not die, but live and declare the works of the Lord.'

The congregation, made up of mainly elderly ladies and gentlemen, obediently repeated the verse in unison. They had not spoken it twice before I heard a howling in the back of the room, like wind in a tunnel.

'Do not be worried,' assured the teacher, Brother Derek. 'That's just the spirit of death leaving.'

I see elderly women fall back on their chairs, writhe on the floor and foam at the mouth. I watch as people line up on the school assembly stage and their legs grow out to be even where one had been longer than the other. I look around at these respectable people. There was no room for showmanship. No lights, no drums. Just grandmothers spasming on the floor. I can find no reasonable explanation.

So I go outside for a while just to think and then I am crying and running and crying and running. My dad says he remembers the impact that day had on me. He thinks maybe that's what put me off going to church. The problem is it's one of the only things that still disturb me. In all my exploration of Christianity, I had never seen anything more real.

*

Growing up, we knew that demons were everywhere. Jesus Christ, of course, had been a proficient exorcist, efficient and swift. In the eighties, demons were behind every tree. The excesses of the times drew moralistic evangelists to their ostentatious displays, like public hangings, each preacher lining up to be the executioner. Nowadays, the American Baptists haven't let us down—www.godhatesfags.com—but the prettiest churches don't talk about demons. They prefer the word 'spirit', because it sounds more like they're life coaches than missionaries.

For those who didn't grow up around exorcisms, the story runs roughly like this. God made Lucifer, the most beautiful and high up angel of them all. Then Lucifer decided he wanted to be God. So God threw him out of heaven and he became Satan, forever to be punished for his grandiosity.

This begets the age-old question of *why* God *why* did you make Lucifer if you knew what he was going to do? Hillsong will tell you that God can't do anything wrong by you. All bad things come from the 'Enemy'. God is good, Jesus is fun.

This is a slight problem if you're a fundamentalist Christian and you believe the whole bible, not just the cool bits. In Psalms 78:49, God judged Israel 'by sending evil angels among them'. In Judges 9:23, 'God sent an evil spirit between Abimelech and the men of Shechem'. In 1 Kings 22:22, God sent a 'lying spirit' in the mouth of the false prophets to send Ahab to his death. The Lord himself made Pharaoh's heart hard and Satan personally entered the heart of Judas at showtime. Then of course there was King Saul, tormented by an evil spirit sent from the Lord. No one's safe.

At the time of his attempted coup, however, Lucifer managed to get a third of the regular angels onside and they were cast out with him into hell.

The rebellion didn't stop there. There were some who had come down from heaven, quite early on in Genesis, and mated with the prettiest girls, explaining why we have giants in the world. Lucifer had already been dealt with, though, when history began with Adam and Eve. Lucifer, now known as Satan, first appears in the bible with them.

According to fundamentalists, angels are men. There are no babies playing harps on clouds. They are plain-clothes men, who turn up inconspicuously to help you or surround you invisibly and protect you. Unlike their former colleagues the demons, they neither oppress you (live around you) or possess you (live inside you) or even control you (make you do what you don't want to). They're just passive good guys, like Tom Hanks. Or, if you grow up in a Jewish South African fundamentalist Christian home, they're God's servants, created to do our bidding.

Demons, on the other hand, who used to be angels, seem to have a lot more power and certainly get ten times the attention from the pulpit. These days they tend to be referred to as 'spiritual attack', but that's just a nice way of saying demons. Back in the Iron Maiden eighties they were Satan's servants.

Satan is only one being and can only be in one place at one time. He prowls the earth, the bible says, looking to kill, steal and destroy. He doesn't turn up in person very often, though. He usually sends his demons to do his work.

My home church Hills didn't do much public demon casting out, but the stories abounded. Some kids from youth group would go into the city to hand out sandwiches to homeless people and come back with stories of places they had been, where vases flew around rooms. 'You could just feel the demons,' they would say.

Some of the streetkids started coming to church, although they seemed to return to the world after not too long. One girl told me that she had had seven demons cast out of her when she got saved. 'I know this stuff is real,' she told me, 'I used to be heavily into the occult. I could knock you over from the other side of the room by looking at you.' That was enough to scare me. This was a girl who was from out there in the world.

We never did exorcisms at Hills, except by accident, at the end of an emotional service. Demon activity usually happened at some secondary event. At a youth rally, a drug addict might have demons come out. Maybe in a prayer group, or at counselling. No one doubted it.

Demons don't have fixed names any more than their counterpart angels do. They don't have a set job description except to get souls to hell. And any way they can do it, they will. Which is why you have to be so careful.

In the eighties, the spirit of rock'n'roll was ripping the nation apart, or that's how we understood it. Although my own clash with this specific spirit (who I believe looks like Steve Tyler from Aerosmith) occurred somewhat independently of the program,

Pat Mesiti was at that time travelling around the country and going on television making bonfires of albums. It was a spiritual battle he was fighting. He played records backwards, and we heard proof that playing Queen's 'Bohemian Rhapsody' this way revealed the words 'it's fun to smoke marijuana'.

Pat has since renounced this misbehaviour. He thinks he was being silly. All of this hoo-ha was before Hills became Hillsong, and the demons of the beat were found to be profitable. Demons that make you rich and famous get to stay, in Jesus's name.

Now, getting possessed doesn't just happen to you, and for Pentecostals, who are baptised in the Holy Spirit, you would think it impossible. Yet I never heard any of the girls at school talk about any exorcisms they had seen up the road at St Matt's. Pentecostals love demon wrestling.

Of course, just like everything else, it's your fault you've got demons. If you're not saved, then you belong to Satan anyway, so he's allowed to do what he wants with you. You live in your own filth by your choice, so don't come crying to me when life doesn't come up roses. The wages of sin is death. You're lucky to be reading this if you're unsaved. You people have demons like dandruff.

For saved people, it's different. They have been forgiven and made new. Jesus won over Satan on the cross and demons have to leave you alone. However, they will try. Who can blame them? They appear to work on some sort of commission as well, since I was told they hang out at hospitals, cemeteries and heavy metal concerts. It's best to stay home.

There are two ways they can get you: either you've brought it on yourself, or it's an inherited problem.

Deliberate sin can bring in demons because rebellion is like the sin of witchcraft. So to disobey your husband or to rob God of his tithe is to step outside your spiritual protection. We can't help you if you're going to choose the road to hell.

Involvement in the occult will guarantee you demons since that's practically begging them to come over. What, you may ask, is the occult? Anything with foreign gods, not just Satan. Christians, I have always known, should have nothing to do with ouija boards, tarot cards, astronomy, astrology, palm reading, rebirthing, tea-leaf reading, mediums, psychics, runes, naturopathy, acupuncture, iridology or incense. And there are many, many more. As an aside, taking drugs will instantly open your mind as a demon playground, though only illegal drugs will do this. Valium's fine.

If someone in your family did any of these things, it may be that you are suffering because of this heritage. It is important to renounce any of the above involvements, as well as Freemasonry, Scientology, yoga, meditation, hypnotherapy and anything else you can think of. The general rule is to go back three generations, to be safe, and renounce everything those people did.

How do you know if someone has demons, or if you yourself might have picked a couple up? Simple. Demons will either oppress you externally or possess you internally. The demon will cause the object of its attack to be unable to stop a certain behaviour. The violent offender, the incurable drug addict, the chain smoker, the adulterer: they may be dealing with the spirits of violence, drugs, nicotine and lust, respectively. Demons don't have names, but they will find you at your weak spot and work on you there. Scared yet? I was.

The person with demons will do their utmost to stop their behaviour. They will pray, fast, read their bible. They will be honest with those close to them. They will attend programs and counselling and still find themselves doing the same thing over. There seems to be nothing they can do to change. That's because it's a spiritual battle, a bondage that needs to be broken.

Luckily, Jesus gave all his charges the authority to cast out demons, so anyone can do it. Home exorcisms are not a problem. Satan has been defeated and his demons have to go. Once you have identified that someone has a demon, you too can get it out.

Demons should be commanded to leave in the name of Jesus, because they tremble at that name. They don't always go quietly.

I'm told that the demons that come out of Maori people in New Zealand can take days to leave. Curiously, I'm told the same thing about African-American people too. In fact, anyone who also comes from a non-Christian country is bound to have demons. Africans practise voodoo, Hindus worship many gods, and the list goes on. If you're going to come here to our nice clean white church, we don't want your foreign gods coming with you.

Souvenirs can also bring you demons, while we're on the subject. If you've been to one of these godless nations and brought home some totem or carving that worships one of their gods, you're in big trouble too. It may just sit nicely on the dresser, but Derek Prince's wife Ruth got a set of severe migraines that wouldn't go away until she got rid of a headscarf she'd been wearing from one of these evil places. You have to be vigilant.

With the world at war, and the horrific stories we hear on the news every day, you might think there'd be a list of demons so long now it would be hard to name them all. This does not seem to be the case.

The most popular demon for the last ten years or so is the demon of homosexuality. It is a difficult one to expel.

Tell the demon in a very firm voice to leave. Say, I command you, you spirit of homosexuality, to leave in the name of Jesus. After that, wait.

The response that is most hoped for is a violent one. After all, it's a big deal and demons are nasty. They may yell back at you in another language or voice. Don't be deterred. Coughing, choking, writhing, heavy breathing, spinning around the room, you name it, it's proof the demon's gone, once the person settles down again.

If nothing happens, further prayer is required. And more intense prayer, often louder. Pushier. You tell that demon to leave. It doesn't want to. You have to make it.

The demon of homosexuality takes three to four hours to leave, give or take an hour. Tales are told of people changing voices, changing character and generally being weird while the demon wrestles with its host. The more entrenched the behaviour, the longer it might take to get rid of the demon. Not that this happened in the bible, it's just the way things are now.

This happened to Michael, whose Italian mother was bitterly disappointed that she would have no grandchildren. She twisted the pastor's arm and, for three or four hours, they prayed and interceded over Michael and his tortured soul. Eventually, Michael concedes, he did hyperventilate a bit, and slip onto the floor. He's also got epilepsy so that didn't help.

After it was over Michael felt better, and tried to keep on the straight and narrow. After some months, he found his mind wandering back to those thoughts again.

Michael had three exorcisms. Eventually the pastor told him there was nothing more he could do. The demons were clearly gone. It was Michael who was allowing these thoughts to go on.

I myself have never been exorcised, although several people have made some lazy attempts. I think they didn't know what to name the beings inside me that made them so uncomfortable and nobody had the time to fight with these things. I remain unexorcised. Or spirited. Depends what side you're sitting on.

Chapter 7

INTO TEMPTATION

He said, 'My name is Love.'
Then straight the first did turn himself to me
And cried, 'He lieth, for his name is Shame,
But I am Love, and I was wont to be
Alone in this fair garden, till he came
Unasked by night; I am true Love, I fill
The hearts of boy and girl with mutual flame.'
Then sighing, said the other, 'Have thy will,
I am the love that dare not speak its name.'

— Lord Alfred Douglas, 'Two Loves' (1894)

I'd like to say I eventually stopped going to church because I found a higher ground. I'd love to be self-righteous and say I left due to my principles, but the obvious erosion of so many of them would make that a joke too.

I, like so many others, in the most uneventful and non-spectacular way, left because the love of a human being outside the walls blew away the love I thought I'd had inside the walls.

My parents were tired by the time I finished high school. Supportive and loving as they were, I had worn them down over the years. At least I managed to spare them the morbid idea that God was a joke being played on all of us, because that would have broken their hearts. Rather, I spent my time debating with them, arguing over the details of life, straining to exert intellectual independence, emotional freedom of choice and to get out of wherever it was we were living. I had moved every few years of my life, and I now live with an inbuilt travelling bug that causes me to want to wander shortly after I settle somewhere.

The northwest districts of Sydney have gone gangbusters since those days, particularly since Hillsong and friends moved in. They are, in my experience, some of the most Siberian suburbs in Sydney. In the endless acres of housing developments, there are buses that seem to cruise by every few days. If you don't drive, you don't leave. There's no beach and no bush. I have no idea why so many people want to live there. In my teenage years I thought I might simply cease to exist in the nothingness of Cherrybrook if I didn't keep alert. It is a sound beyond that of silence; it is how snow-blindness feels.

I had to get away. I had been such a good girl. I had done all the right things as best I could. And I deserved to go out and play.

It was tradition in 1989 for a frightening majority of kids from New South Wales to go to Surfers Paradise in Queensland for a week of 'partying' after the HSC was finished. Some of the cool kids had started to tolerate my weird personality in a positive way, and there was room for me at late notice.

I went in for the kill. I put my foot down. I told Fred and Elaine that I should go and that there was no evidence to suggest that I shouldn't be able to go away for a week *like everybody else* and not come back dead or possessed, since I was actually old enough to vote.

I don't remember exactly how I did it, and some people may wonder why I didn't just go regardless. Well, biblically, I had to honour and obey my parents. I couldn't go to Surfers without their consent or I would be stepping outside of God's will and I would be hit by a bus by lunchtime. The only way around this was to break their will, slowly, torturously, and without mercy. That way, once they said yes, there would be one less deliberate sin next to my name in the Lamb's Book of Life on Judgement Day.

It had been a long eighteen years living with me. Maybe they knew they weren't getting out of this one easy and cut their losses.

Finally, I was granted my technicality. They weren't going to disown me if I went and, giving some indication of consent which I took as blessing, I ran off to pack.

The minute the train left for Queensland, I became a different person. My mother believed for a long time that had she not relented, things could have turned out differently for me. I knew for a fact, one I couldn't articulate, that I had to go away. I know for a fact now that if I hadn't, something more violently explosive might have happened as I chewed away at my cocoon. It was just as well that it was some girls from high school and not a bikie gang. In short, my raw naïveté forced me to depend on the kindness of strangers, and while the majority of people could see me a mile coming, most of the strangers didn't take me for too great a ride. Lucky for me. Sassy but green is a dangerous combination.

Nineteen eighty-nine was still back in the good old days when there were smoking carriages. Nearly everyone we knew piled into that carriage and we met a whole bunch of people we didn't. The difference between smoking and non-smoking carriages was night and day. The smokers were playing guitar and singing. The non-smokers seemed to be spending all of their time restraining themselves from breaking into cross-stitch. The smokers had better-looking people having a better time, and smokers are still much more fun.

There's something I forgot to mention: my holiday was only to last for ten days. I was simply taking a holiday from my life, not changing it. It was the first of December and we were booked for six nights at the backpackers in Surfers, then I was going with a couple of girls to Great Keppel Island for a few more days. And then straight back home to normal life.

I left without any doubt that it would be good to get away from all the stress of the previous two years, get away from my parents and hang out with my friends, stay up late, have my mother not know where I was and smoke as many cigarettes as I wanted. Then, I would come home, open my exam results three weeks later and find out when (not if, when, please God, when?) I started law school. The rest of my life would be history.

So it wouldn't matter to smoke. It was only for a week. I loved smoking. My grandmother's sitting room had been littered with chain-smoking aunties who were a hundred years old in the shade, and cared nothing for talk of tumours. They sipped their sherries and demanded someone find them an ashtray. The room stank and no one noticed.

I got myself a full pack for Surfers Paradise. I was amazed after we arrived that I needed another one after a day. Cigarettes were $2.80. I bought more of them. For everyone.

For five nights and days, I wandered around the Gold Coast with the seasoned smokers from school. I slept almost not at all. I had never been anywhere by myself and I was not going to miss a moment. I didn't want to drink with them. Alcohol has only ever made me sleepy. During the night we went clubbing, and during the day we went shopping and to the beach. It was mild, really mild. We kissed boys, we went swimming at night, they drank and smoked, I smoked. And I didn't have to go home.

You're supposed to go to church when you're somewhere else, but there was no chance of that happening. I told myself that even though I was deliberately sinning by not paying attention to my Christian imperatives, it was likely I would survive and be able to do a collective repentance when I got back to Sydney. It would make for a change. Instead of the same old boring daily chitchat God and I had been involved in, where I asked the same questions and he gave the same responses, maybe it would be novel to take a whole bunch of sins back and work on an entire episode rather than the singular, often fleeting moments I repented of every day. I asked God what he thought of this over a cigarette but knew that my very insubordination was enough to have me struck down. So I got on with my adventure.

By the sixth night, I was ready for something new. The girls had found a little more fun in drinking than I did, and clearly it made them somewhat sleepy as well. I found this tedious. They planned to go on that Friday night to a nuts and bolts party where people pair up according to whatever tag they get.

I decided to go it alone. Six days away from home, and I was feeling like a bit of a natural. The big bad terrible world had turned out to be not as menacing as I had been warned. Rather than treacherous animals, the boys had turned out to be dopey, and the girls were friendly. Strangers were as much fun as I had secretly imagined. Everyone was actually way too interested in themselves to set upon and lure me into their evil ways. You get guaranteed all your life that the minute you step outside the Kingdom, evil men and wicked women will corrupt you and defile you before the light changes to green. Promises, promises.

I was feeling a lot less contaminated than expected and a lot less guilty. Intellectually, though, I knew it wasn't going to be long before I had to face God and explain what exactly I had been thinking and doing. That, however, was still a week away.

I wandered around on my own by the beach that afternoon and then hung out with some guys back at the hostel who were playing cards. I had made up my mind to stay out on my own that night, and meet up with the girls after their party was over at about midnight. So when the sun started going down and the boys wanted to buy alcohol, I tagged along.

I don't remember much more of that night. I know I drank a bottle of champagne. I know that somewhere in the night one of those boys, Roger, and I made out. I found out the next day that after their party, the girls had had an intervention with one of our gang who was outed as an anorexic. She had walked out on all of them, explaining what they could do with their interventions. There was drama everywhere. I was due to leave for Great Keppel. And I really liked the boy.

He walked with me down the street that afternoon and held my hand, like he was proud of me. Like I was a regular girl. I knew I liked him in the sunshine as well as the night, but I didn't think much of giving him my phone number. He was, after all, an atheist, and something that happened on holiday.

I was exhausted by the time we got to Great Keppel Island. It was exquisite and magical but I hadn't slept in days. We met a bunch of new people and they were great, but I was tired. And I was starting to wonder whether Roger would call me. I missed him. That was silly, of course. He was due to self-destruct like a *Mission Impossible* tape in five days. Still, I was sort of yearning.

I got home from the top of Australia and slept for a day. When I woke up, everything looked the same and felt the same. It was good to be back. My parents were relieved I hadn't been shot with any of the devil's poison arrows and I'd even picked up a little colour, so I looked healthy enough.

A few days later, Roger called. He was working behind the counter in a bottle shop and liked having a full-time job. He wanted to go out with me. I wanted to go out with him. We were together for two years.

A couple of weeks after that, my HSC exam results arrived. I scored higher than I had thought I needed to do my course. It was a week later that the real shock came. Both of my applications for law school had been rejected. I had missed out by five points.

I sat like Moses outside the Promised Land. I knew it was my fault. I had chosen flesh over spirit. I had not fought. I had sinned and sinned some more. I had reaped what I had sown. All of that work and I had blown it on schoolies week, right when God was guiding the HSC markers' hands and minds. Like Moses, I had wandered around and around in the stinking hot desert. And just as everyone else was hearing how it was full of milk and honey, one act of pride and I die on the mountain outside the city walls. It seemed it couldn't end any other way. I got what I deserved.

On a multitude of levels I was baffled. It still didn't make sense that the formula hadn't worked. I had combined the ingredients, followed the instructions, and my soufflé had risen and then collapsed.

These triple-tested, can't-fail recipes needed to be quadruply tested, it appeared. The bible works for everyone else but me. Their soufflés rise the first time.

I had been over it thoroughly. Commit to the Lord whatever you do and your plans will succeed. I had placed emphasis on each word, and examined all possible meanings. I had scrupulously, obsessively scrubbed every nook and cranny of my not-so-dusty heart and I had made every choice, up until Surfers, with the utmost of care.

Had I missed out on law school and my future as the attorney-general because of a few packets of cigarettes and kissing a boy who didn't love Jesus? Had God let go of me after all we'd been through because of schoolies? Why not? He'd dumped Moses for less.

I am an original test case for the 'name it and claim it' movement. We had heard so many stories of people who pinned photos of cars on their fridges, or made a list of the perfect spouse, and God had delivered to them their details. All I wanted was a lousy law degree. I wanted to fight for justice. Why didn't my plans succeed? I now had no idea what to do with my life. So I did what every directionless reject does and signed up for an Arts degree.

By that time it was mid-January and I was deeply, heavily in love.

Roger was an Irish atheist from Sydney's inner city. His parents divorced when he was twelve and he lived with his mother, who managed a supermarket. They were proudly working class, and Roger had no academic aspirations at all. He boasted of how he and his friends had gone out all night before exams. None of these things meant anything to me. He was lovely. And he was lovely to me.

The boys at Hills were looking for a wife, and found me immediately wanting. I had had so little to do with them because of that, although social occasions sometimes let me get near enough to have a closer view of the men of our future. I couldn't see anything.

I thought I did have a lot to offer someone if they weren't looking for a housemaid. As a Jewish South African princess, I can't cook or clean properly. And, as Joan Rivers says, I don't exercise—if God had wanted me to bend over he would have put diamonds on the floor. But this boy didn't want a helper or a companion. He wanted to be with me, exactly the way I was. He didn't see my sin. He saw me. I couldn't see me, and wondered what he was looking at.

I fell in love with him in the purest and simplest way. I have always been a cynic, but I had brought with me a heart that was a blank slate when it came to romance. I had harboured serious crushes on boys I could never have, and suddenly here in front of me was a live one. School was over. This was a real boyfriend.

We were never supposed to be serious, of course. He was supposed to be a trial boyfriend, before I got the one that God had waiting around the corner. I also knew that by not trusting God and waiting I was wrecking my chances of meeting him.

He was such a nice guy, though, and we got on so well. We were like playmates. We had a lot of fun together, we laughed a lot, and we went to places I'd never been before. Was it wrong to love him? He was obviously a test of my faith. He didn't seem sent by Satan, but there was no way he'd been sent by God. Only the fool has said in his heart there is no God. But he was so good to me and so easy to be around.

Roger, as it turned out, had no issues with my religion despite my self-destruction over his lack thereof. He was impressed and intrigued that I had unusually high standards for an eighteen-year-old and had no intention of compromising them.

I announced clearly that there was going to be no sex and Roger had no problem with that, which only severely confused matters. We had been taught that men were sex-hungry creatures and that women had to laughingly accept it. Young girls weren't sexual; they were merely responsible for whether or not their relationships turned sexual, young men being the way nature made them. Why then was this atheist bound for hell treating me so much better than the Christian boys had been treating my Christian girlfriends?

I gave up. I loved it in his arms. I loved the touch of his skin, his kiss, and the way it felt when he held me. For a long time it was enough for both of us. My heart opened up to him in a way I didn't understand, nor did I care to. For the few hours I spent with him every weekend, there was peace inside me. Something finally felt right, natural, and I was no longer all by myself.

We spent hours on the phone every night. We talked and talked about our worlds. We got very close, but I faced a no-win dilemma. My conscience gnawed at me constantly. I hadn't returned to the normal life I'd told myself I would; I was now in deeper trouble. Within a month, only an act of God would have pried me away from him. How was this going to be resolved? It *had* to go one way or another. So I ended it.

When you're going to be a virgin until you get married, you automatically block out anything to do with sexuality because it's useless information. Suddenly, here I was having feelings that I had expected to wait a very long time for. Only months before meeting Roger, I had known I would have to wait for some compatible Christian to arrive, fall in love with me, me fall in love with him, date, recognise each other as the one, go through the planning of a wedding, get dressed up, go to Port Macquarie on honeymoon and then get feelings like these. It was years away. Now I had myself a man.

It seemed after a while, four months to be exact, that it was ridiculous not to have sex. I loved him. Nothing about him made me feel bad. His love made me feel good. And since I had already made my booking for hell, I may as well check in.

I knew that once my virginity was gone, I was useless in my old community. Used goods. All Christian boys deserve a virgin on their wedding day. It is an essential dowry. I knew I was disqualifying myself from the competition back at Hills. Anything other than virgin is slut. And as for the idea that you chose sex willingly? Even worse. That's about as attractive as twice-divorced with six kids. We knew there were girls who had been seduced by boys and lived a lifetime of regret. Even if they did eventually find someone understanding, it was never 'the same'. Most of these girls wondered what they had been thinking.

I knew exactly what I was thinking.

I announced there was going to be sex. Roger agreed. And while I had no idea what this process would involve or what all the talk was about, I knew it had to be taken care of. Fence-sitting gets very painful. If I was going to hell, I was going to have a good time. Or at least find out what a good time was. The pleasure of sin lasts for a season, so let's see how long that season lasts. I have a knack for stretching things out beyond anything reasonable.

I no longer had any proof of either of the worlds I now knew. Roger never pressured me at all for sex, but he did pressure me to use logic and common sense over emotion. He did not hesitate to explain that the Old Testament was a storybook, and that the New Testament was a method of social control. I found his lack of fear amazing. Having lived a life based on detailed and programmed fears, I couldn't relate to his disregard for the Almighty. I knew he had never known God, but he also held no interest in meeting him, despite my protests. He wasn't disturbed by it. He had little time for it. I was fascinated and worried. He made a lot of sense, but the god of this age had blinded his mind. Listening to him was akin to walking in the counsel of the wicked. Come out from every unclean thing!

The disposal of my hymen coincided with the disposal of my commitment to the cause. It was something I refused to repent for. I told God that I was sorry I couldn't repent but that I would rather be truthful than break promises. In any case, he would have known I was lying if I had promised to change, so there seemed no way around it.

During so much of my time at Hills I was a doubter. When I was at church, it was mainly okay. But when I wasn't there, my mind was at war. I had been sincere. Deeply disturbed, but sincere.

After the door to sex opened, I was a hypocrite. There was now tangible sin in my life to address. Finally. I had something to make me understand why I was being punished. I had done a lot of time—at least now I had a crime to go with it.

In church I watched my friend's ex-boyfriend tilt back and raise his hands to God like he was an Old Testament prophet, straining with his eyes shut to see his Creator. Nobody imagined that he was the reason my friend was so distressed and her body so wrecked from countless morning-after pills. He hadn't missed a beat. He looked just as holy.

I couldn't be like him. I couldn't purposely go out and do something and then play that role. It would be ridiculous. I'd rather be held up in the main marketplace as the lowest of sinners than pretend to be something I'm not.

I had enrolled in Biblical Studies at uni. There, I heard lecturers talk of the bible as a book; not the divine word of God, just a text like any other. The blatant inconsistencies were acknowledged. No one was taking it in any way seriously. Telling people Jesus was alive was like reporting your recent Elvis sighting. It was the sort of thing best kept to oneself.

For me, it was getting all too much again. I never turned my back on God and went running into the warm embrace of Satan. I didn't renounce. I simply stepped aside. If God was real, he would reclaim me. I had fought long enough to remind him I was there. If he wasn't real then, essentially, nothing would change. In any case, I hadn't heard from him in so long, I'd stopped making a place for him at the table. I wished he'd had the guts to fire me, but he refused to take my calls. I never quit being a Christian. I just stopped showing up to work.

NINA

> The feminist agenda is not about equal rights for women. It is about a socialist, anti-family political movement that encourages women to leave their husbands, kill their children, practise witchcraft, destroy capitalism and become lesbians.
>
> —Pat Robertson, quoted in 'Equal rights initiative in Iowa attacked', *Washington Post*, 23 August 1992

She sat in that massive lecture hall with an orange and blue and white scarf around her dark brown bob. She was eating an apple with the ferocity of Eve and reading *Sense and Sensibility* the same way. I was stunned. Neither Austen nor winter fruit has that effect on me. The room was crowded, first year Literature. I had had more than enough English by that stage but didn't know what other subject to take. Neither it appeared did the other 1500 Arts students wandering around Sydney Uni in 1990. Nor did any of us appear to care. Hundreds of barely adult nomads crammed in, latecomers sitting in the aisles, wondering where and who they were.

She left *Sense and Sensibility* behind. I was unable to relate to the specifics of her passion, *Pride and Prejudice* having been compulsory study the year before. To each her own. I picked the book up and carried it around until I next spotted this needle in the haystack of first years.

Two weeks later, there she was. Picking up things and carrying them around until they become spontaneously useful is a skill I developed playing computer games. This was no exception. Nina was very grateful to have her book back.

My newly birthed interest in feminism bonded us immediately. After high school, Nina had chosen to do an English language degree merely for the love of it. She was accompanied by her partner in life, Alex, who, while not quite as brilliant as Nina, was equally passionate about English literature.

But these were tough times for Nina and Alex. He had developed a penchant for a stranger and dramatically left his childhood sweetheart. We would approach those English lectures strategically, so that she could spy on him incognito.

Nina took me to her shared terrace house in Glebe where she lived happily and independently away from home. Her mother had died when she was a baby, and she had been raised by her wonderful father and stepmother. She was always gracious, modest to the point of secrecy, kind, generous and open. She was a vegetarian, and gave me couscous and tofu. She waitressed to help pay the rent and she studied harder than I've ever seen anyone study. And she was breathtakingly brilliant. The kind of mind you can't ever hope to have, but you can hope to be around.

She showed me feminism. She was passionate and determined. She said words like rape and period and hymen as though they were words that we were allowed to say, just like any others. Her feminism was extreme, when I look back on it, and for that I am eternally grateful. This little fundamentalist was hardly going to be attracted to a merely middle of the road version of events. I liked the things she said. The feminism that I developed for myself was never about men at all. It was about the quality of life for women. It was about justice, choice, acceptance and merit. The school of thought I had come from was about rivalry, marriageability and willingness to work to the male vision. We talked and we talked and we talked. And I grew sharply in my understanding. It was Nina who explained sociology to me; I couldn't understand what the lecturers were saying.

I had come from a thinking of black and white. It took years to train my mind to allow for the flexibility that most concepts, when examined with any sophistication, require, and to think three-dimensionally outside of the unerring Word of God, which commanded two-dimensional obedience. I have seen fundamentalist kids go on to real world universities and colleges and learn in precisely the same style that they were taught in church. Good and evil, right and wrong, black and white. It doesn't allow for much original thought. Maybe it sounds like a great idea to be the best doctor for Jesus, but it means you end up practising only one kind of medicine.

Nina was spiritual, much more spiritual than I felt, and seemingly much more rewarded. She never really defined herself, but she meditated and performed benign rituals of freezing notes, or burning candles and writing poetry. She dreamed dreams and saw visions. And she practised the rituals and beliefs of the native Americans. She read animal cards. When a spider came to live in her shower for three days she left it there, careful not to disturb the energy of creativity that spiders are said to bring.

I was stunned. I had never experienced anything like this before. She wasn't simply dabbling in the occult as a naïve teenager; she was begging for demons. She was not only refusing her salvation, she was blatantly pursuing pagan rites. And here was the hard part: she was repeatedly successful. Why, I could never understand. Why would God bless her like this, on her way to hell, worshipping idols? I knew the gifts of God were without repentance, and that the pleasure of her sin would last only for a season and that season may even be her whole life but still, I couldn't work it out. Was I to wait for her fall?

The worst part was that despite her denial of the Lord Jesus she was so much happier than I was. Even though she faced each day without God's hand on her life, she was carrying on unconcerned. Her life seemed so normal for her, so real, that I could not imagine her undertaking the confession, repentance and discipleship that were necessary for happiness.

Nina had hard times, too. She grieved the loss of her boyfriend, argued with her parents, and had to move house when the lease expired. But instead of being led by the Holy Spirit to the house where she felt God wanted her to be in his perfect will, she arranged the whole thing under the guidance of her dead mother. She made a list of her requirements and conjured up Natalie, who wasted little time in directing her straight to the house she had asked for. Including a bath with legs. To my incredulous brain, it seemed awfully similar to a technique I had watched all my life. I found it impossible to argue against her success. If we shall know them by their fruits, what the hell do we make of the heathen with orchards full?

For the first time in my life, I was forced to accept that someone was happy without Jesus. Even if the devil was appearing to Nina as an angel of light, deceiving her with false spirits, it sure looked like a much easier cross to bear. I knew of course that this was how Satan makes sin appear. He makes it look so appealing, normal even, and that's the trick behind it. He's clever, that Satan. He knows your weak points. That's why he puts certain people in your path, to lead you astray, to steal your truth, rob you of your salvation and destroy your life. But Nina taught me more in a month than five years of night church had, and there was no choice. I could no longer take seriously my private insistence that she was miserable in some subconscious and perversely secret way, and that any day now they'd find nothing but a pile of salt. Worse still, my faith was beginning to bore me senseless, like an invalid relative that I no longer wished to visit. Hers was dynamic, personal, individual and, even more shocking, self-defined. She saved so much time by being indifferent to the amazing grace that wretches like me depended on.

It was in her authenticity, her struggles, her determination and her passion that I learned inspiration. I had never known any other way to be inspired than by leaders and ideas we'd been told to be inspired by. But this came out of nowhere and, like all those other greedy curiosities, snowballed. Imagine if one day I could be like Nina, think freely without guilt, and be brave enough to risk the wrath of God by doing what seemed right to me regardless of what the bible said. And feel good about it.

But I knew that was the sound of the devil following me to uni. I knew I had let him in, and that I had to pay for it. After I dropped out in first year to get married, Nina carried on to do an honours and then a PhD thesis and is now a professor at a major university.

Chapter 8

IT'S HARD TO BE A SAINT IN THE CITY

> If we deliberately keep on sinning after we have received the knowledge of the truth, no sacrifice for sins is left, but only a fearful expectation of judgement and of raging fire that will consume the enemies of God.
>
> Anyone who rejected the law of Moses died without mercy on the testimony of two or three witnesses.
>
> How much more severely do you think a man deserves to be punished who has trampled the Son of God underfoot, who has treated as an unholy thing the blood of the covenant that sanctified him, and who has insulted the Spirit of grace?
>
> For we know him who said, 'It is mine to avenge; I will repay' and again, 'The Lord will judge his people.' It is a dreadful thing to fall into the hands of the living God.
>
> —Hebrews 10:26–31

By the time I had unpacked, the marriage was over. These were the days before prosperity theology. In 1991, a girl had only one meaningful dowry in the Christian Life Centres, and I had left mine somewhere in Sydney's southwest. Who the fifty shekels were supposed to go to I'm not sure, but I had little choice except to follow him who had purchased me. I was long since tainted goods.

So I left my family, who felt I had left them anyway the day I boarded the train to Surfers Paradise. I formally quit my Arts degree after a year and a half at Sydney University, which only brought my attendance down by one day a month but was a lot cheaper. I left my part-time job showering old people in nursing homes, which had been the most practical experience I'd ever had in the real world. I left my cat and my room and all my friends and married Roger, my first boyfriend, who had just joined the army and was about to be posted. The registry office at Births, Deaths and Marriages was half empty on a Monday afternoon. My mother wore black. My father chuckled uncomfortably the way one does at vaudeville and checked his watch. In 1991, I was a June bride.

My career as a military wife was short-lived, and for that I think there may be a god. Adelaide is a beautiful city, but two nineteen-year-olds woke up there one morning and realised they were married to each other, and that one of them was in the army. Five months after the $200 wedding (including petrol, flowers and beers following), I only had one institution to disentangle myself from.

I tried to be brave for the budgie, Rosalita, as my dad drove the two of us home from the airport that post-marriage Saturday afternoon, telling me it was a good time to move on. He didn't understand I was history—or was I? At twenty I had done everything a Christian girl was apparently capable of doing. I'd been married. Now what? It was pure excitement stomped on by the knowledge of my own futility. There is a path that seems right to men, but in the end it leads to death.

The next afternoon, I found Jewels at the house where she was living. She was nannying for a pastor and his family and, while we were kicking around, the doorbell rang. In came Brian and Bobbie, who lived around the corner.

'Hello,' they greeted me. 'Where have you been?'

Having not felt particularly missed since I'd left, I knew then that caring was not their forte. Still, in 1991, they were my family's clergy. I decided to roll the pastoral dice for them one more time.

'Well,' I looked at them both, wishing I didn't have to explain, 'I got married to my boyfriend, who I loved very much, because he joined the army and we got posted to Adelaide and then we had a big fight and he told me he didn't love me, and then we broke up and now I'm back in Sydney with nothing.'

They looked at me like deer in the headlights, said 'oh', and meandered into the other room. Nothing. Not a 'Sorry for your loss' or 'That's too bad, we'll set you up with someone from bible college'. Nothing. And thus, no longer the property of my father or my husband or of any use to the church, I was sort of free again.

Having sold my soul for freedom, and having waited so long for the opportunity, I was determined to get every penny's worth. My choices had stunned me more than they had the people around me. I knew that I would have bet my life not long before that none of these things would ever, *could* ever happen. I would not have let them. And yet, here I was on the broad path, trudging with all the others, on the road to Destruction.

My twenties, or the 1990s as they are more commonly known, were more like Alice's trip to Wonderland. Having leapt through the looking glass, I found myself drinking tea with some very queer folk.

The research shows that I was a textbook case for the children who emerge from highly restrictive thought-control groups and cults. All I knew was that even though I could no longer claim born-again freak status, I was still a freak. I didn't know any of the rules of the new game. And this time, I had no excuse for not fitting in with the heathen. I was now one of them, but they still didn't know what to make of me. And I was clueless.

So I emerged into the outside world like a wombat into a nightclub, socially autistic and loving every minute of it. Having secured a full-time job washing old people again, I moved out to a terrace in Paddington and it was downhill from thereon.

In the early days, I was still heavily time-disoriented. I had grown up knowing that the Rapture could come at any minute. Since there were 2000 years from Adam to Moses, and 2000 years from Moses to Jesus, we knew there would be 2000 years until the Rapture when, after a trumpet call from the skies, all Christians get caught up in a cloud in the twinkling of an eye.

Two men will be working in the field and one will disappear. Which is why evangelical Christians should not be given driver's licences.

My ten-day post-HSC holiday extended on for ten years, but I deeply, deeply believed that God was going to get me one day. The Christians kept telling me and I knew it was true. What he was going to do with me, I had no idea. But I could always hear the clock ticking. I was terrified and I stayed terrified.

When you are working in the end-times framework, planning is difficult. It feels like you have a terminal illness for Jesus. I had never expected to see the end of school, or to be around long enough to get married and have children. Why were we spending our days studying, working, if Jesus was due any minute? It seemed for most of my life like nothing mattered and everything mattered at the same time.

Having lived under a clock that possibly had only seconds left, I was fascinated by people who were able to project five or ten years into the future. Even though I didn't go to church, it was obvious what was happening around us was still straight out of the book of Revelation. The move to a one-world economy, a cashless society, barcodes, microchips. One of the greatest hopes the devil has is for you not to believe in him. Yet you can't help but see his work.

Boundaries are not something that are in the Christian vocabulary. I had grown up being dared, challenged and ignited into evangelising the world. We heard countless glorious testimonies about chance meetings that changed futures. And as God is not a lover of men, I didn't believe I was supposed to have favourites either. Status and wealth means nothing to a true believer. It can't get them into heaven. We were never supposed to be afraid of heads of government or corporations. They were a soul for Jesus like everyone else, and meeting one of us might be the only opportunity they got to hear the gospel. I'll talk to anyone, any time. And that, in itself, explains almost all of the trouble I got into in my twenties.

The brave new world did not come with an instruction manual the way the scared old world had. I debuted with no other way of making decisions. Freefalling, I clung to the bible for as long as I could with horrific results. We had been told the bible would work no matter what, no matter where. It was not to be.

This world I had entered contained so many problems that the bible had never mentioned. If you know that God's hand is *off* your life, how do you know what choices to make? How do you choose your future if you're not consulting the one who created it, the one who wants to 'prosper you', not to harm you, who has plans to give you hope and a future? I seemed ridiculous to myself and I trudged on.

I was and remain unable to stop being curious about other people's lives. My life had turned out to be a huge surprise party filled with eternal pain. I could no longer justify holding anybody's life against them, either. There I was, offspring that fundamentalist parents longed for, mutated into a Christian horror movie. I couldn't explain how it had happened and I was convinced that other people had stories to tell as well. I wanted to know them all. I wanted to know why they were the way they were, and where they thought they were going when they died.

But the book is never enough for me, no. I have to see the movie. And then, I have to step into the scene. I have to breathe the air. I can't just do as the Romans, I have to become a Roman. Only then, it seems, am I satisfied with what the Romans were saying in the first place.

I was detoxed to a great extent from poisonous Christianity by the Salvation Army.

Realising I was now unemployable outside of nursing homes, I resigned myself to going back to 'study'. This time I wanted a job title. The course content of Social Work sounded like me, although I had no idea what it involved. At twenty-one I started uni again and, three and a half years later, I answered an ad for welfare workers in a women's refuge that asked for an understanding of Christian principles. Having been raised by the masters, I sold

Christianity to outsiders at that job interview for the first time without selling my integrity. Over the five years that I worked for the Army, I saw gallons of venom drained from my blood stream, eventually leaving only the scar where the Pentecostals had first entered.

There was nothing that these tambourine-wielding Protestants with kind hearts could teach me, I had thought. I knew their stuff and a whole lot more. We do tend to feel rather generous as trained Pentecostals when working with Other Generalised Christians. We know they're blessed to have us around. We smile because they don't even realise it yet.

The only criteria for accommodation at the refuge was being homeless, female and over eighteen years old. It housed an average of 200 women a year for short-term stays, and so I witnessed the Salvation Army work with over 1000 women, as well as the clients from other services. And I saw the Christianity I had always wondered about. Maybe I saw the Christianity that Frank Houston and Andrew Evans had seen in their earlier visions.

And it was there that I saw Grace. There were problems with personalities and power. There were favourites and there were clients and staff who fell through the gaps. There was never enough money for milk and that made it hard sometimes. I read their doctrine and there were no kooky subclauses. They weren't Mormons or Jehovah's Witnesses, they weren't even Seventh Day Adventists, who sit on the Pentecostal periphery as honorary citizens. They weren't at all Catholic. And they weren't dreary like Anglicans, or wishy-washy like the Uniting Church. Some of the Majors were very old, but their musty Christianity was real. It was doctrinally very biblical.

The Salvation Army liked the refuge ladies to be well groomed and not use bad language. They liked things to be just so, and for clients not to lounge around in pyjamas. The women were never asked about sexuality, and the workers hold the girl who comes back crying from the abortion, or from visiting her violent boyfriend, and support her in her choices. And in my dimmest memories of deciding to follow Jesus, I remembered grace being the way of showing God's love without judgement. Nowadays Grace is the Kylie of Hillsong: every family has at least one child with the name, just for good luck.

I watched the Salvos stretch themselves and their aching budgets to manage what the government couldn't or wouldn't, because the Christians will. The wandering mentally ill, the confused battered wife, the repeat-offending junkie, and the people that simply no one loves enough any more.

Without brochures or big screens or breast implants, they were streets ahead of the people I'd been told were the only Winning Team. While Hillsong girls are busying themselves with being a helper/companion, the Salvation Army has ordained women to equal positions with men since its foundation. They have had a policy on the environment and the church's responsibility to the earth God gave them since 1992. In the services they provide, they follow the models of best practice. A Salvation Army officer may not want their pregnant client to proceed with a termination, but service provision comes before evangelism.

They made me feel a lot saner about my social justice mission. Apparently I wasn't the only one who had heard Jesus say we should help people, not just bring them to church.

What made it bittersweet was knowing that they were not going to be willing or able to dull the second blade of my double-edged sword. Clearly Hills had been strange and superficial, but throughout my twenties I didn't have much to do with it. Christianity was stranger, and I was still scared of hell. I knew the Salvos weren't interested in eternal questioning, not when there was soup to be ladled. But the questions had become like pieces of furniture in my mental living room. On the outside I looked, lived and acted not unlike everyone else. On the inside I was coming home to a nagging ex-wife full of complaints about our marriage and reminders of my failings. Maybe the Salvos had the answer. Maybe God was real and palatable in this more true-to-life charity model.

But why make Lucifer? Why make war? Why curse a fig tree for not being in season? And how could I ever hope to rekindle my love for an indefensible text which had stripped me of survival skills?

The nineties were punctuated by technology and globalism. For me, they were a roller-coaster of morbid curiosity and terror-filled guilt, success and failure and living between two regimes, one that didn't want me and the other, the broad path to hell, that made me feel like a fool. And the year 2000 was approaching.

Chapter 9

MONEY CHANGES EVERYTHING

> Every promise in the Book is mine/ Every chapter, every verse, every line/ I'm standing on His Word divine/ Every promise in the Book is mine.
>
> —Pentecostal hymn

Why shouldn't Brian have a mobile phone? Hey, who was I to say he shouldn't? It just seemed weird. He was a pastor, wasn't he, not a businessman, and in those dark days of 1991 almost no one had a mobile phone. It was strange to see Brian with one.

I was at Hills for a baby dedication. It had been more than a while, and my absence had gone from noticeable to presumed. To me, it felt like my disappearance was from God Himself and His Family. I had chosen sin, and surrendered to all my weaknesses. Satan had won, for all intents and purposes. There was unresolved sin in my life, and I was not willing to change it. I knew I was weak, but I was resigned to it. There's an old evangelical question: if Jesus came back tonight, *would you be ready*? I knew I wasn't, so I prayed the Lord would tarry till I figured out what to do with him.

Still, in the early nineties I liked to turn up occasionally at Hills and hope that no one noticed I was unclean. They had never *said* I was unclean. But you can tell you are, and I knew they wondered what kind of a testimony I would bring back when I returned from the world and its depravity, back home to God.

It's amazing how a couple of years can change things. Nearly all the pastors in my teenage years had moustaches. Being a moustache hater, it's something that stays with you. Well, there we were and gone was Brian's broom. It was replaced with a ponytail, just like all the other pastors. I told Jewels it was a Colombian drug dealer look, because they were all starting to go bald at the same time.

There were only a few thousand people at Brian's church. And there he was with a mobile phone. And a ponytail. And a coldness I sensed where he felt one step further away. I assumed it was me; I was the one who had left, after all. I never said Brian can't have a mobile. It's just a moment I had when I knew things were different.

And behind the scenes, things had indeed changed.

Not long before, leadership had decided that paying rent for a building was money down the drain, and with a fast-growing church it was time to be financially solid. Pastor Phil Pringle had been impressed by American Howard Cargill's fundraising presentation to his congregation at Christian City Church and recommended that Brian meet with Cargill. 'You don't make money out of offerings, Brian,' Phil is reported to have said, 'you make it from bible colleges.' Educational institutions, any buildings that are deemed for education, are the ones that get the biggest tax breaks.

I remember the special presentation morning in 1988 where we were told how blessed we were to have this opportunity. With pride, Pastor Brian told us that Hills would pay $50,000 to an American expert who would teach us how to raise funds for the new building. Those were the days when we had visions of filling Sydney's Entertainment Centre, with a capacity of 11,000 people. But no one was going to call us dreamers. Eleven thousand was nothing. Brian wanted to fill football stadiums.

I was only sixteen and not a financial guru, but I did wonder whether $50,000 was a lot of money just to get the guy out here, before they bought any bricks. Still, at sixteen, who was I to question such things? Men who discussed financial planning were surely none of my concern. They must know what they are doing.

As for paying an American to teach them how to get money out of people, well, this also made me wonder. Surely there had to be some decent homegrown boys who could do the same thing. But, more than that, why did we need someone to teach us how to get money out of people? Shouldn't God lead them to give? Again, what would I know?

The campaign was a success, but by the time the building was up and running I was long gone. It was another three years before Brian bought his phone and got rid of that god-awful moustache.

It wasn't the mobile phone that bothered me, per se. It was the change from the feel of pastor to that of chief executive officer. (I even remember thinking, maybe Brian got a mobile so distressed people can call him after hours or when he's away. He is the senior pastor, after all.) As for the Colombian drug dealer look, with the boys in ponytails, I wondered why men in their thirties were growing their hair. Considering their new serious ministerial status, it seemed a bit immature. One pastor later told me that he woke up one morning and said, 'I'm thirty-seven and I have a ponytail.' He cut it off, but suffered a verbal thrashing for 'attempting to change the church's image without permission'.

The metamorphosis had long begun. By the time that phone showed up, Pastor Butch Plumber and his wife Betty, some new American friends of Brian and Bobbie's, had already been in town from the US of A.

Butch and Betty were loaded. Australian AoG eyes and mouths widened with the understanding of the American way. Butch was rich and Betty was sexy and they ran a huge church. Maybe that Salvation Army 'church-mouse-poor' model was too limited. Maybe it did take money to reach souls. Maybe the Americans were on to something.

Brian and Bobbie flew to the US to stay with Butch and Betty. There, Butch introduced them to another pastor, Bayless Conley, and then the Houstons met Casey Treat and his wife, Wendy, who were based in Seattle. Casey was a bike-riding ex-drug user. If Butch was rich, Casey was royal. Even in the days when the

Houstons first met the Treats, Casey had two Mercs and two bikes.

Casey and Brian and Wendy and Bobbie became the very best of friends and they still are. Casey loved Brian, took him out and showed him what life could be like.

When couples are recruited into Amway, they are all treated pretty much the same. An upline couple will take them under their wing, supervise and show them the ropes until they can do it on their own. They are lavished with ostentatiousness. They are shown the way their lives could be, if only they choose to make the cleverest decision of their lives.

Whatever Brian liked, Casey bought him. Money was no object. Casey Treat bought Brian Houston his famous Harley Davidson. When Brian and Bobbie arrived back in Australia from their big trip to America, their staff was shocked. Brian had left in his grey suit with his pink tie, and the couple stepped off the plane looking like they had been shopping on Rodeo Drive. Speaking at Hillsong on 27 January 2003, Brian explained what happened:

See, about 1990, around 1989, 1990, 1991, I went, our church was a much younger church, six, seven, eight years old. It was growing, it was doing good, but really, there was so much more that we, and that I, as a leader, needed to take this church to where I believe God wanted it to go, and I remember specifically sitting in the back of a big pastors' conference in South Africa feeling anonymous and lost but so deeply impacted by what was happening there.

And around that same time, as I remember—I was in South Africa getting impacted at a pastors' conference and Bobbie and I were, y'know, just absolutely mouths open at what God was doing, just so enlarged—and something happened on the inside and around the same time in Seattle I went to a pastors' conference there and it deeply affected and impacted my life in a way that I believe transformed my capacity as a leader, it's a supernatural thing, completely changed it. But you see, if you put no value in who God is then there's no real value in what God does. So you'd probably be more interested in which end of the aeroplane I was sitting in, and believe me, in those days it was that *end whereas these days it's often nearer the middle toward the front, but do you hear what I'm saying?*

I really believe that one of the ways that you know that you know who God is is that you put value on what God does, which is anything of spiritual significance.

Prosperity gospel isn't anything new. It's just since the nineties that it's been really lapped up by a lot of the Western world as a standard part of Christianity. The late eighties were just awful for fundamentalist Christians. Nobody we thought normal had anything to do with the Praise The Lord (PTL) Ministry and Jimmy and Tammy Faye Bakker dramas. They were living extravagant lives and exploiting people shamelessly. It was obviously a very strange type of Christianity to us, with all that TV and make-up on Tammy Faye's face. We were simple suburban Christian folk.

Brian had visited the Reverend Dr Robert Schuller's Crystal Cathedral in Garden Grove, California, years before and had not liked it. He didn't relate to the prosperity gospel. His own parents had lived by God's provision, not by having thousands in the bank. Frank had run a church in one of the most impoverished suburbs in Sydney where the homeless, the sick, the crazy, were all welcome. Frank was a frontline man. The bigger Satan's attack on people's lives, the more they would benefit from the power of God. Frank and Hazel were never about money. They were about winning souls to Christ. Money was something the world demanded. Revival doesn't take place in Schuller's big Babylonian tower. Everybody knew that. Revival starts in people's hearts.

Jimmy Swaggart's fall was hard to digest. What his cousin Jerry Lee Lewis could do on a piano, Jimmy could do with a pulpit. He could work a crowd from one side of the globe to the other. He could make you feel so close to hell and so close to your sinful, blackened heart that you could actually feel the flicker of the flames at your feet. And as wildly as he could expose your sin for the world to see, as well as he could shout at your demons and at you for letting them stay, he could cry. And he could sing. He could lay down his own burden at the cross right before you, and it was common for Jimmy to weep openly about the sweet grace of Jesus.

Jimmy Swaggart wasn't interested in diamond-encrusted kennels like the Bakkers. He was interested in the morality of people's lives, and about having their disgusting heathen hearts washed by the precious blood of our Lord, a saving we never deserved but could spend eternity thanking God for.

He was also interested in cheap nasty prostitutes, it turned out, and quite a number of them. He gave his ultimate life performance sobbing for forgiveness before his congregation as the rest of the world watched on and wondered, as I had started to, if these people were crazy.

Maybe somebody realised that no one was ever going to successfully preach the 'be pure like me' sermon any more if Jimmy couldn't. So the preachers changed the tune halfway through the song. 'Be rich like me' was the new clanging of church bells.

The Word of Faith movement had laid the perfect groundwork for prosperity gospel. It was as simple as ABC, and I don't think they'd planned it at all. Number one, all of the bible is the Word of God and can be taken literally. Number two, you can take any verse of the bible and apply it to your life. Therefore, number three, you can take any verse of the bible and decide that that's the one that counts, not the other ones. And finally, number four, we've been wrong about money all this time, when you look at the verses we can show you here.

Kenneth and Gloria Copeland were keen to share their brand of the health and wealth gospel which they aired on the *Believer's Voice of Victory* every day in Fort Worth, Texas. Ken Copeland had already prophesied over Sydney in 1988 that 'twelve months from today you will look on this city and say one of two things. "We are seeing the grandest outpouring of the Holy Spirit that we have ever seen or how many more disasters can we stand? And it's more up to you than it is to me saith the Lord 'cause I'm ready."'

Whatever happened, the Copelands relocated their Australian office from Sydney to Brisbane in 1995 and ran a conference while they were there, which my parents went to. At the time, I thought it was good for old people to get out in the sun, and I didn't know much about Kenneth and his lovely wife, Gloria, until my mother called me. The Lord wanted me to have a brand-new washing machine, she announced. The Lord, my mother and I all knew how much I needed a washing machine at the time, so there wasn't much argument.

'Funny you should say that,' I told her. 'I think he really wants me to have a car, as well.' When the Lord is speaking to my mother, you never know what might happen. He ended up only wanting me to have a washing machine.

My parents had been to a prosperity conference where they had learned that God wanted them to be wealthy. Jesus had come to give us life in abundance, hadn't he?

Among my friends, my parents were endearingly referred to as Fred and Elaine after the Nile family, who were the high-profile Christian political extremists of the time. No one at uni knew about the tongues or the demons; they thought Christianity was weird enough, especially for a Jew. Then again, when prosperity theology came in and my new washing machine arrived, some kids started wishing their parents would convert.

I didn't know my parents' own church was saturated with the same ideas. I had no idea that the Treats and the Houstons were riding high on the Copeland trail, much as Brian denied the similarities. And I never guessed they could win with that approach. My Year 8 science teacher had told me Jesus was practically a communist. Not any more. Australia was in for a brand-new Jesus, one wearing Gucci loafers where his sandals used to be.

Chapter 10

EIGHT IS ENOUGH

My little boy's father is a gifted artist. Brought up in Sydney's other bible belt, the Sutherland Shire, he was adopted out by his Maori parents as a baby.

I have always had a soft spot for gorgeous Maori boys. They are the greatest diet you can ever go on. All you have to do is stand next to one and you look like Tinkerbell. This one had golden skin, big strong arms when I met him, a giant with a gentle voice and a dusty old Holden ute. It made me feel safe enough to go to dinner and actually eat.

It was during the main course that he told me about his years on Ritalin as a boy, and his off-the-charts IQ score—not things I usually talk about on a date, but he was serious. In any case, it didn't really matter. I'd been very hungry and my chicken caesar salad was extraordinary. He talked about art, and didn't mind how much I ate.

Being a complicated neurotic type, I have always chosen boys who seem simple. Nice Aussie boys who want nothing more than to check the surf. I figure they're so happy, they can make my life simple as well. The problem is that Martin Bryant is the stereotype I end up with. Blond ringlets and psychopathic tendencies.

And, true to form, the easygoing artist ended up having more personalities than Sybil. The twist with this one was that he admitted it. He was surrounded, he insisted, by seven spirits who had taught him his art.

Maybe I should have paid more attention to this than to my salad. Perhaps the signs were there. Anyway, religion must have come up in conversation because after dinner he said, 'I want to take you back to where I live and show you why I believe in God.'

It was a unique pick-up line, I thought. Still, it made a change from 'I just want to hold you' so I decided, with my full belly, that I may as well go to wherever it was he lived. I had never been anywhere near Cronulla so I got in the front of the ute and imagined I was Daisy Duke all the way there.

His house was a million miles away from the city and, as we stomped through his dark back garden to the shed, the novelty of this nonsense spiritual exercise was wearing off. The spirits, he said, gave him dreams. They had taught him to carve. And at the age of twenty-four, having never been to New Zealand, he began to create traditional pieces out of bone and jade and wood. At night the spirits would show him how, and by day he would teach himself.

Finally, he said, the spirits had shown him whalebone on a beach in his dreams. For four months of weekends, he and his ex-wife had driven up and down the coastline until he found eighty kilograms of whalebone washed up. And there it sat in the shed.

The work he showed me was beautiful, but all this spirit talk made me nervous. Weren't they going to hell for voodoo like all the other natives? Was I even safe being around this stuff?

All I remember is that I went to work the next day and I felt that nauseating falling-in-love feeling. A month later, right when the pregnancy test came back positive, I had to move house anyway. I changed my plans suddenly and moved in with him instead.

The spirits, however, were not always noble and they weren't often kind. Matt was terrorised by violent nightmares and would wake up with his spirits yelling at him that he was a failure, threatening him, berating him and humiliating him. It was an unusual predicament. It wasn't something I felt I could chat about at the antenatal classes we attended. I tried my hardest to understand how he saw life and, just when I would get an understanding, one of the spirits would say something to him and I'd be back to square one.

The spirits didn't like me. They made fun of me to him. I wasn't too worried in the beginning. Initially it's difficult to imagine that this is going to be long-term. And I thought that, whatever they were, voices or fragments or imaginary, I could perhaps get them to like me. Maybe if I hung around and they got to know me, they might change their minds. I asked questions about them. It was me, after all, who had invaded their home; maybe I could decorate it to their liking, make some of their favourite snacks. But nothing made them happy. I was not who they would have chosen, he translated. He thought I was beautiful, they said I was ugly. Tell that one to *Cosmopolitan*.

The nightmares were horrible. He slept badly. He was always sick or sleeping, when he wasn't working or wrestling voices. I was also doing a lot of sleeping. I was pregnant, crying and sleeping. My first baby and I had not just a troubled boyfriend but his seven companions as well.

Often, the gentle giant and I got along well. When the spirits went quiet, it was good. But we also spent a lot of time fighting, and he would go to the workshop and carve while I cried and slept. I wanted to run away from all of them, but the crying and the pregnancy made me so so tired. I had to do something.

I hated it, but I had to do it. It was different this time: I was going to have a child. This time it wasn't just me I had to take responsibility for. I hadn't ended up at a really bad after-party; I was inflicting this on someone else.

I had asked him if he wanted the spirits gone. He said that he couldn't remember or in fact imagine life without them. They were as helpful to him creatively as they were debilitating with their torment. I didn't know what to do. He hadn't called them voices. He had called them spirits. This seemed different from mental illness, which I didn't know much about then. He said it was spiritual. I was miserable and scared, and I was wondering whom one goes to to deal with such things. He refused to see a psychiatrist. I figured I had a choice between a dark, incense-filled room in the inner city, or I could go back to familiarity. Were these the wages of my sin? I didn't care any more. I just knew I was stuck, more stuck than I'd ever been, and the baby kept growing bigger.

If Michael Murphy hadn't been the local pastor, I probably couldn't have done it. But Mike, the wonderful Mike and Val, had been heading a large congregation in Sutherland not far from where we lived for years. If I was going to drag myself back to church, it made it so much easier to contemplate with the Murphys there. Surely they would help explain what the hell was going on.

I went into the church and I saw them. Theirs was a much smaller, plainer hall than Hillsong's, much more intimate. I approached the Murphys and told them a bit of the story. I needed some kind of help. Was this a demon thing? I asked. It was my fault I was in this situation, I knew that, but I assumed that demon infestation was something that required immediate action. As an unwed, backslidden mother-to-be, I didn't feel I had the authority to exorcise anyone.

It was 1998. The days of the old church picnic might have been long gone, but I was still seriously naïve. I believed that if they discovered I had evil spirits at my house, then someone would be around right away to get rid of them. This was no reported sighting, or a hunch. I had dobbed in Legion himself because they were many.

But nobody came over to cast out the demons or even for a cup of tea. This distressed Matt, who'd been listening to wonderings out loud I'd been having and was now open to having these spirits addressed. He still wasn't interested in doing it via anti-psychotic medication. The last time he had tried that, the spirits had taken over and suppressed him altogether.

Instead of Pastor Michael or Val's guidance, I was allocated Jeremy, who was some sort of leader at their church. Jeremy was forty-two, recently married to a 21-year-old and had a baby girl. He would call every couple of weeks to check up on me.

Jeremy was going to be it for pastoral care so I kept chatting to him, in case an emergency arose in the future. Maybe if Matt's head actually started spinning they might say something to the demons. I had as much in common with Jeremy as I would with any house brick, and while I knew it wasn't Mike and Val's fault they were busy, I wondered what they'd been thinking.

Since no one did ghostbusting at the church any more, Matt saw about forty spirits in the room when Sam was born, and later relayed that one reached down and with its claw released the cord that was wrapped around our baby's neck. By this time, sleep was my national goal. I hated them. I wanted out. But not before a nap.

Having a baby, especially a first-born son, is a big deal for a Pentecostal Jew with a Maori partner. With some downloaded prayers, my mother and I made sure the *boychik* got a minimal bris in the surgery of the Sutherland medical centre that was prepared to perform the procedure. For me, though, it wasn't enough. I had always liked the idea of the Pentecostal 'baby dedication'. Rather than a formal ceremony where an infant is christened, the fundamentalists teach that water baptism happens by choice following salvation. So they skip the water and pray a prayer that will see the baby born again before you know it. In my frightened newborn mother's logic, I decided better safe than sorry. Instead of leaving him on the foothpath for Satan, dedicating him to God couldn't be such a bad thing.

This would have to take place at Hillsong. It was the only church I knew, even at the age of twenty-eight. Fred and Elaine still attended, having survived the usual judgement reserved for grandparents of illegitimate babies. I felt it was right to do what the Christians do, in the way my parents are Christians.

I got sad and scared. A few days before the dedication I called up Donna, still a pastor, and asked her if my baby could possibly be accepted before God. Of course he could, she told me. Why wouldn't any baby be? Do you think your children are different to mine?

Was I stupid to stand on stage before all those Christians, their knowing that I was a relative whore? She said I was being silly, and was so kind and understanding I decided to enjoy the dedication rather than fear it.

So we traipsed—Matt, Sam, them and me—all the way from the Sutherland Shire to the Hills Shire, from God's country to God's country, and stood on stage next to the other couples each with their bundles of joy, waiting in turn for the blessing. I prayed that the spirits wouldn't go ballistic and embarrass everyone in some unforeseen way. They didn't. They behaved. By chance, Brian was on shift that week, which was great. I'm one of those people that prefers being operated on by the head surgeon, and if my baby was getting handed over to God, if I was putting my hand up for this, I wanted the okay to come from the boss.

Every year, Brian does a hundred thousand baby dedications and faces each couple one by one. When he came to us, he smiled with surprise. He hadn't seen me for a long time.

'Hello,' he said warmly.

'Hello,' I replied nervously.

'Who's this?' he smiled at Sam. We chatted briefly. After he prayed for Sam to have happiness, health and a determination to serve God, Brian gave a hearty Amen. He looked at Matt, whose eyes were black with psychosis and fear, and said, 'May he play rugby for Australia.' Brian smiled at the congregation. He looked back at Matt. 'I mean, New Zealand,' he said and laughed, and my dad and the whole football-loving crowd laughed with him.

I had survived. Sam was safe from hell. I moved out six months later and went back to the Hills district to live near Jewels.

Chapter 11

FREE AT LAST, FREE AT LAST, THANK GOD ALMIGHTY, WE'RE FREE AT LAST

> And if anyone *offends* (Greek, *skandalizo*, to scandalise, to put a stumbling block or impediment in the way upon which another may trip and fall, metaphor to offend, to entice to sin, to cause a person to begin to distrust and desert one whom he ought to trust and obey, to cause to fall away, to cause one to judge unfavourably or unjustly of another) one of these children who believe in me it would be better for him to tie a millstone around his neck and throw himself into the sea.
>
> —Matthew 18:6

A couple of weeks before it was announced at Hillsong, I found out about Pat. I decided to go and watch the proceedings. I figured I could sit through a morning service if there was something of interest at the end. It was a sin of a sexual nature that was to bring him undone, but the details were unclear.

It was around then that I started catching on to the set-up, or so I thought. The way the service is put together. The music that day was particularly hopeful, upbeat, positive. The sermon explicitly laid a foundation.

Pastor Robert Fergusson, from Hillsong in the city, speaks with a lovely Jude Law type of English accent and is very soothing to listen to. He spoke about the events of September 11, and how much fear was now in society. He relayed a scary incident on a plane that he'd been through, and was troubled that this was the world we were living in. It was a confidence-building message, delivered smoothly and generously to an audience of Sienna Millers.

This was interesting, as I had heard the preaching right after 11 September 2001. I went along again back then, wanting to see if Hillsong took a stand, if they would realise the impact of the disaster and reassure the people. They didn't. In those days, of course, Brian Houston did not show the support for Prime Minister Howard, and by extension for his good friend President Bush, that he does now.

It was only in August of 2002 that Robert chose to speak of these things, coinciding with the foreboding announcement of Pat Mesiti's removal. Finally, after nearly a year, I heard what I'd waited to hear. It was going to be all right. We didn't have to worry about a thing. There was no need for fear; God was in control.

Pastor Robert finished and, after a quick song, a smiling Brian took the stage. He complimented his crowd and, before saying goodbye, made a request.

'If you're a part of this church, we'd like you to stay behind for an announcement. If you feel you're part of this church, please stay, otherwise have a great day, because this announcement won't mean much to you.'

I sat very still. I wanted to throw up. I had watched these men over the years, seen their intimate friendships grow, indulged them in their references to each other from the pulpit. When you hear someone's voice over and over for years, you get familiar with the tones. When you listen to public speakers often enough, the sensing of genuine emotion becomes more acute. Having heard so much insincerity, it's clear when people are real. Brian's voice sounded like this was hard and he was sad.

The people who didn't know or didn't care shuffled out, possibly only to kick themselves a few hours later. Then it was quiet. If I wanted to throw up, how was everyone else doing? And where was Pat?

Brian explained that Pat Mesiti, a pastor on the team and one of his oldest friends, had been caught by someone on staff engaging in 'a pattern of immoral behaviour'. Pat recognised the problem and accepted that he should stand down from his role as a pastor, as is standard AoG policy.

Brian turned to a waiting Bobbie and took her hand. 'We want everyone to know that our marriage is still strong,' he said. Who knew what that had to do with the price of fish, but with reassurance and a prayer request for Pat and his family, the big announcement was over.

I didn't know whether to throw up or ask for my money back. If that's public acknowledgement and accountability from the men of God, if that's what caused the emotion in Brian's voice, well, I had not yet begun to feel sick.

Outside the walls, I found it was no different. What happened with Pat? I wanted to know. He'd been friends with my dad, who didn't know and refused to get engaged in the melodrama. And the Hillsong members didn't really care either.

I couldn't understand it—this was Pat. We had followed him as a group on buses to youth rallies, supporting his dream of getting all the young people saved in Australia. He had drawn us to him and kept us close for years. Why hadn't he put his face to this side of his life? This man was running family and marriage seminars. What had he actually done?

It hurt. I felt cheated. One of the supermen just got shot or shot himself and we didn't know why. How's his family, for God's sake? Where were the anecdotes about his relatives? Where was his little nonna now?

'Why do you want to know?' I was asked. 'God's forgiven him. It's none of our business.' How did they know God had forgiven him? Were they there? I was sure he was sorry now. But did his being sorry mean it was none of our business? There had been no coming clean. Why make an announcement unless it's to come clean? Why not just stay dirty? I couldn't figure it out. Why wouldn't they name what he had done? What was 'a pattern of immoral behaviour'? Surely a plain old affair wasn't a pattern? That didn't make sense.

It was a Hillsonger, Saskia, sick of my endless questions, who sent me to Pastor Philip Powell's website, and there I found the answers. On a message board, people were discussing this very issue. Christians themselves were arguing back and forth about what Pat Mesiti could have done and why no one was discussing it.

Soon after, it hit the press. The *Sydney Morning Herald* ran several stories on the million-dollar ministry that had to be shut down. I got more from the *Herald* than from asking people at Hillsong who were there. Prostitutes and phone sex. We never found out who paid for it all.

I investigated a lot more of that site. There were lots of articles about Hillsong. The webmaster, Philip Powell, was a preacher himself who had been on the AoG National Executive until 1992 and had left on principle. He spent the next ten years telling people what he'd seen then and what he now saw in the church.

I had read the article on Frank some time before. The penny just hadn't dropped. A couple of months later, however, I went back to it. This time I mentioned it to Jewels.

'I know I've been away for a while,' I said, 'but I didn't know Frank got in trouble too. How come you never mentioned Frank?' She said that she'd never heard.

Odd. There on the internet in black and white was a lengthy article on the history of the Houston family. The writer suggested that Frank had not moved to Australia on the basis of a vision but to escape disciplinary action after some bad behaviour. It was written there as if it were old news.

Not so. Jewels called her friend Megan to check it out. Megan was Brian's personal assistant. When Jewels called back, she said Megan had told Pastor Brian, who had responded immediately. 'I'm going to resolve this thing this weekend,' he had said.

This sounded like good news. It had been three months since the last scandal. I was ready to sit through another morning service. Time for another trip to Pleasantville.

The message didn't set the stage for what was about to happen. By this time, it seemed, Brian didn't know what sort of foundation to lay. The rumours were that Frank Houston had been involved in paedophilia.

It's not like there wasn't a precedent. Australia had just had an identical scenario unfold in the Anglican Church. After the Archbishop of Brisbane had been appointed governor-general, he faced allegations of failing to act on cases of sexual abuse by church workers.

The public was furious at what had happened and demanded the GG's resignation. The climate had changed. Sex offenders were not the only ones being held accountable in the clergy. It was those in high authority who had looked the other way or kept their secrets who were judged even more cruel.

Brian Houston would have to have been living in a cave to miss the news. The GG was an old friend of the prime minister's, and the revelation was an embarrassment to all concerned, as well as the church. The pre-terrorist witch-hunt for paedophiles had been on for years. Now the public were informed that these weren't isolated incidents: it had taken a broad network of powerful people to cover up the unspeakable acts, first admitted in the Catholic Church and then by the Anglicans.

During that time I was doing a TAFE course on therapy with children who have been sexually assaulted. It was a year-long course, and elaborated on some theories I had covered in social work. Predator and prey. The ongoing preventative research was on the process of grooming, the way in which a predator sets up its prey. Studies with offenders reveal a consistent pattern. A perpetrator can't risk the victim telling someone. A child is thus prepared and groomed. This takes time but perpetrators, who are patient, are willing to wait for years for an opportunity. Often, a perpetrator will set up where children are, at schools or youth groups or in a family role. The child's trust needs to be gained. They are made to feel special, more special than others. They are given gifts, and told they are the favourite.

Gradually, the perpetrator starts introducing new behaviour to confuse the child, who isn't sure whether a touch is accidental or not. Boundaries are eroded so slowly that by the time an act of clear violation takes place the child is too often uncertain, guilty and appreciative of the positive attention to resist. If they do, threats of harm may follow. The perpetrator hopes a child will be too frightened or confused to tell anyone. A single act of abuse can set the dynamic and become familiar, intertwined with love and affection. The prey is caught in a trap set by a much more skilful predator.

Brian Houston stood on stage that day in November 2002 to describe what he later told the press was the hardest time of his life. He also told the media that he had been completely open and honest with his church and had used words like 'predator' and 'sex offender'. That simply didn't happen, at least not on that day. I was sitting still this time, objectively, as it were. I hadn't really known Frank. It was different from the way it had been with Pat. This time I was watching without the same emotion.

Brian began swiftly. 'About two years ago, George Aghajanian received a phone call from someone making some allegations about my father. I did the toughest thing of my life and went around to my father and confronted him. He broke down and confessed that the allegations were true.

'I immediately stepped aside and let the investigators from the National Executive do their job. My father was found guilty of "serious moral failure" and his credentials were taken away from him.' (At this point I was waiting for the punchline, and had a near-irresistible urge to yell out like the boys used to do in the old days, 'What did he DO, Brian?') 'This has devastated my family. We haven't told our daughter yet, but the boys know and they're doing okay. My son came into my room the other night, and he said, "Dad, I still love Jesus."

'You know, my dad loved God. And while he was deeply repentant for the mistakes he had made, it didn't change his love for God.'

Once again, Brian took Bobbie's hand and asked the church to pray for them and for their family, given the ordeal they had just been through.

That was it. The entire congregation responded by giving Brian and Bobbie Houston a standing ovation.

Rather than a huge statement from the pulpit, this was a tiny one. There was no demand for righteousness, no zero tolerance stance on abuse of children. There was no plea for forgiveness from those wronged, no promise that the giant congregation would join together to prevent this from ever happening again. That policies would be put in place so that everyone in leadership understood the signs and their responsibilities.

There wasn't even a naming of the crime, simply an appeal for prayer for the Houstons.

My blood skipped from boiling to mercury. Watching people get had is upsetting at the best of times; watching them applaud a cover-up was heartbreaking. To digest having a paedophile for a patriarch so readily is no mean feat. How do you get people to comply like this?

At exactly the same time as I was furious, I was as peaceful as daybreak. I had never felt so close to God. Hillsong was boasting a 12,000-strong congregation at the time. All I could hear in my head was '12,000 people are wrong and I'm right'. I knew that I understood nothing of God, but that Jesus was nothing like this. And if he was, I didn't want to play at all any more.

I felt little and insignificant. I was out of place. I had not been invited, and yet I was sitting there with the greatest liberation flying through my heart. I felt freer than the whole room put together. I felt born again.

I ran up to my lecturer the next time I saw her. 'Is it possible,' I dared, 'to groom an entire congregation?' There seemed no other way to explain the standing ovation.

'Of course it is,' she answered.

Had Brian done it on purpose? Who knows? Perhaps he had simply learnt at his father's knee how to get trusting people to comply with his demands. Except his father's dynamics had affected individuals. Brian's decisions were to affect multitudes.

HOLD ME, THRILL ME,
KISS ME, KILL ME

Chapter 12

WALK THIS WAY

> When you meet the friendliest people you have ever known, who introduce you to the most loving group of people you've ever encountered, and you find the leader to be the most inspired, caring, compassionate and understanding person you've ever met, and then you learn the cause of the group is something you never dared hope could be accomplished, and all of this sounds too good to be true—it probably is too good to be true! Don't give up your education, your hopes and ambitions to follow a rainbow.
>
> —Jeannie Mills,
> *Six Years with God: life inside Rev. Jim Jones' temple* (1979)

Vilma Ryan didn't feel like she was being recruited. The 68-year-old elder of the Wiradjuri people had seen mission managers come and go. She was working in the Riverstone Aboriginal Community Association (RACA) in Sydney's west when a young Indigenous girl working for Emerge, Hillsong's welfare arm, invited her to their neighbourhood centre.

At the meeting the director of Hillsong Emerge, Leigh Coleman, a welfare worker and Louise Markus (Hillsong member and local MP) were all present. They spoke to Vilma about a joint application for a government grant for RACA. Vilma knew that without Hillsong's name, the association alone could never be awarded a substantial amount.

Through the course of the conversation, Vilma was wary. She remembers continuing to try to find what was behind their enthusiasm. They looked like mission managers, she thought, but maybe they were different. They seemed very understanding.

While talking, Vilma opened up about her daughter, whom she had lost years previously to drugs, leaving behind a young child and a truckload of grief. Still, she didn't trust these strangers. She asked them in a number of ways about their personal ties with the church. How long have you been in Hillsong? How did you get involved in this religion? What has happened in your life to turn you to God?

Vilma says they avoided answering until she confronted them directly. 'I've been upfront with you,' she said. 'Why can't you be upfront with me?'

Leigh Coleman looked nervous. He glanced at Mrs Markus and the Emerge worker. He told Vilma he'd spent time in Kings Cross in the seventies at the same time her daughter was there as a drug user, he presumed. Then he became a Christian and Look at Him Now.

Vilma was surprised by his willingness to discuss these things in front of the others. She felt there was common ground with the new breed of mission manager and thought maybe these ones weren't so bad.

Vilma concedes being impressed by the way the representatives from Emerge treated her and other employees at RACA. They were taken to dinner at the Superdome in Sydney's Olympic Park, but they never talked about God. They didn't force their Christianity down the throat of the Indigenous people. They were much easier to work with than Vilma had anticipated.

The submission for the grant went in after many hours of work with Emerge's professional writer. RACA openly shared its information with its newfound partners. The last Vilma heard was that the application had been unsuccessful. Only weeks later did she find out that a second, very different application, one that RACA knew nothing about, had gained approval. Hillsong's new submission writer used ideas and letters of support without RACA's permission, and competing with seventeen other community groups had received $414,479 in the National Community Crime Prevention Program out of $1,700,000 being allocated. The successful grant contained statements RACA would not have endorsed such as Hillsong Emerge's assertion that the local area was 'overrun by gangs of aboriginal youth'.

When Vilma confronted Leigh Coleman, she says he told her he would write RACA a cheque for $280,000 not to make a fuss. (Hillsong Emerge said later that Coleman promised funds 'as an act of good faith'.) 'I don't sell my soul for $280,000,' Vilma told me. She contacted every media outlet and member of parliament who took an interest. After NSW Labor parliamentarian Ian West supported her plight and the issue was raised in federal parliament, the federal justice minister removed the funding from Hillsong Emerge in February 2006.[1]

RACA ended up with nothing, but Vilma remains undeterred. 'I felt as though I let this white man, Leigh Coleman, into our community and he dudded us, but he did it through me,' she told the *Koori Mail*. Instead of hiding, though, Vilma is committed to preventing Hillsong repeating their mistakes. If it can happen to her, she says, it can happen to anyone.

Vilma's experience is not uncommon. The Moonies are trained in exactly the same way, as are all cult devotees. Recruitment success ultimately depends on the quality of personal interaction with could-be members. The recruiter first learns something about the potential recruit. Then, to demonstrate that they have shared interests, the recruiter mirrors their target's opinions. So, when an invitation to a workshop or a dinner is extended, it seems that the recruiter has something genuine to offer, based on the apparent compatibility of their beliefs or interests.

Recruitment is vital for AoG church survival. The Hillsong church-planting DVD encourages everyone to 'plant a church, plant a church, plant a church' in the same way greenies might tell everyone on earth to plant a tree. The most curious statement is this: 'If we don't plant churches the church will die.' You don't hear the Dalai Lama saying this, but the AoG aren't kidding. Sure there are 18,000 people at Hillsong, but it's unlikely that they're the same 18,000 for very long at all.

The average membership of an AoG church is around two years. The turnover is large and constant. There are also a significant number who stay for around three months before the infatuation dies. The pattern is similar to any love affair. Psychologists have long advised people to refrain from marriage or heavy commitments before two years have elapsed. This is because the 'in love' feeling wears off after time, the neurochemicals stop, and the participants are left with the reality of another human being.

Another myth that abounds in AoG churches like Hillsong is that every seat is being occupied by a brand-new believer, who once was lost but now is found. Instead, the huge volume of attendees is also made up of an unmeasurable number of people who had a Christian upbringing, already know the stories and join Hillsong as a perceived extension of their own beliefs.

In evangelical circles this form of poaching is called 'fleecing the flock'. Youth rallies and healing services are particularly useful in attracting curious strays or disillusioned visitors from mainstream, established churches. In country towns, where competition for pew-sitters is fierce, recruitment from other Christian groups is essential for numbers, growth and any reported success.

'They must be stupid' is the reason given for cult involvement from many on the outside. Only the mentally ill, gullible or lonely would ever find themselves in a cult. Up close, nothing could be further from the truth. Most people are recruited at home by a family member.

Everyone is susceptible to the recruitment techniques of cult members, because cult members are trained to work with everyone. Central to recruitment training is the ability to home in on personality traits and sensitive issues in individuals. Members are generally matched to the demographic that will respond best to their own. Once an individual (or group) is engaged in a conversation with someone who they feel relates to them, they are open to recruitment techniques. Apparently hellfire and damnation as an introduction wasn't having the mass appeal intended. The new fundamentalist Christian is your new best friend. Even before you know they're a Christian! That's because their recruitment techniques are more sophisticated than ever.

Hillsong has literally countless courses, programs and community services currently in place all over Australia and the world. Whatever the shopfront sign says, the doors are open to get the maximum number of customers into the church building that funds it. Once you're in the building, it's much easier to get you saved. Your membership can't be activated until you're born again, but the recruiters don't tell you that initially. They tell you about an art class, or a mothers' group, or a lifestyle course they go to where the people are friendly, particularly to newcomers. This is called 'love bombing' according to cult psychologist Dr Margaret Singer. The flooding of attention, flattery and companionship is not as spontaneous as it seems but is rather a means to smother recruits and new members and to offer them acceptance. As Ian West MP explained in the NSW parliament: 'I am also concerned about some practices at Hillsong in regard to "shining", which is an intense and concerted show of feigned affection by a group of people towards an individual whom they seek to recruit or otherwise influence.'

The people who are the most likely to get into such discussions with strangers are overwhelmingly people who are going through some sort of transitional stage in their life. This is why university evangelism is so strong. Eighteen-year-olds with freedom are often able for the first time to create their own belief systems. The next most common time in which an adult converts is after a relationship breakdown. While anyone can be seduced by a charismatic personality, recruitment is much more probable if you were questioning your own truth anyway.

The black and whites of fundamentalist Christianity make it easily digestible for people who are in any way psychologically disadvantaged. The message is simple, repetitive and emotionally based. Those with alcohol or drug-related brain damage, acquired brain injuries, mental illness, children, the elderly and victims of violence may not have the cognitive functioning required to decipher the simple propaganda they are fed.

Having chronic pain, a terminal illness or a major drug habit can also make it harder to tell what's real. Faith-healing evangelists are predators of a particularly twisted variety. They are well aware of the desperation in their audiences. They know that some people will do anything at all if they believe it will cure them or their sick child, no matter how poverty-stricken they are. God may be their only hope. If God wants proof of their faith, and clearly he does, then they should be willing to show him their sacrifices in dollars.

In Australia, where poverty is not at the crisis rate of America's, we can afford to be more altruistic. We like to think of ourselves as contributors to our community. That participating in a Hillsong group will better the world. As Labor adviser Monika Wheeler said in a speech outlining where the ALP was losing young people to Hillsong, 'One problem that we have is that people who are going to Hillsong services think that they are doing something for society.'

Chapter 13

LAST NIGHT A DJ SAVED MY LIFE

My friends all had their salvation dates written in special pen and special writing in the front of their bibles. That glorious day when they met Jesus for the first time. There was a bit of Christian family snobbery among the teenagers about that, or at least there was for me. You know, with some of them, if they hadn't been in the right place at the right time they would have ended up like the rest of their unsaved family, who are all still going to hell. Not like us from Christian homes, we always were and always will be.

Still, I was kind of jealous. I didn't really know when I had become a Christian. There was no late-night tap on the shoulder, no whisper from heaven, no nothing. I never knew any different. I had nothing to convert from. I had decided to follow Jesus all the way to nursery school and there had been no turning back.

At church, we Christian kids were deemed the most blessed, having never smelt the odour of our own original sin. We had been born to Christian parents and had never known any life other than the abundant one that God had in store for us from the word Go. Not like those kids from broken homes. They were too busy praying for their unsaved step-parents and half-sisters to come to church and leave their fleshly ways behind. I never got saved from anything. With all of my earliest memories come the knowledge that Jesus was Lord, and that the whole world had better know about it.

When somebody tells the story of their conversion, it's called a testimony. And every convert has a testimony, we were told, a story of how Jesus saved them from their horrible old life. As a

Christian kid, I was in a state of constant gratitude for a salvation I couldn't put my finger on. This blurriness wasn't relevant, since we were told that the kids born into Christian homes had a lifetime of knowing God as the best testimony of all. Thus, even though I had no pulled-out-of-the-gutter story to tell, it did make me feel a little like Christian royalty.

Hills Christian Life Centre was all geared towards getting saved. In my day, people would ask if so-and-so was 'saved'. Is her family saved? When did you get saved? This word 'saved' has now been replaced with the more palatable 'churched'. Do they go to church? Are they churched or unchurched? Let's get out there and reach the unchurched of this generation.

Most people are converted when they are between the ages of ten and eighteen, when their values, cognition and decision-making abilities are neither fixed nor independent from their upbringing. They're easy pickings.

The adults are harder, because the older they get the more educated they become. Grown-ups also have life experience that conflicts with Christian doctrine. Most young adults get converted at university, and usually conversions of adults over twenty-five happen to those suffering relationship breakdown. Being grief-stricken is a perfect place to find God.

What is getting saved? Why was that song at Hills 'I'm Saved (S.A.V.E.D.)' such a winner? Because it's the wedding day of Christianity.

If you missed all of the allusions to salvation during the songs, or the message at Hills, or all the references to the difficulties and sadnesses of our unsaved friends and relatives who, for some reason known only to the Lord, continue to resist salvation, you couldn't miss the altar call. It's the grand finale of the meeting. Even if just one unsaved piece of trash repents, the angels in heaven rejoice, and it was worth everyone turning up to church.

I've wondered if maybe I kept leaving university in the last week of semester because I'm inherently frightened of the altar call, for it is down at the altar that God meets you, shakes your hand and pulls you swiftly over the great chasm between heaven and hell. Powerful things happen at the altar.

Believing in Jesus isn't enough. You have to commit to him. You have to get saved from your sin, the universal human condition. This is where the Pentecostals shine, where the boys are separated from the men. The number of salvations—the number of people who put up their hand when the invitation to meet Jesus is given, the number of people who trail down the aisles, down the stairs slowly, hesitant and hopeful, down to the front row to stand by the supportive New Christian pastors—is the equivalent of the number of notches in a gunslinger's belt.

At Hills, you knew when the altar call was coming. I never thought of it as a set-up then, except you knew when the message was over because the preacher would say 'Musicians please', and quietly and steadily, with heads down, the musicians would file back up on stage and play soft elevator music. The preacher would then start the spiel. Almost invariably, it would go like this: 'You know, we've had a great time today, worshipping God, learning about his greatness. We have a good time in this church, we love God, but that's because we can worship freely because we know him as our God. I'd like everyone to bow their heads and close their eyes, just for a minute. Just keep your eyes shut, to give those around you privacy.'

At this point, I would often leave for a bathroom break, to give those around me privacy and to avoid the rush. Having been saved a hundred thousand times in these meetings, it seemed expedient to me to wrap up without going through unnecessary prayers. When I did stick around, though, I wondered about the catch. Everyone was supposed to have their eyes shut for privacy. However, when the preacher said, 'If you'd like to meet Jesus and have him as your personal friend, Lord and Saviour, please raise your hand,' it seemed a bit odd that they would then say, 'Please raise them straight up in the air so the ushers can see them.' Or: 'We've got three on this side, how about some people come meet the Lord on this side of the auditorium? There's no one in the middle section at all wants to get saved today? Come on, people, let's meet Jesus.' There must be laws of spiritual as well as acoustic symmetry in these buildings.

With everyone except the trusted leaders having their eyes shut, all you have to do to get saved, they tell you, is raise your hand to the Lord. But once it went up there was no turning back. I knew inside at a young age that no one had told these people that after they had put their unsuspecting palms heavenward, they were shot ducks. They had a big target on their forehead and there was no going home. Not yet. They didn't know what they were in for, but everyone knew it was for their own good.

Once they put their hands back down, they would be told to 'c'mon down the front'. If they didn't, well, the ushers knew where they were. Now, who wants to go back on a commitment like that, in front of a room full of people? Nobody I ever saw while peeking ever changed their minds on Jesus, especially not when the preacher indicated to the ushers that there were slow movers who needed some encouragement.

And so down they would trail. At youth rallies they walk hand in hand, girls and girls, boys and girls, dudes on their own, groups of them sometimes, hundreds of them all over the stadium, down to the front to rid their young lawless lives of their sinful ways. And to start making a difference in their high school.

You can do it anywhere. You can get saved in a hotel room, flicking through cable TV channels and deciding to try God one last time before you overdose. You can get saved at McDonald's. You may get led to the Lord by your parents, your brother, your best friend, a total stranger. Jesus will meet you wherever you're at, whoever you are—he died for you, all you have to do is ask him into your life. The rest is easy. It's called the Sinner's Prayer and when you pray it, you get the gift of salvation. You get saved. That's when you become a child of God, and you are born again.

There's no better time to get saved than right now, here, tonight, in God's house with his people around you. There's no reason to wait, to spend another day hellbound, without having

Jesus as your best friend. Come on, people, come on down, is there anybody else who wants to meet Jesus? Maybe you used to be a Christian and you want to come back to the Lord. Come back to him. Come home. He's waiting for you. He's been waiting all this time. He never left you and you know he loves you.

At the altar there is weeping and there is repentance. There is salvation. People recount vivid testimonies about what happens at the altar. How a simple prayer changed their whole life.

Chapter 14

WILL YOU MISS ME WHEN YOU'RE SOBER?

I was the last person who wanted to suggest Hillsong was a cult. Me, a wretched backslider, the ultimate example of what Pastor Brian refers to as 'hurt, negative, bitter, with a wounded spirit, lashing out'. Except, every time I checked, I didn't feel any of those things. At all.

No one had assaulted me in my time at Hills. They weren't mean to me. They didn't go out of their way to befriend me, but I had always felt it was me who didn't fit the program. After the Pat and Frank episodes, I knew it was the program, not me.

A psychologist colleague of mine who is a devout Christian called Hillsong a you-know-what ('cult' is a very bad word in the Christian world). She said that the permeation of Hillsong music was dividing her small Anglican congregation. 'If I wanted to go to Hillsong, I'd go to Hillsong,' she vented one day, 'but I don't because it's a cult.' I hadn't said it, she had.

So I dipped an apprehensive toe into the fascinating pool of cult theory to see if any of it was relevant to Hillsong. It was all Hillsong.

Beneath the surface of cult research you find very little difference between the major theorists' conclusions. The researchers agree on all the criteria necessary for an organisation or a group to be considered to have the qualities of a cult, thought-reform program or mind-control system. They just categorise the process differently. One analysis of twelve-step groups, the most famous of which is Alcoholics Anonymous, suggests one hundred different signs, though psychologist Edgar Schein has suggested belief change happens in only three steps: unfreezing, changing, refreezing.

Getting people to change their belief systems and to behave differently than they did before is a lot easier than it appears. There is no need for whips and chains. Psychological control is agreed to be the most powerful force driving any other form of control, such as physical or financial. Possession is nine-tenths of the law.

What all the experts conclude is that there are definitive ways of creating change in human thought, attitudes and the resulting behaviour. Physical disorientation, sleep deprivation, isolation, the inducing of extreme emotional states, particularly guilt and fear, are some of the basic techniques that will weaken mental strength and increase compliance. It works in domestic violence situations, as a primitive torture method, and in cults. It's effective, but it's nothing new.

The only people who disagree with a relatively uniform body of knowledge are those suggesting that adults cannot be manipulated. Adults, it is argued, are responsible and aware of the choices that they make. Journalists report that no one at Hillsong has a gun demanding money. This is true. So what inspires people to devote so much of their time and money to a group so soon after joining? How do you find yourself applauding the senior pastor's cover-up of his father's sexual misuse of the same role and powers? It's actually not hard. Most importantly, whatever you call it, no one who has been brainwashed believes they've been brainwashed.

The Western world first heard the term 'brainwashing' in 1951 from American journalist Edward Hunter. He had learned, via people coming to Hong Kong from China, that the communist process of ridding people of the vestiges of their old belief system was called colloquially *hse nao*, meaning literally 'wash brain' or 'cleansing the mind'. Current mainstream theorists maintain that 'brainwashing' is an extreme event and only takes place in severe circumstances where people who are facing direct physical threat change their beliefs for survival. The notorious kidnapping of heiress Patty Hearst, who later participated in a bank robbery, is one such example. Despite their compliance with brainwashing, the victim knows who is the enemy.

In 1956 psychiatrist Dr Robert Lifton came up with the idea of 'thought reform' after examining how the Koreans changed their political mindset. He looked specifically at how non-violent measures were able to create and sustain brand-new belief systems and behaviours in individuals and communities. He developed eight criteria that, carried out in order and in combination, have been shown to produce measurable thought reform: Milieu Control, Mystical Manipulation, Demand for Purity, Culture of Confession, Sacred Science, Loading the Language, Doctrine over Person and Dispensing of Existence.[1]

Out of all the research, I chose to examine Dr Lifton's eight criteria more closely because he's a forefather, so it's like quoting from the King James Version, Old not New. Many of the more recent theorists based their work on his foundation.

There is ongoing debate about consent. Some experts in the seventies and eighties were involved in deprogramming people involved in cults at the request of their family. As this often required the physical removal of a person from their environment, some individuals considered themselves kidnapped and subsequent lawsuits bankrupted the professionals involved. At times, consent is in the eye of the consenter.

Consent can be hard to measure or define. One approach is to inspect whether there is deception involved. What I think I'm agreeing to, and what I'm really agreeing to. Sales contracts allow a 'cooling off' period, in consideration of impulsive decision-making. In any case, influence, persuasion and coercion can be honest. They become dishonest when the power equation is way off keel, when an individual or group's true agenda is not presented initially and nor are the obligations and requirements involved in what is being offered.

There are several expressions of thought reform, after all, that we welcome, fund, encourage, demand and expect. We privilege good education for this reason. We want our children to learn some habits and not others. The best schools isolate children and indoctrinate them appropriately.

We enjoy the gimmicks of advertising and marketing no matter how sneaky. We like going shopping to be like the pretty people in their beautiful houses on TV. We congratulate ourselves on how much choice we have.

We accept political propaganda as part of the cultural furniture, no matter how frightening or loaded it is. Politicians use all of the same techniques as evangelists, it seems, only with better paid advisers. We see through them. We're smart.

We are cynical and world-weary. Can't shock us. There's nothing we don't know, we've seen it all before. We know people lie, get caught and lie again. We understand that our society is full of all kinds of manipulations and trends. We live in an age when the buyer had better beware, because there's no sympathy out there. Since we have so many freedoms and options, we think we're very clever. We think we're consenting to everything we do. No one makes decisions based on emotions any more. That would be ignorant.

Because we can isolate muscle groups and Blackberry our time, we assume we know everything about life and people. We believe we are rational decision-makers. Everybody's an internet-educated expert. We know we're smarter than ever before and, thanks to Oprah and therapy, much more in tune with our real emotions. Especially about the big stuff. We know what's true. We live in the age of consent.

We also don't dare to acknowledge the influence that thought-reform systems have had on us. It has worked for politicians and demagogues down the ages. Does this mean that Hillsong is no better than the Moonies? It all comes down to what you consider to be an individual's capacity to consent.

LIFTON'S EIGHT CRITERIA FOR THOUGHT REFORM

Milieu control

This involves the control of information and communication both within the environment and, ultimately, within the individual, resulting in a significant degree of isolation from society at large.

The only thing that is missing for me is the dance music and the dealers, although in the good old days there were plenty of people with eyes rolled back in their head. I guess a double-shot of white chocolate mocha coffee from Gloria Jean's outside might do the same. Apart from that, Hillsong provides everything else that a good nightclub should, and it does it with the finest and most expensive of equipment.

If there were Christian dance music, I'd have stayed. It's another thing evangelicals must contact the gay community about: they're missing the best music. My bet is that they're not far off as there is Christian dance music now, just not in the actual churches. It goes 'doof doof doof Christ is the future, doof doof doof Christ is the future'. Suddenly I feel like jumping up on the podium and giving a special offering for no reason at all.

Are the people using these techniques aware of the science behind what they do? Hillsong is not a meeting place of rocket scientists. Curiously, most of those who have been close to the men at the top report that they generally have no idea of the actual effect a church service has on people's lives. They're not doing it on purpose; they just know it works. It's worked for generations.

Puritan and Calvanist Jonathan Edwards did it first in 1735 at Northhampton, Massachusetts church meetings that were heralded as 'the First Great Awakening'. He worked the crowd into a frenzy of evangelistic terror, preaching a turn-or-burn message that would make any Southern Baptist proud. His failure was that his dramatics incited too much fear, and several people went on to commit suicide. Presbyterian minister Charles Finney outdid Edwards four years later using the same methods, inspiring the crowd but implanting messages of hope and salvation in people's minds rather than damnation and punishment. He had much more favourable success and retention rates.

Originally, preaching was the focus of the Pentecostal church. When a musical item was performed, pastors sat alongside the stage to watch. Piece by piece, the preaching proportion of the stage was reduced, and the musical elements expanded. The pulpit is now the visitor to a platform arranged around instruments and sheet-music stands. Hillsong's new building was acoustically designed for album recordings.

Hillsong has done for Christian music what the Dixie Chicks did for country and western: made it blond, sexy and mainstream. This is no accident. As the Hillsong music conference became more successful, so did the 'church'. When musical director Geoff Bullock left in 1995, it was a perfect opportunity to throw young, fair, female Darlene Zschech out of the back-up frying pan and into the leaders' fire. The gracious and lovely Darlene replaced Geoff's masculine profile on the frontline with one that had never been so damn cute. Darlene is now an international Christian star in her own right, a preacher, and still calls Hillsong church home.

Neither Darlene nor any of the spin-off music ministries were around for Hillsong's real 'praise and worship' beginnings. Geoff Bullock and some friends were dope-smoking musicians before they met Jesus. They used to sit around and try to recreate the music of ELO and Genesis. When they became Christians, Geoff simply recreated the same music style for 'praise and worship'. As the eighties progressed, music teams adapted to the tastes of the public using similar styles and riffs. Pub rock was big in Australia at the time, and the music team used as much of it as they could to keep the crowds rolling to church.

Hillsong 'worship' music takes up between a third and half of the time spent in the building at a service. The 'bring them to church' instruction is not just to get them saved. When you are ushered into the auditorium, like entering a giant concert stadium, you are in a completely controlled sensory zone. The music is useful for getting you to the building and keeping you there long enough for recruitment purposes.

American hypnotist Dick Sutphen says that the techniques used in 'trance-inducing churches' are the same as the ones he uses to induce patients into an hypnotic state. The difference, he argues, is that his patients are aware they are being hypnotised.

A repetitive beat, ideally ranging from 45 to 72 beats per minute (a rhythm close to the beat of the human heart), is very hypnotic and can generate an eyes-open altered state of consciousness in a very high percentage of people. And, once you are in an alpha state, you are at least 25 times as suggestible as you would be in full beta consciousness. The music is probably the same for every service, or incorporates the same beat, and many of the people will go into an altered state almost immediately upon entering the sanctuary. Subconsciously, they recall their state of mind from previous services and respond according to the post-hypnotic programming.

Very simply, the basis of persuasion is always to access your right *brain. The left half of your brain is analytical and rational. The right side is creative and imaginative. So, the idea is to distract the left brain and keep it busy …*

Thought-stopping *techniques are used to cause the mind to go 'flat'. These are altered state of consciousness techniques that initially induce calmness by giving the mind something simple to deal with and focusing awareness. Continued use brings on a feeling of elation and eventually hallucination. The result is the reduction of thought and eventually, if used long enough, the cessation of all thought and withdrawal from everyone and everything except that which the controllers direct. The takeover is then complete. It is important to be aware that when members or participants are instructed to use thought-stopping techniques, they are told that they will benefit by so doing: they will become 'better soldiers' or 'find enlightenment'.*

There are three primary techniques used for thought stopping. The first is marching*: the thump, thump, thump beat literally generates self-hypnosis and thus great susceptibility to suggestion.*

The second thought-stopping technique is meditation. *If you spend an hour to an hour and a half a day in meditation, after a few weeks, there is a great probability that you will not return to full beta consciousness and you will remain in a fixed state of alpha for as long as you continue to meditate. I'm not saying this is bad—if you do it yourself. It may be very beneficial. But it is a fact that you are causing your mind to go flat. I've worked with meditators on an EEG machine and the results are conclusive: the more you meditate, the flatter your mind becomes until eventually, and especially if used to excess or in combination with decognition, all thought ceases.*

The third thought-stopping technique is chanting, *and often chanting in meditation. 'Speaking in tongues' could also be included in this category.*[2]

After 45 minutes of music, a message is repeated to a ready audience. Is it coincidence that Brian used the word 'purpose' 124 times in fifty-three minutes during his opening address to the public at the 2005 International AoG Conference? Possibly, until I counted Pastor Ashley Evans from Paradise Church doing the same thing at the same conference with the word 'authority', this time 141 usages in fifty-two minutes.

Sometimes the visiting pastors yell so harshly, I'd do anything they say to get them to stop screaming at me.

Mystical manipulation

There is manipulation of experiences that appear spontaneous but in fact were planned and orchestrated by the group or its leaders in order to demonstrate divine authority or spiritual advancement or some special gift or talent that will then allow the leader to reinterpret events, scripture, and experiences as he or she wishes.

All thought-reform programs use mystical manipulation. Pentecostals are defined by signs and wonders and, whether or not they abound, you will be convinced they're there anyway.

The Lord said to Moses and Aaron, 'When Pharaoh says to you, "Perform a miracle", then say to Aaron, "Take your staff and throw it down before Pharaoh" and it will become a snake'.

So Moses and Aaron went to Pharaoh and did just as the Lord commanded. Aaron threw his staff down in front of Pharaoh and his officials, and it became a snake. Pharaoh then summoned the wise men and sorcerers, and the Egyptian magicians who did the same things by their secret arts. Each one threw down his staff and it became a snake. But Aaron's staff swallowed up their staffs. Yet Pharaoh's heart became hard and he would not listen, just as the Lord had said. (Exodus 7:18–13)

In the holy-roller days of the fifties and sixties, evangelists had demons flying all over the circus top. Crowds were sweaty and excited, all revved up for revival, leaping out of wheelchairs and sickbeds. It was easier then to demonstrate the power, the greatness and the wrath of Almighty God.

These days, as long as the conference is running smoothly and the sound system doesn't fail, it's evidence that God is here tonight, Amen? Can't you just feel him? I tell you, he's doing some amazing things tonight and he's already done some powerful works in the lives of people tonight. Our God is a great God, isn't he? And all the believers said?

Amen.

God shows up the most at the end which is why, traditionally, it's always kind of okay to be late for church. It's always after the people have worshipped that the signs and wonders follow. The 2006 Colour Your World conference invitation arrived from Hillsong with the news that the final week was already booked out. No surprise. The biggest blessings come as a finale, like the closing night of a concert tour.

In the small church times, it was easy to prove that God was there. Someone would prophesy something, the choir would sing with extra heart, someone would start speaking in tongues who never did before. Modern times made it harder to get people to do these sorts of publicly embarrassing things when from out of nowhere came the most unusual phenomenon. Then the games began.

Like the origins of World War I, there is debate about at which moment the Toronto Blessing started. What is certain is that Dr Rodney Howard-Browne, a South African evangelist who settled in the States in 1987, made it internationally famous in the nineties. Howard-Browne is reported to have been preaching just outside of Albany, New York in April 1989 when holy laughter broke out. People began laughing, swaying, crying and acting as if they were drunk: 'Worshippers are overcome by laughing, weeping, groaning, shaking, falling and, to the chagrin of some, noise-making that has been described as "a cross between a jungle and a farmyard." But of greater significance are the reports of changed lives: healings, restored relationships and increased fervor for God.'[3]

On 20 January 1994, several revival meetings were held at a small church located in a Toronto industrial complex. The 'holy' laughter broke out there as well. Preacher Randy Clark had spent time with Howard-Browne the previous year. Following this, it was believed that whosoever visited the Toronto Airport Vineyard Church in Canada would receive the Toronto Blessing. When they returned, they would bring back Godgerms, and all the people in their home church would start laughing and crying and rolling around as well.

This international Christian Mexican wave infiltrated the majority of Pentecostal churches around the world, with the endorsement by all of Pentecostalism's big brass as the twentieth century's best Sign and Wonder. The Christian channel TBN broadcast it, televangelist Benny Hinn sold its mysticism to his audiences, and the Vineyard Movement capitalised on it. It was marketed as a cleansing of God's church before his return and as a more liberal alternative to the moralistic Assemblies of God.

'My little nine-year-old daughter Jordan came to the first night service and Rodney laid hands on her,' said (Oral Roberts' son) Richard Roberts. 'She fell to the ground and laughed for an hour and 45 minutes. When we tried putting her to bed, she fell out laughing. We finally had to put her in the bathtub.'[4] The Toronto Blessing reinforced every participant's belief that the Spirit was alive and well and living in their church. It spread like wildfire, despite being denounced by other Pentecostal churches, until the late nineties when it burnt out, although outbreaks are still reported in small congregations.

Spontaneous eruptions of the supernatural are unmeasurable, and not directly profitable. Prosperity is the real Pentecostal stigmata: money in the bank shows that you've had a tangible spiritual encounter with God and church leaderships hope it rubs off like Toronto.

Demand for purity

The world is viewed as black and white and the members are constantly exhorted to conform to the ideology of the group and strive for perfection. The induction of guilt and/or shame is a powerful control device used here.

Good Christians are supposed to be *in* the world, since God made it for everyone to enjoy, but not *of* the world, meaning they shouldn't share its flesh-driven values. You can mix with the sinners, but you mustn't wish you were one of them.

Fundamentalist Christians have brought the demand for a spotless Bride of Christ to a new and improved, stain-removing best. It's no longer about getting down to the sinner's level, it's about making sure the doors are locked so tightly none of the bad guys can get in.

It was always a case of Us vs Them. The difference now is that We used to feel sorry for Them, and cheer on the day when They might be converted. Now, We are threatened by Them, the Great Unsaved, because They might take Our Freedom, Our Families, Our Profit Margins.

Christians have to be very protective of who they let in. Brian made this confusingly clear when he spoke at the beginning of 2005 on 'who you should sit with'. He explained that We are supposed to be the salt of the earth, so We should interact with Them. And it's all right, he went on to say, to stand with people and talk, as he himself had done at the kids' footy barbecues where the language turned ugly. You can walk with Them, you can stand with Them, but you can't sit with Them. When you sit with Them, then you're a part of Them.

Maybe that was my problem. I was more Them than Us and that became increasingly obvious as the years went by. I liked Them much better. They had aisles of diversity in their super-store. We were so homogenous in our one-shop town, it was like making conversation with drone bees at the hive. The extraordinary part was most of Them said that We could join in Their reindeer games. Which meant They were more inclusive and understanding than We ever were. And We were supposed to be the ones loving Them!

Nothing much has changed. Jewels will suffer for being in this book. I understand we're not supposed to be friends with people who aren't friends with Our Destiny. This has been bugging me. I have always felt that I was a friend of Jewels's destiny, whatever that may be. Besides, if We were so sure what Our Destinies were, We'd be fortune-tellers, wouldn't We?

It takes constant work to stay uncluttered by the rest of the world. It means you have to let a lot of people go. If they're not for you, they're against you. Mustn't let people get in the way of Destiny. Whoever They may be.

Culture of confession

Sins, as defined by the group, are to be confessed either to a personal monitor or publicly to the group. There is no confidentiality; members' 'sins', 'attitudes', and 'faults' are discussed and exploited by the leaders.

My best friend knew that Santa was coming to town. When she was three, she was so obsessed with Santa's omnipresence that she thought he could see her everywhere including the toilet, leading to a nasty trip to the doctor's office.

I was the same about God up until only recently. When you have a biblical worldview, there's no escape. As a good Christian, I did nothing wrong, so there was nothing to see when people saw through me. As a bad Christian, I knew everybody could see through me and what a hopeless, futile backslider they saw. Either way, I knew that everyone knew everything about me by looking at me. So I've always been a great confessor of sins. To anyone who looks at me oddly.

Not ever having been a new Christian, I never went through the deprogramming of my 'old' life. Thought-reform programs and fundamentalist churches get new participants to confess all their wrongdoings, so that they can always be recalled as the labels from their past: former alcoholic, former adulterer, former Catholic, former homosexual, all of them crowd pleasers. This inevitably leads to a culture of continual confession. That way, leaving is only going back to that former life like a dog returning to his vomit, the bible says. Everybody else then knows exactly what we're dealing with. Confidentiality has never been a strong point in the Assemblies of God, and there's a fine reason for that.

More than life or money itself, Pentecostals love gossip. They couldn't exist without it. They are the original network marketers. All out of a sincere desire to please God. They don't call it gossip. The bible says gossip is bad. Initially, when you get saved, they call it 'confession as a sign of genuine repentance'. After all, repentance means to turn away from your old life, so you better tell us what your old life was like. A few times, if it's interesting.

Then there's follow-up to see how you're going. New Christian follow-up, post-surgery follow-up, new baby follow-up. It's called pastoral care. Concern. We want to know what's been going on for you. Because we pray for you. And we still remember where you came from, all that time ago.

Once you decide to join a home bible study or cell group, it's called sharing with family. You can tell everybody in your cosy home meeting your marriage problems or your financial troubles. Bible study leaders are able to take their concerns back to leadership because that's called accountability.

The majority of people will only ever confess once to a superior, particularly if either the superior or the confessor has an important church role in leadership. Most pastors have nothing to offer but their own advice. Their expertise stems from wanting a successful church. Marriage and financial troubles look bad in a church that is supposed to be blemish-free for presentation to Christ. The Pentecostal ideal is that once you are saved, you disappear into an abyss of joy. You're saved, what else do you need? You're forgiven and your problems are solved. The end.

Should you choose to confess to the pastor that you're still wrestling with sin, it's unlikely you will do it again. Not when confidentiality expires within the hour, and then you find yourself rostered on less often for choir practice. Luckily, Hillsong is one big family so if you need to unburden, you have plenty of relatives around.

Sacred science

The group's doctrine or ideology is considered to be the ultimate Truth, beyond all questioning or dispute. Truth is not to be found outside the group. The leader, as the spokesperson for God or for all humanity, is likewise above criticism.

Once a Pentecostal convert has been thoroughly disoriented, they must begin a very important phase called 'the renewing of the mind'. One's dirty old fleshly mind is full of sinful thoughts that must be cleaned out immediately.

This process of indoctrination has as many arms as an octopus, all vital for survival in this new, previously unrealised spiritual world. We know that Satan will try to get you back any way he can, so you have to keep yourself pure in body, surroundings and thought. Satan loves to attack people in the mind.

Once you know Jesus you know Truth and, as he said, the Truth will set you free. The exciting part is that there is even more Truth. And it's all available here right outside in the gift shop.

The fundamentalists were once heavily criticised by the liberals for being so polarised, so black and white about the bible. Fundies have always taken their texts literally as God-breathed scripture, so that not a jot or tittle should be moved.

The Prosperity Rat Pack don't need to worry about such criticisms. They don't bother with the bible much. Sermons aren't even messages any more. Speakers just sort of morph into personal feel-good chats. As reference points, AoG pastors mainly quote other pastors' books and conferences, celebrities who appear noble, movie clips, stories their friends told them, stuff that happened last conference and, my personal favourite, 'someone once said'. It's as useful as listening to the dream I had three weeks ago. Any reference to the Christian bible is purely coincidental.

Tammy Faye Bakker once said you can educate yourself right out of a relationship with God. Despite the below-average education level of most evangelists, even in theology, there is a long-held fear of 'secular' thinking. Many Hillsongers derive their beliefs about the world from anecdotal evidence, pastors' ad-libbing and books written by Christians. The concept of applying usual logic to spirituality is abhorrent. My thoughts are not your thoughts, neither are your ways my ways declares the Lord. Yet, despite the limited objective information that they receive, fundamentalists are happy to lap up irrationality like mother's milk. Bobbie Houston, when getting 'real' about sex, used Facts for back-up.

Fact number one. God gave man and woman to each other.

Fact number two. Sexual union is not abhorrent to God.

Fact number three. Sexual intimacy is the God-ordained consummating act of marriage.

Fact: Because it is a God-ordained, whatever, it is very, very authoritative.

Fact: A healthy sex life is evidence—underline that—of unity and intimacy. Satan so knows this.

She elaborated.

Here's some facts for Kingdom women living under a mandate.

Fact: We the church in this generation live in a sexually saturated society. You and I have a job to correct it.

Fact: A generation is emerging who are literally the fruit of a society that has had no moral fibre. That makes their behaviour a little scary. If they're unredeemed, though, it's not their fault.[5]

Ad-libbing, the new fundamentalists will lay claim to anything as the truth. Their truth is the only truth, but the sources are infinite. Celebrities or atheist philosophers used to be quoted only for sinfulness; now, if they say something we like, we can whack them on a poster, right next to a New Testament promise.

These are open-minded fundamentalist days. Science is not a dirty word. Pentecostals are not weirdos who don't believe in taking their children to doctors. As soon as they're sick, they're straight to the finest hospitals, asking you to pray God guides the medical team. Pray the medication works, pray the nurses are well staffed, pray the scars don't show, pray the insurance company pays. And then pray for healing, if you've got time.

Current scientific thinking is in all AoG stories now. Everyone loves a sentence that starts with 'Psychologists say' or 'The research shows', and Hillsong has wasted no time in cutting and pasting such clips. They will go so far as to quote Einstein's or Stephen Hawking's view on the universe if it's catchy enough.

But science and Hillsong are only ever married by Hallmark. The progression of logical thought is derailed, as is every other method of gathering knowledge. Don't ask Hillsong about the earth's real age. They don't like it. They don't know what to say. Stephen Hawking may swear by it, but we're not here to talk about Stephen Hawking and the world's lies. Satan is the father of lies. We're here to talk about Jesus. The author of Truth, found in the Word of God and in your hearts, now that you're one of us. He's our Saviour. What other questions do you have?

Is it fair to blame the leaders for their followers' haphazard responses to logical questions? I say yes. It's hardly intelligent design.

Loading the language

The group interprets or uses words and phrases in new ways so that often the outside world does not understand. This jargon consists of thought-terminating clichés, which serve to alter members' thought processes to conform to the group's way of thinking.

Jesus said that on Judgement Day we will be held accountable for every idle word we've spoken in our lives. This means I need to book a Judgement Week special, if any are going, because it's going to be one long day otherwise.

The book of Proverbs says that life and death is in the power of the tongue. Half of modern evangelism is based on this alone. What you say is what you get. Blab it and grab it. Faith words vs fear words. You could kill yourself if you say the wrong thing.

You might think this would encourage some people to practise what they preach, yet mass evangelism is the most verbose, babbling brook witnessed in the history of Christianity, if not the world.

All thought-reform groups 'load the language', creating communication that only insiders understand and which subtly saturates the entire culture. All these years, when I was filling out forms, I honestly believed English was my only language. When you look at it, though, I've been fluent in Christianese all my life.

Christianese is a language that is harder to learn than most people realise. If you're born into it, it's second nature. To outsiders and newcomers it can be baffling, and hard to understand. Christianese has many dialects throughout the world, and if you weren't at last week's camp or conference you could miss out on a spontaneous new in-joke that will lead to an 'old saying'.

This list contains phrases you might encounter when going to Hillsong, but it can also be useful for listening to a TV evangelist or when setting foot in a neighbourhood fundamentalist meeting.

Awesome: Originally a Valley Girl word, now used in Hillsong as a high holy word
God: Santadaddy
Jesus: The guy behind the Christmas spectacular
Holy Spirit: Any sort of rush you might feel during the Christmas spectacular
The/your/our/God's Church: Hillsong
Saved: Converted to Pentecostalism
Unsaved: Everyone else

Unchurched (previously *Unsaved*): Those who are not 'locked into' a church and therefore can't be saved
Backslider: Person who used to go to Hillsong but doesn't any more (see *Unsaved*)
Laying on of hands: Originally for healing. Popular at youth services; can lead to marriage
Slain in the Spirit: Having the Holy Spirit take a hold of you so strongly that you fall backwards; often induced by laying on of hands
Catchers: People who catch those who are Slain in the Spirit so that they don't hit their head and can spend comfortable passed-out time with God
Carpet time: The time between going unconscious and when you wake up and go back to your seat
Gone to be with Jesus: Died
Immorality: Anything at all to do with sex outside of marriage
A lifestyle We don't approve of: Gay
Drug addicts: People who don't dress as nicely as we do
Girl: Any female from infancy to retirement
Man: Any male from infancy to retirement
Doing life: Living, since people are too busy to do lunch any more
Girlfriends: Women who attend Hillsong women's events, not to be confused with same-sex partnership. Girlfriends do life together; the alternative is *not* boyfriends doing life together
Family: Someone related to you who isn't gay, except for adopted children who aren't related to you but are still family as long as they're not gay. Non-biological relationships can't be counted as family except for heterosexual spouses. And people who believe what you believe. Or give money to the building fund. Or who have a franchise of Gloria Jean's Coffees
In the scale of eternity: Deciding whether or not you should do life with some people, not others
The Enemy: Satan. 'The Enemy' sounds less nasty the way KFC sounds better than Kentucky Fried Chicken

Manifest: To behave as if demons are controlling you, for example, 'I showed my parents my bad report card and they started manifesting'
Spiritual battle: Conflict with those who won't think like you or your interpretation of the bible
The Throne Zone: Heaven
Resources: CDs, DVDs, books by pastors
The Word of God: Resources
Blessed (v): Given money to: 'They've blessed our church'
Blessing (n): Source of money: 'They've been a real blessing to us'
Blessed to be a blessing: Getting money to give it away
Generous: Giving lots of money to the church
Presence of God: The feeling of anticipation a crowd gets before a band comes on stage
Worship: Singing along to Hillsong songs, CDs or DVDs, at Hillsong, at home or in the car
Hope: The gamble that faith is real
Faith: The reason for all the things that don't make any sense
Love: Feeling really special on the inside about anything at all; being nice to someone
Grace: The whitewash process by which we only talk about the positive and no one has to be accountable for anything, for example, 'When are you going to get a hold of the concept of grace?'
Legalist: Anyone who disagrees with leadership
Suffering for Jesus: Missing your connecting flight
Salvation: Turning a bad business idea into a good business idea
Peace: Knowing your investments are secure
Miracle: Anything that goes your way without trying too hard
God's will: The plans of the AoG
Kingdom ventures: The work of the AoG
Church planting: Colonisation by the AoG
New Christian: Convert who hasn't been to bible college
On fire for God: Totally brainwashed and ready to go to bible college
Bible college: Tax haven

International leadership bible college: International tax haven
Challenge: Convince/bully, for example, pastor feels challenged at a conference to challenge his congregation to do something, usually to do with church growth
Power: The right to challenge other people
Purpose: Justification for self-obsessed behaviour
Purpose driven: Unashamedly self-obsessed
Vision: Expected net profit, hallucination
Praise: Dividends
Partnership: Joint venture
Pathways: Networks
Frozen chosen: Congregants who won't follow instructions quickly enough
Discouraged: Wondering why these formulas aren't working out
Doubting God: Realising the formulas are never going to work out
Developing a negative, critical, defeatist attitude: Asking leadership why you've been told a bunch of lies
Now worshipping at another church: Left in disgust and outrage over being conned
Faithfulness to God's will: Willing to put up with any amount of bad treatment from leadership and still go back to church
We want you to have a free bible: Quick! Jump on our mailing list!
Bring your friends: Recruit as actively as you can
Bring your family: Take no prisoners
We want to welcome them to church too: We can't believe how much untapped cash is out there
Great to see you, have an awesome week, we love you so much, bless you heaps: Please get out of the auditorium as soon as you can before the next service starts

Doctrine over person

Members' personal experiences are subordinated to the sacred science and any contrary experiences must be denied or reinterpreted to fit the ideology of the group.

It's important, then, once you're in and you've thrown it out, not to bring it back again, except for special occasions like testimonies. Why would you look back? Your entire life can now be seen clearly through your new eyes, guided by your leaders' wise old ones.

What you thought was harmless experimentation as a teenager was actually very dangerous. It explains a lot of the choices you've made since, and if you look back you've reaped what you've sown.

The Pentecostal heartbeat is the word 'choice'. The world is a level playing field. People are where they are because of choices they or their ancestors made. Once you hear the good news of the gospel, the choice between life and death is yours. Turn or burn. This predicament nearly finished me off my whole life. The logic goes like this: because God loves us, he wants us to want to love him, therefore he gives us 'free will'. If we freely choose to decline his offer, we go to hell. Thus, there is only one choice to make with free will. You have to get with the program because there is no other on offer.

After the first introductory choice, you're on your own. 'You are a result of your choices' is the Pentecostal waiver form. You're a Christian now, so if it goes bad from here you've only got yourself to blame. Look at the brand-new life package you got *for free* just by accepting Jesus. If you choose to do anything other than walk in the light, you are choosing your old life and you will get the consequence of your choices. If you choose to live like us, then you too can furnish this life package with all the things you said you were dreaming about before. Things God wants for you, if you'll let him. Things like a happy marriage, kids who love God and financial success. Then, when you're rich, you can reach your individual potential. Or you can go back to Satan's service. Entirely up to you.

Does that mean you have to give up everything when you become a Christian? Hell no, that's what grace is for. Not long ago, it was atonement through the sacrifice of Jesus Christ as opposed to having to observe every letter of the law like the Israelites. You don't earn salvation by being good enough for God. No one's good enough for God! God forgives through grace. Any time you ask a member of the AoG to show the books or you mention a name from the past, they go glaze-eyed and talk about grace covering everything bad, like shaking an Etch-A-Sketch. All gone.

Dispensing of existence

The group has the prerogative to decide who has the right to exist and who does not. This is usually not literal but means that those in the outside world are not saved, unenlightened, unconscious and they must be converted to the group's ideology. If they do not join the group or are critical of the group, then they must be rejected by the members. Thus, the outside world loses all credibility. In conjunction, should any member leave the group, he or she must be rejected also.

Being part of the Cause can take up a lot of time. Being a member of a big international family calls for a lot of devotion, if you're truly interested in seeing people affected and lives changed. Pastor Brian says it's selfish not to share the gift of salvation with others. No one forces you to get involved, though you will be encouraged.

For starters, it's still traditional to go to Hillsong twice a weekend, which is easier now there's Saturday night services. Then there's a bible study group on a weeknight. Also your gender-based meeting on a Thursday morning. There are courses to attend. There are camps for the kids, and monthly leadership and volunteer meetings for those who are either or both. There are always conferences, album recordings, vision nights and prayer meetings to support if you want to make a difference. And that's before you take on anything extracurricular like car park duties, or helping out in the call centre.

Volunteering is an important part of serving at Hillsong. Pastor Brian has suggested that one weekend be spent at church and the alternate one volunteering. The 'volunteer spirit', as he calls it, is vital to Hillsong. The conference every July uses three to four thousand volunteers, many of whom take a week off work to be there day and night.

Then again, should you wish to spend your entire life at Hillsong, that can be arranged. If you were considering any serious responsibility, time with your family is history. Rehearsals and meetings are all compulsory, frequent and long.

Cult theorists argue that exhausting people helps maintain control. If all they're craving is sleep and to see their kids, they're not as likely to care where all the money's going, or how nonsensical the ideologies are. The AoG calls it a commitment to the things of God.

It's silly to live far away from the main building when you go there all the time, so a lot of people move closer. It's also a way to see your new family, since you don't have that much in common with your old friends anymore. Your new friends are the people you do the most with, share the most with, and sometimes even work the most with.

The Hillsong business directory has over 1000 entries. If, rather than unchurched expertise, you require a Christian plumber or a Christian accountant or a Christian whitegoods specialist, fear not. The Hillsong business directory guarantees you need never do business with a non-Pentecostal again.

The motivation to see your church succeed grows every day. With every facet of your life changing for the better, safely away from the old you, there is nothing and no one you won't sacrifice to see success. And with prosperity stories pouring out of the resources and the pulpit, working for the man somehow doesn't make sense.

Why get up every morning to waste your life working for an unsaved boss, who is almost certainly not a friend of your destiny? He doesn't know what it means to serve the living God. Suddenly it becomes much more meaningful to give up an empty career in exchange for something supernatural and exciting.

There is a plethora of roles for the enthusiast: washing the many windows of the many buildings, organising registrations for up-and-coming events, and every pastor needs a personal assistant. If, in the beginning, you can't get a paid job, never mind. You can go to bible college or volunteer or both while you're waiting. Then you're practically guaranteed a spot somewhere in good time, once you're out of the trenches. If you refuse to relinquish all ties with the outside world by maintaining your own independent business, make sure it's got a Christian theme and make sure it's listed in the directory.

Now that you've ensured that your old family knows who you are now, your new family knows who you once were and you no longer have any real idea who you are at all, the process is complete. Leaving is not so simple.

Moving to another church used to be like going to a different restaurant, take it or leave it. Leaving a thought-reform program is laden with 'exit costs', those things you have to give up to leave or even to doubt the leader. All those business contacts, all that family, all the love, and truth and cash that's been invested with passion. It's hard to get up and just walk away from everything you've seen and experienced for yourself. And the more time you spend there, the harder it is to remember the old you.

But why would you want to remember that life anyway? Why would you hanker for your old life of sin when Jesus died for freedom like this?

ONLY THE GOOD DIE YOUNG

Jordie was my med student's best friend. My tall, blond med student, there on the other side of the church room, dreamy thing, always had his bouncy best friend next to him. That's all I ever knew Jordie as. I had had my eye on that about-to-be doctor since I was sixteen and he is, of course, a specialist now and still unmarried. Oh, the agony. But Jordie, as I've said, was his best friend. Popular, outgoing, a Chosen One. Nice guy. His mop of curly hair reminded me of the guy from Simply Red. I never really knew him much, though the other girls did. I didn't understand why they weren't trying harder to marry the doctor. Clearly none of them had Jewish mothers.

I didn't know Jordie well by the time he came to my house, but I had known him through the others all those years in between. I caught up with him at one of the gang's overpriced thirtieth birthday dinners and made some off-the-cuff remark about Hillsong merchandising. I was rambling. 'I see sheets,' I said, 'with Hillsong on them, I see crockery with the logo, and most of all I see the amusement park.'

'There are some people,' he had commented, 'who probably would agree with you, quite seriously.'

I had never heard any disloyalty coming out of any of their mouths. They were all there that night, the faces that I had seen since I was sixteen.

A bunch of them had gone through bible college together, and most of them were still impenetrable. But he wasn't.

A few of us ended up back at his fancy city apartment. I was delighted to be among the A-list again. The Spirit really does seem to fall in the front rows. Here I was, the infidel, having drinks with the favourites.

He was happy at that time but, then, he never stopped seeming happy. We decided we should have lunch but, both living very busy lives—his successful and international, mine humdrum and decidedly local—it was six months before we managed to catch up.

Platonic relationships with Christian boys are the best, when you can actually find a real one. It's novel. This was a lovely man, with no shortage of dates with beautiful women. And he was one of those guys where you close your eyes and try really hard but you know you can never be attracted to him, much less marry him, regardless of how wonderful a husband he would make. Sad, but true.

When a lunch date was finally set, again at his apartment, I turned up, oblivious as ever, having no idea what I was in for. Gone was the healthy, happy character who'd been the same since forever. In front of me was a relative skeleton, and the spirit of Tigger was dwindling into Eeyore.

'How come you've lost fifty kilos?' I said. He turned away, tears in his eyes. Good start.

He got us each a drink and began his story. I don't know to this day why he told me. I don't know why he involved me in his life. He didn't know me apart from the consensus that I was the difficult one, the one the girls hung on to, who he'd never really talked to because he'd never wanted to date me. Courting is important to Hillsong men. There's not much time to waste on girls as friends.

He had no need for my input. His whole life was successful in so many ways, and he had way more friends than time, having always been one of those people who can talk to anyone. He had money to burn and the power and influence we had been raised to believe we could wield. He was changing the world and making money and a fine reputation out of it.

So here was this well liked and loved man in front of me, swaying as he fixed our drinks. Skinny. Calm but edgy, if that makes sense.

He told me he'd been randomly attacked by two men at an ATM two months before. He couldn't tell me all of it, but he told me enough. His bid for freedom, only to be dragged back by his attackers. The way he dropped his key down a grate so they couldn't get into his building. Then suddenly being released after all those hours.

Where was God? I thought it but never said it. Where was God? This person had put in years of his life to the Cause—creatively, inventively, passionately—to reach people because he was spirited and determined to do it. Where was the God that he had preached about from the pulpits? Where was God for those twelve hours?

There was to be no vengeance. His attackers had threatened him sufficiently not to report it. And here sat Jordie, honestly, openly, all that money, all that success, all that devotion, and he did not know what to do in the next five minutes.

It is a humbling experience to sit next to a broken human being. They do not struggle, they do not argue. They exist broken, not even waiting for an eleventh-hour reprieve, just waiting to find out what to do next. Hope has not gone for good, but it has taken long-service leave, and its substitute is often a simple, cold despair.

I didn't know what to say—there seemed nothing to be said—and so when he had finished he took me out on the balcony and showed me most of Sydney's angles through his binoculars. He pointed out the houses in the next streets. He had been watching them. The views were really overwhelming, stretching one side of the city to the other, but he wasn't very interested in the city's breadth. He was fixated on the houses in the next couple of streets. Was he paranoid? He was jumpy, edgy, a little manic almost. Surely he was post-traumatic. It made perfect sense. Poor guy, struggling without any professional help, surrounded by well-meaning Christians, I thought. After quite a while doing alley analysis, we came back in from the balcony and I said very little about it and went home.

Weight loss, not working, flashbacks, jumpy, out of character, thought disorder—I began to research post-traumatic stress disorder to find out where he could get information or something, maybe a victims of crime counsellor. He was clearly not doing well. Still, I always assumed that he had more resources and support than he could handle. He was already talking about avoiding family phone calls. He was fine, as far as he was concerned, and wanted to be left alone a lot. Which made sense. It had been a devastating ordeal.

I found out after I talked with him why the others had been friends with him all these years. I never saw anyone other than someone his mother would be proud of, even in his clearly most confusing and dark times. Arrogant, inconsiderate and rude, sure, but in that adorable, Pentecostal, laugh it off way. Make a joke out of it and everything will be all right.

A month later he called me asking to stay. His flatmate had thrown him out of the fancy apartment because of his bizarre behaviour. No stranger to bizarre behaviour myself, I offered him a spare room. He chose the couch.

He stayed there for a month, coming and going and sleeping. When he woke up, I would feed him if I was there. I figured getting his strength up was priority one. He slept long and deep. Good, I thought, more strength, more time to heal.

Often he wasn't there but I made sure not to ask questions. I thought it was respectful, and it was. Whatever he was going through, the pressure from people who cared was intensifying it. So I tried to care nonchalantly, as it were. Be there when needed, nothing more.

He would sleep for sixteen or seventeen hours at a stretch. When he was awake, he was dazed. He was still fun, still funny, still quick, still insightful, but he was dreamy or preoccupied or something. He would tell me stories about the A-list and things that he had seen and been through with the people behind the curtain. I was furious. He wasn't. I never saw hatred in him, just a more cynical approach. I had never heard stories such as these. He was resigned to them, and had reasonable explanations for all. The pastors, he told me, were so wrapped up in the ministry tour that they did not have a connection to reality. They were so far removed that we couldn't expect them to behave like regular folk. But overall they were good guys.

He ran out one night to see his grandmother, who was dying in a nursing home not far from my house. How he got into the nursing home that late I don't know, but it was typical of him. When she died a couple of weeks later, he gave a eulogy that left everybody weeping.

After Jordie left my house he went to his close friends, a couple who took him in and supported him for months, I'm told—I had little to do with him. He gained weight, went back to work and not long after met a girl. About a year later, they got married. Things had been looking up for a while. Times were still hard, his mind wouldn't leave him alone, but life was starting over for real. It wasn't going to be all okay, but at least it was going.

I met him a couple of times for coffee and he still seemed dazed but resigned to getting on with it and mustering up all the enthusiasm he could for his next overseas project, which was bound for success. He was focused on his wife and there was no need to rehash the past, so I didn't nag for an update. He seemed to have moved on, and so there was truly very little room for me in his life now.

Then I got a call that he was dead; a drug overdose. I assumed it was a bad reaction to a crazy experiment that zany people might do. I was wrong, and I had been very, very wrong about him.

They tell me that it doesn't matter that we will never know how it all came about, but to me it does. Someone sold him the drugs and someone knows what happened. Most of us never even knew he took drugs at all until he was dead.

Maybe it was my arrogance that got in the way. I had identified that he was post-traumatic, and that to me explained all his behaviour. I've worked in this field long enough to know post-trauma when I see it in one of my friends, thank you very much.

But not a roaring drug addiction. I wasn't the only one who missed it. He told so few people anything because of the shame, the confusion.

The funeral was beautiful, everyone wept. Yet there was an understanding, an unspoken relief almost. He had been broken beyond healing. The Lord had taken him to heaven to peace.

A friend of Jordie's widow said to me, 'You work with these things, don't you? He had a relapse. He was fighting so hard. It was God saying, "It's okay, you don't have to fight any more."'

Thirty-one years old and too hard for God. This goes against everything we had understood God to be. Through Christ all things are possible. God created the universe with a spoken word—nothing is too hard for him. He who did not spare his own son but gave him up, will he not then give us all things? Is there some time when we are supposed to gracefully let go? I am grateful every day that nobody gracefully let go of me. Because there were too many times that I would damn well have gone, ungracefully, kicking, screaming and cursing, I would have gone with the greatest of joy. So many of us would at different times, wouldn't we?

Is Jordie one of those cases we just can't account for? Is he one of those questions we'll have to ask God when we get to heaven? Is there a bible college with the answer to this that someone could refer me to?

It isn't good enough for me that he's dead and that that's the best outcome, really. It isn't good enough that he was way more ashamed than most anyone because of the mantle on his shoulders. Whatever happened—and they keep reminding me that we will never know—he died alone and without the real help that just might have saved him. Why couldn't he find it?

The God I was told about could have performed a miracle, a transformation, turned his life around, upside down and brought him out of Egypt's bondage. But what happens after you get to the Promised Land, when you've swallowed all the milk and honey you can handle and more? Then what? Once you have maxed out your life, and blessed many with your blessing, then what? How do you cope with reality?

His wife was serene at the funeral. She was graceful and strong.

She wasn't angry or unresolved like I am. She stood proudly and said that, in her grief, Isaiah was all she could find for comfort, for in chapter 57 it says:

The righteous perish and no one ponders it in his heart;
Devout men are taken away, and no one understands
That the righteous are taken away to be spared from evil.
Those who walk uprightly enter into peace; they find rest as they lie in death.

I had never met her but the admiration welled up, again, for her strength during the unfathomable. The Christians were convinced of Jordie's newfound happiness. I'm still not. The state provides welfare that shuns the hard cases. Wasn't Jesus supposed to be different like that? And with my friend's private-school education, his mastery of language and his buoyant personality, with all that love and all that support, how much harder, then, will the really hard cases be?

He was clever and shifty, a storyteller, a prankster, an actor and a preacher. In the end he lied to almost everyone and told different lies to different people. There was little that anybody really could have done. He was determined and headstrong and spoilt. Those who loved him are not alone in asking why and how this happened. It happens in every drug death.

Still, it haunts me. My own insecurity, my own arrogance, did they get in the way? Almost no one would have thought he would take drugs. He knew this and used it as every middle-class drug user does to get away with it for as long as he possibly could. Still no one suspected. And if they did, they scoffed at the idea. He and my mother are about as likely to be injecting drug users, I would have thought, but I have been forced to scrutinise my mother now.

It's none of my business, really. I can lay no claim to this grief. I just wish I had recognised humanity in Christians for what it really is instead of what we are told it is. Or could be. If only we try harder. Or let God in more. Make God bigger. Reach our potential. Have all God's got for you. I thought the cream of the crop was special, too special to get hurt, and even more dangerous, untouchable.

It is what it is and, yes, we may never know. But if I can do all things through Christ who strengthens me and if two or more are gathered together in his name it will be done, then why wasn't it? And more than that, when they buried him, why wasn't anybody else asking?

Alava Shalom (M.H.D.S.R.I.P)

ALL ALONG THE WATCHTOWER

Chapter 15

HOLLABACK GIRL

> In the case of the girls, one watched them turning into matrons before they had become women. They began to manifest a curious and really rather terrifying single-mindedness. For the girls also saw the evidence on the Avenue, knew what the price would be, for them, of one misstep, knew that they had to be protected and that we were the only protection there was. They understood that they must act as God's decoys, saving the souls of the boys for Jesus and binding the bodies of the boys in marriage. For this was the beginning of our burning time.
>
> And I began to feel in the boys a curious, wary, bewildered despair, as though they were now settling in for the long, hard winter of life.
>
> —James Baldwin, *The Fire Next Time* (1963)

> Wanting to be a good Christian, Elaine always forgave him. She told herself: this time it's different. This time he's really sorry. He even prayed with me! I know he's really changed and that he's seeking God this time.
>
> —Dr Margaret Josephson Rinck,
> *Christian Men who Hate Women* (1990)

It started as a conversation with my next-door neighbour. He told me his work colleague went to Hillsong to pick up girls.

'Is he a Christian?' I asked, yet another layer of my green skin starting to peel.

'No,' he laughed at me, shaking his head.

'So he goes to Hillsong for the sole purpose of picking up girls?' I was in shock.

'Yes,' he tried to explain, 'all that music, lights, it's like a dance party.'

Then Sam de Brito from the *Sunday Telegraph* wrote about his friend Benny, who had recently converted to Christianity and was attending Hillsong.

'You could do a lot worse than hook up with a Christian girl,' Benny said. 'At least you know she'd be honest, she's living a good life and, if things get tough, she's not just gonna bail out but work on it with you in front of her community.'

But it was when Miranda Devine, also in the *Sunday Telegraph*, wrote three months later that I realised this approach was a common one. Due to the male terror that is arising from this century's female coldness towards them, the Stronger Sex are choosing weaker women and overtly trying to break the spirit of those who would survive. 'My friends are seriously considering quitting the bar and nightclub scene and dating girls from Hillsong,' a young bachelor is quoted. 'The women out there are mystifying.'

Once again, the winner is Sydney. We have a brand of cheerleaders all of our own. The Hillsong Girls. Don't Christian girls wear denim skirts and white blouses? Not these ones. They know that if you don't look great you won't get (as good) a husband, and that if you already have one, to quote Bobbie, he'll leave you 'should the world come knocking on your door'.

Hillsong girls don't take drugs and go out all night. They are generally financially confident, if not well endowed, because they understand prosperity principles. And they know that boys will be boys, so women must submit and obey. That's what they've been taught. All they need is a handsome prince to place a large-carated diamond on their French-manicured finger.

We all know about Catholic girls and their unique gift to the world of dating. Well, so far Protestant girls have made absolutely no contribution. With none of the raciness of those who leap from convent to coven, these girls have generally stayed unsexy, unappealing and, if you did get to fulfil the fantasy of sleeping with one, you usually had to marry them, and then the sex was bitterly, painfully disappointing. But not any more. Now we've got Hillsong girls. Fundamentalist Christian girls with sex appeal. So here's the best part, if you're a boy.

Fundamentalist Christians take the bible literally, so these girls are more than happy to believe that as women, they stay blamed for eating an apple and were created from a man's side, a rib, an afterthought, a helper and companion. Like someone who'll pass you the wrench when you're working on your car.

Most of the New Testament is actually written by the apostle Paul who, in his lack of time for women, explicitly wanted them to shut up and be grateful they got forgiven at all. His letter to Timothy said:

A woman should learn in quietness and full submission. I do not permit a woman to teach or have authority over a man; she must be silent. For Adam was formed first, then Eve. And Adam was not the one deceived; it was the woman who was deceived and became a sinner. But women will be saved through childbearing—if they continue in faith, love and holiness with propriety.

Hillsong girls love this approach. They are A-OK with submitting to a husband's authority. They just hope that when they find the one God intends, they will be acceptable to him.

Their leader in this operation is Bobbie Houston. How to explain the High Pastoress of Hillsong, the Hostess with the Mostest, the Jewel in Brian's Crown? She has to be seen and heard to be believed.

Before I left Hills, Bobbie was the pastor's wife, a sweet, ditzy girl. I remember when she was pregnant with Laura, vaguely. No one knows how she got a pastor's licence. She qualified by nabbing Brian, anyway. That's how it works in the AoG. That's why you want to marry well.

Luckily, Hillsong's female crew know all about it. One of my initial visits doing my early investigations was to a women's morning meeting where one of Bobbie's 'best friends', Wendy

Treat was speaking. One of the first things that came out in Wendy's warm-up was: 'I tell *all* my single girlfriends: don't keep your head low and walk slow, keep your head high and walk by.' My heart sank. I remembered then why I left.

Just this year, American pastor Holly Wagner, creator of God Chicks, recounted to the congregation a vision she had of going to heaven, after she had become intolerant of her husband of twenty-one years. 'But, Lord,' she reported saying, 'I was such a great counsellor and I was a pastor, and I wrote all these books for you.'

'Bummer,' God said to Holly. 'You were supposed to love and support Philip.'

That's it. It's your job, and your eternal responsibility. Your life dreams are cute, but at the end of the day it's all about making his dreams come true.

Bobbie insists that all her 'cheersquad' girls concentrate on Proverbs 31, a highly elitist proverb about a wife of a noble character who is worth far more than rubies. The Proverb 31 woman gets up before dawn and serves her husband, a respected man of the city, by doing her chores appropriately. She has maidservants, which quickly narrows down the amount of women who can realistically fulfil the proverb. But not, from what we see, the number of women who are encouraged and determined to try.

Hillsong girls are well aware of how important being a good wife is. It determines what kind of rib you get to be.

Chapter 16

SAVING ALL MY LOVE FOR YOU

If the entire plot of the Old Testament were made into a movie, it could only be screened in Amsterdam. With storylines so violent and obscene, even to preach against them would require an Adults-Only timeslot. The children of Israel make twenty-first century pornographers look infantile and highly unimaginative.

Given the sordid behaviour of the kings and commoners that preceded them spiritually, fundamentalist Christian sexuality is a curious thing. To witness it in its natural environment is Attenboroughesque: an environment where purity and pathos thrive and reproduce with the most startling of results.

Curiously, though, given this rich history, the sexuality of the fundamentalist is simple and totalitarian. There is no diversity or choice. Your mission, and you must accept it, is to refrain from any sex outside traditional marriage. One member only of the opposite sex, forever. Like the Baptist bumper-sticker about the bible: nothing more, nothing less, nothing else.

There are two exceptions. If your spouse dies, you're allowed to marry again. If they don't, you are with them until death, unless they 'commit adultery'. These days, physical violence is also being considered as a possible third exception, even though Jesus only ever gave the two get-out-of-jail-free cards. No adultery, no divorce.

This is a high standard to maintain, considering recent Christian research shows that American born-again Christians are just as likely to get divorced as non-Christians. Evangelist forefather Oral Roberts appeared on his glamorous colleague Benny Hinn's

TV show saying that since eighty-seven per cent of Americans were affected by divorce, he wasn't going to hold this against them. Even considering that it's near impossible to get eighty-seven per cent of Americans to agree on anything right now, I was still impressed by Oral's generosity of spirit.

Nobody would take me to the men's conference. It only goes for two nights and one day, which makes all the Hillsong girls giggle. They know that men have short attention spans and don't like girly stuff, so you've got to keep it short. The men's conference costs thirty-five dollars as opposed to the women's one hundred dollars, which is about the same difference as for a decent haircut, I guess.

No one would accompany me to the men's meetings on Thursday mornings either, despite my longing for the bacon and eggs they advertised as opposed to the raisin toast and coffee the girls were served in the building next door.

The only insight I got into the secret men's business of the Heterosexual Hillsong Hero was through a monthly email newsletter from the men's group RealMen, at Phil Pringle's Christian City Church. In one month, all my questions were answered. There, among advice about getting sleep and being a good servant, was this:

Men & relationships

Men regularly ask what is kosher for a Christian Man when it comes to sex. What is acceptable and what is not? I have read so many books that don't answer that particular question. They either add to the confusion or create guilt. Let me answer this for you. Sex is about intimacy and men need to know what builds intimacy between a man and a woman.

From a biblical point of view, the bible is silent about this subject. God created sex not only to procreate, but to be enjoyed (not endured). So what is in and what is out (pardon the pun). Anal sex is out because of medical reasons. It can damage the anus and the bowel. Otherwise everything else is acceptable, if both parties are in agreement and enjoy the experience.

The subject is far too extensive for me to answer in a few paragraphs, so if you are wanting to build intimacy with your wife through practical and helpful advice, I recommend you purchase 'A Celebration Of Sex' *by Dr Douglas E. Rosenau. The following link will get you to Nelson Ministry Services Creator site where this and other great books can be purchased.*[1]

As for women, they have not been neglected. Bobbie Houston released a set of three CDs called *Kingdom Women Love Sex*, but because the public took everything the wrong way again, she has renamed it *She Loves and Values Her Sexuality*. Bobbie created this series because she knows the topic is important, which is why she reports one newlywed listened to it eleven times.

Being a Bride of Christ has a dizzying aspect for a Hillsong girl. Having a love affair with Jesus is an established expectation. As Darlene said, you may not have a 'he' that brings out the best in you, but you have the Ultimate He in Jesus.

I don't want to date Jesus. I don't think that was the idea. All that 'Jesus is my boyfriend' music makes me nauseous. I've asked people about this continued urging to 'C'mon, fall in love with Jesus,' and they refer me to the Song of Solomon, a book in the bible depicting the dialogue of two lovers but mentioning nothing about romancing God. I continue to find the whole thing strange.

Sex is never far away from this brand of Christianity. With stunning boldness, Bobbie says in *I'll Have What She's Having*:

In that movie I made reference to at the beginning [When Harry Met Sally], *Sally fakes an orgasm. I looked up orgasm in the dictionary. Now relax, I do know what an orgasm is. I just needed a dictionary definition. Interestingly, it means,* ***height, zenith, summit****. Now, forget the bedroom for the moment. Shouldn't we who are 'in God' reach the summit, zenith, uttermost heights in life? I think so! Shouldn't we who are 'in God' have the genuine experience? When it comes to life, let's not settle for a* ***fake experience****, let's go for the* ***genuine article****.*[2]

But what if being genuine and being yourself is an abomination to God? What do you do then? What if you're an impossible princess?

Fundamentalists know that gay men are everywhere. They know what they look like now. They have earrings, a lisp and wear pink. Most of them either have 'full-blown' AIDS or will get it soon, so it's best not to touch them.

The 'church' cannot accept the gay man. This is not because he should be stoned to death like the bible says. It's because he's the ultimate rule breaker. What about women, though? They don't actually register as human beings, if the truth be known. It's all about men in the Christian hierarchy, and a real man is defined by his income and his family. What if the only use a man has for a pretty wife is to go shopping with her?

Fortunately, there are no homos at Hillsong. There weren't in the Garden of Eden and there sure won't be any in heaven. This raises some obvious concerns. Heaven is going to be full of monogamous heterosexuals with no interior design sense. The venue will be lit with fluorescent lighting and the catering will be homestyle rather than gourmet.

Truly, it's good to know that there are no homosexuals actually standing next to you in church. The way you can tell is that almost everyone is married. Or wants to be. And has children. Anyone who isn't married hasn't found the right girl, but in God's time they will.

These ideas underpin the huge rate of suicide and attempted suicide in fundamentalist churches all around the world. There is no coming out. Ever.

There was only one gay boy at Powerhouse Youth that I can remember, but he says he wasn't gay then. My god he was camp. He maintains he was straight, telling me he 'dated the most beautiful girl in the church'. I only ever saw him hang out with one girl, and they were inseparable best friends.

He wasn't gay back then; he was just doing Hills' artwork for a while. 'I'm the one,' he shrieked at me later, 'who took them from typed newsletters to glossy magazines. I told them, "We can look professional, but it's going to take work!"' The years were long and eventually he realised that he wasn't getting anywhere in Hillsong.

He had made confessions about indiscretions along the way which ruined his career chances in the church. He left Hillsong and the closet and is happy in his new Christian gay identity.

'That stuff they said about Frank Houston isn't true,' he told me. 'It couldn't have been. He was the only one who was nice to me. He would come into my office and sit down with me and ask me how I was. He was the only one who took an interest in me.'

'That's because you were gay,' I said. He didn't like that.

He had done his time in one of the ex-gay ministries that Hillsong used to run, Living Waters. He failed, and is among several who claim that they were the one that led to the program's closure. During those confessional group therapy hours with the sexually deviant—lesbians, gay men, frequent masturbators and the like—he said he'd learnt all he needed to know about the 'lifestyle' he was working so hard to ignore. By the time he came screaming out, he was already well educated in what gay men do.

Homosexuality is a lifestyle. It is something one is constantly doing. Evangelicals are well aware that homosexuals live, sleep and breathe homosexuality, they drink gay tea, think gay thoughts, sleep on gay sheets and spend their whole time plotting to sneak up behind good Christian folk and win them over. They won't be satisfied until everyone is leading the same depraved, perverse, decadent, lust-driven lives they are. They know God can't stand what it is they do, but they just don't care.

To make it worse, as Paul says in Romans, '*even the women* exchanged natural relations for unnatural ones'. There are some very ungrateful ribs out there. Some girls are not impressed by the size of your church or your car. Some of them don't care whether you were dux of the bible college. They don't care how many people you got saved or how good-looking you are. Yes, there are girls out there in the congregation who don't care if you are descended from Brian Houston himself.

Queen Victoria and Pentecostals both plead ignorance when it comes to lesbians. They've never heard of such a thing. They could never imagine how any rib would be able to extricate itself from masculinity's greatness. Lesbians are witches so any gay girl, particularly the pretty ones, must be under a spell to resist the charms of a good Christian man.

Born agains know that gay men are real. They've seen them on the news. They can't believe that these people would carry on with their lifestyle after what clearly took place in both Sodom and Gomorrah.

Gay men are strange monsters who are obsessed with perversity. But in the end gay men are men, which means they still get to be people and not ribs. They can repent and get wives and children.

But the lesbian, on the other hand, does not exist. For if a woman is not actively searching for or serving her husband, she ceases to be. There is no Proverbs 31 lesbian.

Yet, when I went to those girl meetings, I didn't know where to look. Hillsong is a breast church. The uniform consists of manicured hair, nails and face, and a very low-cut top. Interestingly, the girls also tended to wear long skirts or pants, which made everybody's implants really leap out. There is a cosmetic surgeon somewhere in that Hillsong business directory who is laughing all the way to the AoG credit union.

And as Bobbie says, we love to hug and kiss here at women's meetings, you'll never go home from Colour Your World starved for affection. And with all those beautiful girls and hot lights, I found more girl-on-girl action overall than on any given Friday night jelly-wrestling in a red-light public bar.

I never made it to a youth meeting, but the lesbians who did told me they didn't know where to look either. The girls in miniskirts and thigh-high boots are all touchy-feely with each other since everyone's just girlfriends, right? All that music, all that prayer and intimacy and laying on of hands, all that love, all those dreams, all that sisterhood, and so few clothes.

The strange thing about all this puritanical morality and homophobia is that the organisation is damn sexy. The music is sexy, the people are good-looking and the energy is intense. Intimacy runs high with emotion when people are vulnerable and sincerely looking for love. It's like a nightclub where they charge you the door fee after you're already in and sipping a drink.

That's not the only disturbing part. In this community of pure heterosexuality, there are many members who are gay or once were. More homos than you can poke a stick at. Even the stories I verified added up to a disproportionate number. Glamorous people, bright lights, special shows, love, joy and pride in being the well-dressed *you* God made. There's no way the Sydney Mardi Gras was as high camp as Hillsong conference 2005. Plus the Hillsong party goes for five nights, not one.

Frank Houston loved the company of young men. Over-age, but young. He had his golden boys, his disciples, the men he had stay in his home for years at a time, the men he travelled closely with, always young, always good-looking. Some of them became pastors. Some of them he groomed sexually, some he held their hand. Some of them he disciplined. Some of them needed their deviant sexuality purged, taking years, with extreme results. This may appear shocking to some people, but in an organisation whose values are submission and obedience, it's no wonder the sexualities are so perverse.

VERONICA

Weekly movies are $1.10 on Thursdays at my video store. Sam and I go every week. To make things fair, we get seven: three for me, three for him and one 'together' movie. I've already seen everything I want to in this video store. It's not very big and I was still wandering around one Thursday when I met the assistant, Veronica. It was getting cold and I didn't want to be there at all, to be honest. The video store, as I like to call it even in this age, is an adventure for any family, and this Thursday I was exhausted and not looking for new friends.

Veronica was trying to be helpful. At eighteen, she was involuntarily effervescent with youthful energy.

'Are you looking for anything in particular?' she asked.

I sighed. She was standing right there. Who knows, she might even be helpful. 'I'm writing a book,' I started. 'Do you know the Hillsong Church?' 'Yes,' she answered. 'Do you go to the Hillsong Church?' These are my two standard questions.

'No,' she said, 'but my parents are total Hillsongers.'

It turned out to be a strange coincidence. She recommended the movie *Saved* and told me the story of her family.

Her parents had been attending Hillsong for a year and a half and had recently donated their life savings of $100,000 to one of Hillsong's projects. They loved Hillsong and wished Veronica would go with them.

Veronica had other plans. She wanted to be a filmmaker. To do it she needed $10,000. Her parents were happy to pay for her to go to Hillsong's film school for $7000, but wouldn't pay a penny for her to enrol in the course she considered the best in the country. So Veronica was stuck getting paid twelve dollars an hour at the video store when she wasn't working her other job.

I liked Veronica's refusal to be bought. She was in shock at her parents' choices, though. Her father listened to Hillsong CDs and watched the DVDs in all his spare time. He was constantly involved. Her mother loved the women's meetings. Veronica couldn't make sense of her parents' fanaticism. She grew tired of hearing the same CDs over and over and over. For the most part she ignored it, but she said having them on around the house drove her crazy.

I saw her every Thursday and she let me renew the DVDs Sam had shoved under the couch until I found them.

One Thursday, Veronica had news. Her mother had left Hillsong. Without much explanation she had joined a Baptist church down the road. She was reportedly very happy.

Two Thursdays later, Veronica had more news. Her father had woken up and asked for a divorce after thirty years. There seemed to be no reason.

The next Thursday, there was a reason. He was having an affair with a woman from Hillsong. He was moving out on Friday.

Veronica's father rented a house down the road from her mother. The removalists he hired took almost everything out of the family home. It echoes now, she said. He took Veronica's bed, cushions, sheets and all, which had been her eighteenth-birthday present from her mother. Veronica was furious. She doesn't want it back any more.

Veronica's father's girlfriend has a husband. He has shaken Veronica's father's hand and said he approves of her father for his wife. They all attend Hillsong and sit together. Leadership has, so far, been silent.

Veronica's father's girlfriend moved into another house with her children. Veronica's father is paying the rent there as well. He told Veronica's mother he has a new family to support. Which is why he wants half of everything he can get in the divorce. Veronica's mother is not ruling out the possibility that the new couple will want children to celebrate their love.

Veronica doesn't call her father Dad. She said that since she was ten she has called him by his first name. She said they were never close and that she's always been much more concerned for her mother's welfare than her father's. Her mother told Veronica that she shouldn't cut her father out. He's always been your father, she said, and nothing will change that.

Yes, said Veronica, but he's always been a bastard, and nothing will change that.

Chapter 17

LET'S HEAR IT FOR THE BOY

> If a man has a stubborn and rebellious son who does not obey his father and mother and will not listen to them when they discipline him, his father and mother shall take hold of him and bring him to the elders at the gate of his town. They shall say to the elders, 'This son of ours is stubborn and rebellious. He will not obey us. He is a profligate and a drunkard.' Then all the men of his town shall stone him to death. You must purge the evil from among you. All Israel will hear of it and be afraid.
>
> —Deuteronomy 21:18–21

> *Rules for Christian Households*
> Wives, submit to your husbands as is fitting in the Lord. Husbands, love your wives and do not be harsh with them. Children, obey your parents in everything for this pleases the Lord. Fathers, do not embitter your children or they will become discouraged. Slaves, obey your earthly masters in everything; and do it, not only when their eye is on you and to win their favour. But with sincerity of heart and reverence for the Lord ... Masters, provide your slaves with what is right and fair, because you know that you also have a Master in heaven.
>
> —Colossians 3:18–22, 4:1

According to the bible, God is male. He is a Father, a Son, and the Spirit form of him is male. Jesus is a brother, if he is the Son, and we are Children of God. We are joint-heirs with the Son, after all. Which is going to make the reading of the will interesting.

All books of the bible were written by men under the divine inspiration of a male god. It is written to men, with clear instruction on how to handle everything beneath them, which is everything, including the earth, the animals and the she-folk.

Christianity was a very male bastion to begin with and not a whole lot has changed, despite the heroic efforts of women in history to be noticed, even casually, for something other than starching shirts.

Of course women have contributed to Christianity. All that nursing, and caring, and loving and forgiving, and sacrifice and chastity and obedience and poverty, are characteristics that come naturally to women, anyway. As Bobbie says, women are born into the world with open hands for giving. Which frees up a lot of time for men to get on with business.

In Australia, it's an all-male Assemblies of God.The eight members of the National Executive are male, as are all the State members. Reading through the National Executive outline is not so different from trying to meet guys on-line. 'Hi, meet Ian, he's the pastor of a city church with over 300,000 people. He loves changing lives, planting churches and seeing people radically on fire for God. He has a wife called Lindy and three beautiful children, who all go to church even though they're teenagers.'

It's icky. I found myself comparing these men. Some have a bigger church in a smaller city. Some have international ministries. But not to those hot sweaty countries, only to air-conditioned countries like Texas, where the room service is reliable and the bathrooms are sterile. Planting churches overseas, or having raised a couple in your youth group who did, is a winner. That's a real flag in the earth. Claiming other countries for God makes you a pioneer, not just a pastor. It was hard to choose whom I liked best.

As for the wife and family, well, they're terrific. Where would anyone be without them? These marriages must be intact. Watertight. The length of their marriage is related to the strength of their wisdom, particularly in these unstable times. Not everyone makes it any more, ain't that the truth. If you want to make National Executive decisions, boys, the search for the right companion can never start too early. And you must have children.

A rumour abounds that pastors aim to have three kids like Brian and Bobbie. There is not an option of no children, or one child. Even two seems a little ungrateful. Three is nice. A couple of boys, and a girl to provide friends for them to marry. More than three is greedy, really. Although I guess you can never have too many sons.

Most of the churches are run by men. Hillsong is. All of the members of the board of directors of Hillsong Pty Ltd and the church elders are men.

The boys of my generation became men quite early on in the piece. Getting married when you're not much more than twenty is often really cool when you're not much more than twenty. It's not common to find a bachelor floating free for long. As soon as his eligibility comes to light, and if he's a pastor's son, he's snapped up in the twinkling of an eye.

The men of Hillsong are in a terrible bind. They have to rule over their wives, yet demonstrate compassion. They must be metrosexual, but never, ever gay. The beauty of their wives is a reflection on their holiness. She must be the envy of every man and never look sideways at any of them. Without her you have no purpose, no chance at success. And she better be fertile. There's no greater curse on a pastor's photo opportunities than a fruitless marriage. We all know about people who can't have children. There's something they're not telling us, isn't there? Some kind of joint sin they haven't addressed.

At last count, the AoG has planted 1100 churches in Australia by sending out good folk, couples with the call of God on their lives. Everybody wants to be like Brian and Bobbie, except none of these churches has the 18,000 people required to support their lifestyle. Many have only fifty or sixty members, who live in the small town where the church was planted. None of these believers is tithing figures that end with multiple zeroes. Some weeks, the pastor's family lives off a very bare minimum.

Planting a small church in a faraway place isn't easy. If you're a newlywed, it can be a real shock to be thrust out into the wild. Babies turn up, and before you're twenty-five there's a lot to be a man about. As a pastor, you have to learn to cope. It's hard to live off a small income, so church growth is important. It's also better, a lot of the time, not to rock the boat. If church members bother you, or intimidate you with their views, you can't always afford to disagree and take authority. Their absence may mean the difference between paying the bills and not. So you put up with it. You keep your mouth shut, and do your best. Sometimes, it gets hard.

Church growth is a sign of God's blessing. If it's bigger, God is there more. Why else would all those people go? You have to keep working hard for church growth. Then you can put in a praise report at the next conference. Make sure you don't drop out of the loop. At the many conferences you are expected to attend, you still have to look cool and carefree. You have to look strong and successful, which costs money and more stress.

The pressure can creep up. Eventually it's exhausting to work all week as well as pastor a small church. Sometimes it's hard to sustain kindness towards a demanding flock. Strains on the family can start to show.

Men in the AoG will only ask for help as a desperate last resort. Needing help is a sign of not coping. Not coping is a sign of lack of faith. Or an abundance of sin. And not enough hard work. It's this type of person that can develop a negative attitude and become part of the problem, not part of the solution. We can't have leaders who aren't coping. Maybe leadership isn't the right place for you right now. Maybe you need a little time off.

Pastor Brian often says, emphatically, that he does not care to be around negative people. He won't spend time with people who are defeated, and who complain about the way things aren't. Brian likes to be around people who are excited about God, and have a vision and a purpose.

A man says yes as a sign of faith. He doesn't say no because he's not afraid. He is never uncertain. He is in partnership with the Almighty. A real man is committed to the things of God no matter what it costs.

If a man is not careful, he could lose his church. If he shows signs of one weakness, then what others will develop in him? Is he really fit to lead? If he's not, how soon can we get a replacement?

I don't know of any insurance against this kind of thing happening. Like a crooked cop, an ex-pastor has no other training. Twenty-odd years of devotion to the Cause, having been educated in the most highly regarded AoG bible college in the country, counts for absolutely nothing on a résumé. The high-celebrity pastors haven't tied their own shoes since Toronto. The anonymous ones specialise in a field that doesn't exist in the outside world. There was no need for a retirement fund when they started off, not when you have the call of God on your life.

It's important to be a man and make sure you are continually remasculinised. Women are the weaker sex and it is men's responsibility to ensure that doesn't change. There are no brownie points for prowess.

Your masculinity is based on your commitment to your wife, and how long you and your chosen one can stick it out.

The Pentecostals claimed a number of 195,000 in Australia's last census. They said that was more members than the Australian Football League, even though it has over 500,000 members. Still, if sport is the analogy we're left with, then so be it. It becomes difficult to tell the difference anyway between a footy team and a pastoral team after a while. Same bunch of guys running around an auditorium, leather-bound book underarm, making the crowd scream, picking up a sinner, running him all the way down field and kicking him right over the goals, all the while cheergirls going crazy with excitement. The players toss the ball back and forth to each other for an hour or so. There's a halftime show and everyone gets a little tipsy. In football, it's the other team we're fighting. In church, as long as you beat the hell out of the Enemy, you score. Every boy wants to be man of the match, don't they? All men love football, don't they? Brian does. He's the male role model for tens of thousands of men out there. He lectures on husbandry and fathering and the benefits of family. Which is great.

I'm not anti-family. Not by a long shot. I think family is a wonderful saver for government service providers. The last thing we need is more separations with numerous children having picnics with other parents without partners. No thank you. I've heard enough friends crying on the other end of the phone about family law. Personally, I'd like everyone to be just as happy as Larry. So it's not my fault if I have coffee with people and they start fighting. I never planned it that way, and usually have no inkling until someone's yelling at me that I started all this. I was still trying to decipher the Hillsong man's code first-hand when I ended up talking with Jack.

Jack's wife is the loveliest girl in the world. It's the one thing we agree on. That's why he wants to keep her that way. Yet, after one conversation with me in the garden she had come back inside with a different attitude. She was displaying a negative opinion of Hills. He doesn't need that kind of negativity in his household.

Technically, I've known her longer than he has, although he's right. He's the one who loves her and will spend the rest of his life with her. She's the mother of his boys.

She and I had caught up at Colour Your World women's conference a couple of months before I spoke to Jack. She asked me my thoughts. I told her it was the biggest load of rubbish I had come across in a long time. She said you have to learn to filter out the good from the bad.

We met a few weeks later for coffee and talked about everyone from way back when. Her entire family has faithfully attended Hills for twenty years and she knows what became of everyone and anyone. We decided to get our kids together.

Her mother and sister were sitting on the couch when I arrived at her house. I asked her privately if she had warned them. She didn't see what I was worried about. She herself had lots of questions, and while the kids played she called Hillsong a dictatorship. She asked me where the money goes. She wanted to know all about this book.

A couple of hours and a couple of cups of coffee later and it was time to go home. I called her that evening and her husband, Jack, answered the phone. It was eight-thirty, and I asked him if it was too late. He said it was. I just got home and I don't let her talk on the phone after eight-thirty. I'd heard that tone of voice from husbands before. Sometimes I feel like I'm the drunk divorcee from downstairs who's come upstairs to whisper evil into Marylou's innocent ears while Jimmy's out doing an honest day's work.

But this guy was harsh. He wanted nothing to do with negativity, he said. What good did it do him and his family to be a part of such a negative adventure as the book which, in his opinion, would be a passing wind and sell about 150 copies? No one he knew was interested in listening to someone complaining about their life or dredging up the past. Why rehash?

He had been there, he said. He had been obsessed with people who had done him wrong in the church. He realised he had to move on. In fact, he had coffee with Brian just the other day. Brian told him he knew that in the old days he was a tyrant and that Hillsong had made a lot of mistakes. Brian conceded that he had handled Jack's own situation badly. And they had a laugh. That was that. You move on.

It wasn't hurting Hills that he had been angry. It was only hurting him. And as his wife says, you have to get better, not bitter. There's no perfect church, he told me. If this one was ninety per cent good and ten per cent bad, then what more could he hope for? They do so much good stuff, you know, he said.

Why this interest in his wife, he wondered: she's the type, he said, to talk to anyone. She gets caught up in other people's lives. She's a great conversationalist because even strangers feel comfortable with her. So he has to be careful about who she talks to. And who influences her.

He doesn't choose her friends for her, he said, but if he has to make that decision, he will. He can't see why we girls can't talk about our kids and our husbands. Why would we want to talk about something so negative as the book? Men, he told me, don't talk the way women have to. They go to a football game and grunt at each other for hours and call it a good night out. He understands, though, how women are.

The most important things to him were his wife and his family, he said, and he would do anything to protect them. One thing that was not going to be happening was his kids being exposed to such negativity. He knows that Hillsong has its faults, he's seen a lot of things. But the children's program puts a smile on his kids' faces and that's the way he likes it.

He had told his wife that if this friendship with me turned negative he would have to call it off. The decision was confirmed when his boys were in the car with him on the way to soccer after I'd been to their house.

'Why is that lady so angry at church, Daddy?' one was reported to have asked.

My ten-year-old is very inquisitive, he told me. He is curious about everything. I don't need him asking questions like, 'What does "emasculated" mean, Daddy?' he said, the word 'emasculated' causing him audible physical discomfort. (Don't worry, son, that's just a made-up nonsense word. Fear not. Your masculinity is eternal.)

That's when he came in and said to her, 'It's over.'

'Have you made these decisions before?' I asked him.

'Of course I have,' he said.

'And how does she go with them?' I asked.

'She's fine,' he said. 'She knows I know what's best for her.'

'If you're going to be all head of the household and all ...' I started.

His tone changed from charismatic bible college graduate to psycho. 'Are you trying to say I'm not?'

'No,' I said. 'I just want to ask you one favour.'

'What?'

'Would you get her an email address and teach her to use the internet, please?'

He laughed. 'Believe me,' he said, 'I've tried.' He may well have but she was keen as mustard after he'd left for soccer to learn to Google. He's going to kill me when he checks his web history.

I asked him what might happen if she explodes and kills him when he's fifty. 'I'm not the one who gave her the book on serial killers she's reading,' I offered. He didn't seem worried. He'd been in that situation with her older sister. Everyone had to tiptoe around her until he put her in her place. Now they were the greatest of mates because everyone knows where they stand.

Both of their parents have been together forever, his fifty years, hers forty. He looks at his father, he said, and sees a placid man now. Jack, however, knows he himself has a bad temper. Just like her father used to. Now, his dad's the calmest man in the world, but when he was young it was different. Jack's wife understands this, he says, like Bobbie understands Brian.

Part of maturity is moving on, he explained. Focus on the positive. Why dwell on the negative when there's so much good going on? Also, he didn't want their name associated with me and affecting the whole family in Hillsong. It just wasn't worth it. I told him I totally understood, because I did.

I asked him to say hello to her, and I thanked him for taking the time to explain to me why I had to get out of their lives. He said it was a pleasure but that he had missed half the movie. And he had been looking forward to it. It was a Friday night. Saturdays are soccer all day long. And Sundays are for church. I went back downstairs to my apartment to leave Marylou and Jimmy be and pour myself another scotch. I put my hair up in curlers, my slippered feet up on the couch and waited till the bitter, soothing alcohol took me right through until the morning.

DAVID'S PRINCESS

It doesn't say why King David did not lead his army into war. The bible tells us only that in the spring, when kings go off to battle, David instead sent Joab out with his men.

But David remained in Jerusalem.

Getting up from his bed one night, King David took a walk around the roof of his palace. From there, he saw Bathsheba bathing. It says she was very beautiful.

King David made enquiries about her. He was informed that she was the wife of his soldier Uriah, who was away at war for Israel.

David sent messengers to get her. She came to him and he slept with her.

Bathsheba, the beautiful, who brought the King undone. Bathsheba, the adulteress. Bathsheba, the one the King could not resist. Bathsheba, who was not given the choice to resist the King.

When Bathsheba became pregnant, King David did not know what to do. He sent for Uriah, and encouraged him to spend the night with his wife. Loyal Uriah refused to leave the King unguarded and slept at the door of the palace instead.

So King David sent orders for Uriah to be put in the front line where the fighting was fiercest and then for the troops to withdraw from him, so he would be killed. And there on the battlefield, at the orders of his general, Uriah died.

When Uriah's wife heard that her husband was dead, she mourned for him. After the time of mourning was over, David had her brought to his house, and she became his wife and bore him a son. But the thing David had done displeased the Lord.

The Lord's displeasure saw Bathsheba's baby die to punish King David, and so Bathsheba was punished again. Their next child was King Solomon the Wise. David famously begged for the Lord's forgiveness, and the Lord ended up using him for great things including being King Solomon's teacher. But what about Bathsheba?

It doesn't say whether Uriah and Bathsheba had children of their own. It doesn't say if Bathsheba grieved that he was dead, just that she was given her allotted mourning time. Then she became property of the King. How many Bathshebas are there?

Maybe Uriah and Bathsheba had children, and maybe they mourned their father, even if he was a Hittite. What happened when those children grew up? Did they see their countrymen bowing to the King and taking his word as gospel? Did their blood boil when they saw their mother, trapped by the King's whims? Did Bathsheba grow to enjoy being a queen, after some time had passed?

One day, when David has been too glorified, Uriah's children might tell the story of a king who should have been at war with his men, but instead remained in Jerusalem. Yet, with their father long dead, who will listen to Uriah's children in David's kingdom?

Chapter 18

KIDS

I'd like to ask [Marilyn Manson], 'Did I influence you in any way to this lifestyle?' I keep thinking, 'Wow, did I do something I should have done differently?'

—Carolyn Cole, former principal, Heritage Christian School, in Marilyn Manson, *The Long Hard Road Out of Hell* (1998)

I am 10 years old. I only can give a quarter. Please don't underrate me because of my age, I believe strongly in Jesus.

—Letter to TV evangelist, reported by Zira Bransletter in *Tulsa World* (27 April 2003)

One Sunday morning around ten, pyjama-clad, I answer the knock at my door. There, standing, immaculately groomed, are an elderly gentleman, a middle-aged woman and a boy of about nine. Jehovah's Witnesses. I'm too tired. I don't have the energy to play with the J-Dubs. I tell them I can't possibly and shut the door.

As soon as I do, I am struck by the image of the boy. He was hollow-eyed, lost and silent. That terrible look children have when they are in a situation that is, for them, timeless and powerless. While other boys are at soccer, or even in church, he is out, dressed in pants and a long-sleeved collared shirt and a bow-tie with his mother and the old man, doorknocking, recruiting.

I throw on a sweatshirt and walk around the block looking for them. I want to talk to the boy. They'd come to preach to me, so I figured it was only fair. I want to say to him: get your older brother, get someone at school, get *anyone* to Google these people. Find out about them. It's okay, kid, but you haven't got long till you can leave—or have you? But they were gone.

The fundamentalist Christian worldview provides a bizarre perspective on life. Apparently I am an evil parent because I refused to teach my son the Santa story. I had thought it perverse to lie to an infant about a Coca-Cola version of God, only to tell him years later that we'd all been deceiving him for no defensible reason.

And I would find it far stranger to instill the values of the Old Testament into a developing child's psyche at home or via innocent-looking 85-year-old women in scripture classes. The stories of the bible are brutal and unpredictable. A few pages into the book, by Genesis 6, God's heart was filled with regret and he decided to drown the lot of us. The giraffes and tigers looked sweet going in two by two, but I'm still not good with the Noah story. A few months ago, my mother gave me a DVD. 'A friend of your father's makes these,' she said. 'Just show it to Sam.' Sure, Mum, right after *Nightmare on Elm Street*. On the back it reads:

God created the world in six days, the heavens and the earth and every living thing, including Adam, who lives in the Garden of Eden. When God creates Eve from Adam's rib as a companion for Adam, he warns Adam and Eve about the Tree of Knowledge, and to never eat its fruit. A wicked serpent tricks Eve into eating a fruit from the tree and when she gives it to Adam to eat as well, God becomes angry and banishes them from the Garden of Eden and punishes the serpent. In the new mortal world, Eve gives birth to Cain and Abel, who become great friends until they are adults. When Cain suddenly kills Abel out of jealousy, he is cursed to become a restless wanderer of the Earth.[1]

All fundamentalists realise the urgency of controlling the children, and born agains are no exception. I am eternally grateful that my parents sent me to a state high school. Evangelical Christians have a dreadful tendency to send their children to 'Christian' schools or, worse yet, to homeschool them.

While there is an infinite variety of Christian schools worldwide, the evangelical/born-again/Pentecostal school, often advertised as 'non or multi-denominational', is the scariest. Entertainer Marilyn Manson grew up in a devout evangelical family and attended a Christian school. Manson credits it with his loss of faith and much of his gory artistic expression.

Gradually, I began to resent Christian school and doubt everything I was told. It became clear that the suffering they were praying to be released from was a suffering they had imposed on themselves—and now us. The beast they lived in fear of was really themselves: it was man, not some mythological demon, that was going to destroy man in the end. And this beast had been created out of their fear. The seeds of who I am now had been planted.[2]

A Christian education sounds super, but if the school is attached to a church, spiritually or financially, it can make for some close-knit problems. It's one thing if all the kids from church go to school together. It's another if the senior pastor is the principal. One nasty rumour in either the church or the school and a family's reputation can be destroyed.

Born agains believe in indoctrinating children relentlessly. As with smoking, the younger you get 'em started, the harder they find it to quit. According to research published in 2004 by the Barna Group, an organisation specifically devoted to born-again Christian market research, there are 98 million Americans who have received Jesus Christ as their saviour, thirty-eight per cent of adults and thirty-three per cent of teenagers. Around a third of America is saved! One study highlighted the age, circumstances and subsequent values of 992 born-again Christian salvation stories. It is a stark set of demographics. The age at which salvation takes place becomes very significant.

Forty-three per cent of Americans who received Jesus or got saved did so before the age of eighteen. Half of these were led to the Lord by their parents, another twenty per cent by a relative or friend. This group were least likely to get saved via media or at an event or church, which is another reason why fundamentalists promote 'family values'. The most sure-fire way to get people saved is to give birth to them. These early birds are much more likely than those who convert later to stay 'absolutely committed' to Christianity, although they are also less conservative in their spirituality, watch less religious TV and talk about their faith less with their friends than the latecomers.

Thirty-four per cent of born agains got saved between the ages of eighteen and twenty-one. Parental influence on their decision dropped to twenty per cent, which was the same as that of a friend. Other relatives accounted for sixteen per cent, ministers ten per cent, and twenty per cent were triggered by an event. Youth rallies and church take on a meaningful role during young adulthood.

Only twenty-five per cent of American born agains got saved after their twenty-first birthday. These are the people more likely to watch religious TV and discuss matters of faith.

Hillsong pastors preach that if you don't bring your kids to church, you can't expect them to stay saved. The research generally supports this. Hillsong sets itself up as the alternative to hell for all children; without Hillsong your precious bundles will be 'out there in the world' and end up 'on drugs'. How Hillsong knows this I'm not sure, but it's almost guaranteed they'll be 'on drugs' the second Sunday they skip 'church'.

The kids' program at Hillsong is extensive, even including their own life-size costume characters. At Hillsong Kids, or Kidsong, Jesus is fun.

The Hillsong Kids' music is by far the coolest Sunday school music ever. It's got a real mainstream pop feel, sung in the little girl voices that are so popular now. Hillsong Kids also has live album recording sessions. My favourite song is 'Every Move I Make' from *Shout to the Lord Kids* where Hanson meets Roxette. It starts with a great guitar lead that everyone from birth to my age and older can get into, even do their housework to, which wound up happening to me. And I know it's terrific to have the kids up and happy and not fighting on a Sunday morning and, true, this kind of music has made me yearn for Hillsong in ways unseen since Youth Alive rallies. It just made me wonder about consent. It's all very well for adults to subject themselves to trance-like states and hypnosis, but are these kids going to sue when they grow up? Some of the other songs are intense too. 'I Give You My Heart', 'Worship You Forever' and 'Open the Eyes of My Heart', for example.

Not satisfied with just their kids, they want yours as well. And everybody else's. I still get flashbacks of the DVD of Bobbie in Uganda, meeting her orphan and putting a $30 pink Colour Your World t-shirt on her, 'from all the princesses at home', while the other ten children in the room had gaping holes in their clothing.

Closer to home, Hillsong is making sure that it impacts on the young people of Australia with its message, whether or not they are aware of it. Hillsong runs community service programs for children and teenagers of all kinds that at first glance appear apolitical or inoffensively 'Christian'. One such service is Shine, for girls aged twelve to sixteen. Promoted as a course that offers young women self-esteem, Shine currently runs over 150 programs, including in detention centres and high schools, with very positive feedback. Teachers and welfare workers have told me that the girls love the program and the attention they receive.

Shine is explicit in its wishes for female self-discovery:

Shine presents the truth that every girl has intrinsic value and is somebody.

This journey is explored through the concepts of worth, strength & purpose …

I have worth!*—Through skincare, makeup, haircare and nailcare, girls discover their value in their God created uniqueness.*

I have strength!*—Explores the power of choice in each girl's life and reinforces the truth that decisions determine destiny. Covers will-power, feelings, peer pressure, problem solving, etiquette and respect.*

I have purpose!*—Purpose and destiny are examined in the light of looking after themselves; identifying the hopes and dreams they have for their life and the confidence and tools to walk in them.*

Shining.[3]

If only I knew then when I was growing up what I know now. The answer's been nailcare all this time.

Chapter 19

THERE'S NO BUSINESS LIKE SHOW BUSINESS

> His unity is an arrow, it is a shield, when everything is great, and right and correct in God, not perfect, but correct, you know what I'm saying? It's like it is a shield, the enemy cannot, the fiery darts of the Enemy cannot penetrate your lives. And it is also an overshadowing protector, which is what we try and teach you from Malachi about giving when you when you doing what is correct in God, there is a protection over your life, that you don't even have to like, hello, it's just there. So it is a very, very powerful thing. Amen?
>
> —Bobbie Houston,
> *She Loves and Values Her Sexuality* (2004)

If you're still wondering whether an organisation is a cult, try this two-second test: if it's all about recruitment and fundraising, it's a cult. Some longstanding ex-members of Hillsong say it was always about numbers and offerings, that there was always a competitive spirit.

The rivalry was over salvation quotas initially. Pastors would argue over coffee about who had more conversions that year at their church or rally. They were serious, sometimes heated discussions.

The church was a good place to do business. And there were plenty of opportunities to make money right from the start.

It's all due to the trust the Australian government has in charities, namely Christian ones. Conservatives believe that charities operate as a collective Florence Nightingale, and allow them extraordinary tax breaks as a result. Along with educational institutions, religious institutions do not have to pay sales tax. The Assemblies of God could have written this policy in as the fifth gospel. For them it started small with salary packaging and fleet cars.

According to folklore, pastors were always poor and struggling. Ministry is a calling, not a career. If God requires your service, he'll supply your needs. It was called living by faith, and the miraculous abounded. Pastors were paid very little, we knew that.

What we didn't know was the unmatchable unlimited salary packaging operation these boys had. They might take, for example, a \$30,000 salary but receive only \$15,000 in wages. This usually qualified them for social security benefits, and greatly reduced the level of personal income tax paid. The remaining \$15,000 could be used to pay for bills, mortgages, holidays, or anything really in the church's name. No tax on it. This was called the 'pastoral expense account'.

There are no fringe benefits concerns for church or pastor. So where other companies offer a car on top of a cash wage, the employer has to pay fringe benefits income tax on the car. The Australian Tax Office isn't stupid. So when it was time for everyone to get a new car, the Assemblies of God was able to save thirty per cent using their non-taxable expense account. A new car depreciates around ten per cent within seconds of driving it out of the showroom, so within six months the boys were selling the car as a new model at ninety per cent of its original retail price, profiting roughly twenty per cent. Which allowed everybody to improve next round. It's always worthwhile noting which brand of car is mentioned from the pulpit to know which deals have recently been cut for the pastors.

Of course, all churches are allowed this benefit. Not all churches, though, say explicitly that they need more money. By the mid-nineties, the AoG car system had to be toned down a little. Ferraris were a little showy, it was deemed. A number of industries are grateful for the 'name it and claim it' gospel.

None, however, is as successful as the Hillsong industry itself. In order to produce a successful CD in Australia, a musician has to sign a contract with a record company which produces, publishes and markets the album. The performer also has to pay distributors and retailers before any returns are made. Even independent entertainers who produce their own material must pay for distribution and give a commission for retail.

Not Hillsong. They don't even have to pay the performers, or hire a studio. Hillsong is the production house. The majority of the musicians and production technicians are volunteers. The live audiences pay to be a part of the recording. Hillsong is the artist, the record company, the publisher, the distributor and the retailer. The workers don't get paid and no tax is paid on any of these stages of production, the way any other guitarist or band would have to.

Songwriter royalties, the only copyright that needs paying, and some production expenses are subtracted. Apart from that, Hillsong gets all the profit. And it's all tax-free!

Imagine if you could run a financial institution under these conditions. You can and the AoG does. On the Australian Assemblies of God website, an investment account is advertised brightly flashing higher interest rates than competitor banks. Lower interest rates on home loans might be helped by the tax breaks as well as the supportive attendance of the prime minister and the federal treasurer at the primary place of business.

Yet in the terms and conditions on the application form it says that 'the AoG Development fund is designed for investors who wish to promote the charitable and religious purposes of the Assemblies of God in Australia and for whom the considerations of profit are not of primary relevance'. Of course not. 'All profits derived from the activities of the AoG Development fund are used for the wider work of the Assemblies of God in Australia.'

The next point concedes that 'such investments are not specifically secured' but are underwritten by the AoG. The AoG Development Fund is not subject to the normal requirement to have a prospectus and trust deed under Corporations Law, and this scheme has not been examined or approved by the Australian Securities and Investment Commission. In 2004, there was $19.4 million invested in an underwriting body whose annual report for 2003 reveals a surplus of $63,000 in 2003 and net assets of $288,531, compared with a loss of $1 million in 2002.

An organisation or individual needs a thousand dollars minimum to invest. It's not actually a secured investment, but the Assemblies of God guarantees your money so there's no need for that governmental rigmarole. Despite the flashing interest rates, by the time you get down to the fine print you understand that this is not a *money*-making enterprise, no way. It is an opportunity to invest in the work of the Lord. Unfortunately for most of the population, you have to be a Christian in order to take advantage of this offer. That may seem simple to most, but you have to have an affiliation with a Christian church in Australia.

This company has also branched out into mortgages and superannuation. No tax. All completely legal. The fund reserves the right to refuse investment with anyone. The amassing of Christian wealth has begun.

The investments are said to be low risk and high liquidity, such as fleet cars and real estate. It's not clear how many properties are owned by the pastors in the church's names. Or in one of the business's names. Hillsong runs too many other companies and incorporated associations to list. Some, such as Colour Your World, don't seem to be registered businesses at all, while others such as Australian Christian Women NSW Incorporated don't seem to *do* anything at all except organise conferences, yet they are entitled to all the charitable tax concessions.

Leadership Ministries Incorporated (LMI) is the incorporated association through which Brian and Bobbie's pay is channelled. LMI manages the Houstons' properties. Having at least twice sold real estate to their own company, they make a tax-free profit on properties they can keep using. There is also a Life Ministries Inc. in Western Australia which receives the same tax concessions.

Educational institutions are, as mentioned, also exempt from sales tax. Any church, or even an ice-skating rink, could be used as a bible college auditorium either now or in the future. Thus, any purchases made on behalf of this college are also tax-free. Which is strange given that Hillsong rents its current meeting place out to corporate companies privately.

If you have a ministry of your own externally, say, youth or missions, and you had come up with a really cool idea, your merchandising products bought by the church are tax-free. The profits are received back into the ministries, and still no tax.

These are just the formalities. The straight job, as it were, what you put down on paper. But it's the chickenfeed. Everybody knows moonlighting's where the money is.

When a pastor preaches at his own church, he earns his weekly salary. When he preaches at someone else's, he gets a traditional 'love offering' as well. The love offering stems from the days when evangelists travelled in faith, not knowing where they might rest their heads that night or how they might feed the new baby. Because of the sacrificial life they were leading, a visit to your church obviously cost them. The congregation was always happy to dig deep after their tithes, to give a love offering for the visiting pastor. It is still a common practice.

The love offering is pocketed. No one sees it. And the favour will be returned when the hosts appear at the visitor's home church. It's the main reason evangelists travel as often as they can and why they have so many close friends.

Hillsong is indeed a registered company. Its board of directors is the eldership of the church. Brian presides over both, and the Gloria Jean's boss Nabi Saleh is now a clear second. There is nothing on paper to link Gloria Jean's to Hillsong apart from Nabi Saleh himself.

Gloria Jean's is one of Australia's most recent business success stories. Founders Nabi Saleh and Peter Irvine met at Hillsong and decided to open a coffee chain. Their timing was impeccable. With smoking and drinking receding from the picture in these healthy days, especially for born-again Christians, coffee has taken the cultural place of the smoke break and even lunch. Being able to make a cup of coffee is now a very employable skill.

Which is why Gloria Jean's has opened up an outlet at a women's prison that specialises in programs of rehabilitation. Visitors to the jail can buy a full-priced cup of coffee from an inmate who is on wages of about fifty cents an hour. These women are trained up so that on release they are able to get jobs with Gloria Jean's, having graduated from a very cheap traineeship. Gloria Jean's also sponsors Mercy Ministries, Hillsong's young women's rehab, where 'girls in trouble' (or who have 'been involved in lesbianism') can get help. There's no better place than a jail to recruit 'girls in trouble' or train the unemployable for future use, at almost no cost. And of course it offers these women the opportunity to become part of the family that Nabi Saleh says you join when you work for Gloria Jean's.

I contacted the jail's governor and expressed my concern about the recruitment opportunities for the mob from Gloria Jean's, given the connection with Hillsong. After many weeks, I received a clarification. It wasn't that Gloria Jean's had anything to do with Hillsong; it was just that the owners of the particular franchise at the jail attended Hillsong. Sheer coincidence.

There are rumours that Hillsong members get the best franchise locations, but these have never been officially confirmed. Surely it pays to be part of two families, not just one.

Gloria Jean's sponsors Opportunity International, which is behind the micro-enterprise agreements that are operating around Australia and in countries in which foreign gods are worshipped. The United Nations declared 2005 the year of micro-enterprise, and the federal government in Australia wasted no time in endorsing it. The idea is that a big company with lots of money offers people who have no hope of starting their own business a little bit of money to do it. The individual can then become self-sufficient, with a debt to the big company. Labor MP Warren Snowdon described some of the results:

Hillsong Emerge spent $315,000 from a federal government grant to employ seven people for a microcredit program in Sydney that gave just six Indigenous people a loan. The total grant for the microcredit program was $965,421, with ninety-three borrowers across Australia. Only $362,673 of the grant ended up in the hands of Indigenous borrowers. The sum of $610,000 was also spent by Hillsong on projects for 'business development' and 'self-confidence for young women' in Sydney, which was supposed to help Indigenous people find employment.

Answers to questions asked by the federal shadow minister for indigenous affairs, Senator Chris Evans, reveal that, from seventy-four clients, Hillsong Emerge advise that to their knowledge 'none of those assisted have moved to full self-employment'.[1]

*

None of this would ever have been possible without the original sponsors: the tithers. The Old Testament practice of tithing has kept the pastors in frequent flyer points from here to eternity.

Will a man rob God? Yet you rob me.

But you ask, 'How do we rob you?'

In tithes and offerings. You are under a curse—the whole nation of you—because you are robbing me. Bring the whole tithe into the storehouse, that there may be food in my house. Test me in this, says the Lord Almighty, and see if I will not throw open the floodgates of heaven and pour out so much blessing that you will not have enough room for it. Then all the nations will call you blessed, for yours will be a delightful land, says the Lord Almighty. (Malachi 3:8–12)

Malachi, Malachi, Malachi. An international revolution based on five verses in Malachi.

What we were taught was that you better give unless you want to steal from God himself. Plus when you give, God will pour out blessings on you. Easy as pie. If the payout was never guaranteed, there was a clear answer to this. When you sow into something, the harvest doesn't come overnight. You don't plant an avocado seed and expect to find avocadoes the next morning. The Lord doesn't reward impatience. Oh, and the longer you wait, the bigger your harvest will be.

To tithe literally means to give a tenth. This is a complicated Old Testament practice, relevant to certain tribes of Israel. It was never for every man, woman and child, despite being heralded as such by the prosperity proponents. The understanding at Hillsong and in churches like it around the world is that each person should tithe whatever they receive as income. Pocket money, babysitting earnings, wages, Christmas bonuses, all before tax. One must give one's first fruits to God, not the tax department.

Tithing is not just for individuals. Ten per cent pre-tax of what every tiny church makes in the weekly offering goes back to the head office of the Assemblies of God. This is called the National Executive expense account and is used accordingly for the members of the team to travel. It's an expensive role to go around gathering up love offerings, and it's impossible on a meagre pastor's salary.

Offerings are money you want to give above and beyond your tithe. This may be a general offering, or for a specific purpose such as the building fund, overseas missions or a love offering.

Sacrificial offerings occur when the pastor believes that it is appropriate for you to go without something to support a cause. It often comes across as a privilege to be involved in such a special project, such as a building or outreach, and people are willing to sacrifice 'that trip to McDonald's', as it is often referred to, and give the money used for that to the church.

How does one pay tithes and offerings? At Hillsong it couldn't be easier. Not one service that I have ever attended has neglected to mention that the envelopes under your seat, labelled according to offering department, allow you to pay by cash, cheque (made out to 'Hillsong Church'), or that you can fill your credit card details out. The envelopes have the boxes ready to tick against a backdrop of the Sydney Opera House or the Sydney Harbour Bridge. Makes giving an all-round Australian experience.

The offerings are taken upstairs and counted by the counters, then the money is written up and put away into bags. On Monday the armed truck comes and takes the money away.

Where do the millions go? Hillsong says that its books are open and anyone can have a look for themselves. The catch is that they mean anyone who is trusted by the church. And the reports from such people who have asked to see the books describe being looked at up and down and being told they had an attitude problem. In any case, Hillsong conceded an income of $50 million for 2005.

Brian told viewers of ABC TV's *Australian Story* in 2005 that 'sixty per cent of that goes to helping people directly through our programs and our ministries and so on, twenty-eight per cent to buildings and facilities and twelve per cent to administration and running of the ministry'.

Does it go where they say it's going? If, hypothetically, the AoG says that money is going to 'missions' and all the missions money goes to the TV program, does TV count as missionary work? Does the Lord's work include the business-class airfares and five-star accommodation that pastors scratch each other's backs with? Who pays for the restoration processes for the fallen pastors? Do the sacrificial givers know that the AoG spent $100,000 in 1995 on one defamation case that they eventually discontinued?

It doesn't matter. Nationalise the Loss, Personalise the Profit is the virtual bumper-sticker on the fleet cars they're driving.

People talk of envelopes of cash pushed over tables as commission on love offerings. And pastors are looking great.

None of this is a philosophical problem for the new fundamentalist Christian. God wants you to be rich. He called you to live in abundance. Why shouldn't Brian ride a Harley? It's the best way of demonstrating the blessing of God in his life.

How else will the new Christians understand how their lives can be, will be, if they follow this same formula? They have to give in order to receive. They have to tithe and be faithful. And then they too will get their harvest.

It's just that none of the average joes can compete with those tax breaks. God may want them to be rich. They may need more money. But without the government assistance, it's unlikely they'll get it as easily as the leaders do.

IF I WAS A RICH GIRL

> I clearly remember two young men who each had specific dreams and goals for their future. On separate occasions, they each shared their personal vision for their lives with me. Both of them had outstanding business acumen, with the potential of great success in the corporate world.
>
> The first one confidently told me his vision. 'Brian, my ambition is to be a millionaire by the age of 30!' He had set himself a goal and he certainly had the determination and potential to achieve it.
>
> But the vision of the second young man impressed me more. 'Brian,' he said, 'my personal vision is to fund and finance the salvation of the earth.' What a powerful perspective he placed on his gift and talent. To him, money was a tool which could do great things for the Cause of the King and the Kingdom.
>
> —Brian Houston, *For This Cause* (2001)

Prosperity theology is very confusing to me. It's a contradiction in terms, like military intelligence.

Not that I've got anything against going shopping. And I love rich people. Rich people are lots of fun. I've read Paris Hilton's book so many times I can't believe how much fun rich people are having.

Who wouldn't want to be a part of it? Yet, as she says (in her book *Confessions of an Heiress*), 'An heiress would never talk about money. It's boring and only agents, lawyers and managers should ever talk about money.'

Paris is right; it's gauche to talk about money. That's because Paris comes from old money. Not that old, but much older than the prosperity spin-doctors'.

Old-monied people don't discuss money because only the miserly eccentric aunt or the crazy cousin talks about how much things cost, or where the money is hidden.

I am Jewish. This is a religion where your first-born son gets bought back from the synagogue by making a cash donation. You buy the seats you sit at in the synagogue and they engrave your family's name on a gold plate. G-d is indeed a G-d of money. The better a Jew you are, the more money you get. That's the way it works. But ask any Jewish person, and they'll tell you they have no money, they wish they didn't have what they have and that money is a terrible thing. Jews are a constant turnover of old and new money.

New-monied people love talking about money. How much they made, what they spent it on. What new-monied destinations they travelled to. How it's changed their lives. Other new-monied friends they've made. And how much more money they're going to make at this rate. They can't believe how great money turned out to be.

New-monied people talk about money all the time because that's how they think it's made. Expressing one's financial status seems to be related to expressing one's business acumen, in their minds. Recent success seems to make them experts on future investments as well. Oddly, this somehow ends up being about investing in them. Even if their success was contingent on picking the right lotto numbers.

Even though new-monied people appear to love nothing more than to gather together and talk about money, the sad truth is that they actually *need* to do this. Talking about it, visualising it, living it, was often part of the book they read, or workshop they went to. And even when the money's made, they can't stop living it like a 24-hour-a-day infomercial.

Once they've got money, the new-monied don't know what to do with it or how to maintain it. So they write motivational books on how you can become more like them. Or if they're AoG, they start a church.

New-monied people like to talk about how getting money didn't turn out to be as bad as they thought it would be. They didn't hate themselves quite as much as they thought they might, didn't feel themselves changing, and if they did, they surprisingly felt it was for the better. Even if they do find their values becoming a little more conservative of late.

Prosperity proponents always remind you that money is not important to them. Just like Jenny from the Block, they will always tell you that the rocks that they got mean nothing to them. It'll never change the person that they are. They still wear those rocks, though.

According to Brian Houston in his book *You Need More Money*, money is the answer to everything.

It's true!—money is inevitably the bottom line of everything.

What is the answer to hunger? Money! But you may say 'What about food?' But you need money to buy it. What is the short-term solution to poverty? Money! What is the answer to powerlessness in your life? Money! It enables you to be influential.

While money provides many positive solutions, money also has just as many negative responses.

How do you feed a heroin addiction? Money!

What is listed as one of the greatest causes for marriage failure? Money![1]

There used to be a time when Christian preachers used to yell out 'Jesus!' It was the answer to every question they asked the congregation.

'What's the answer to heroin addiction? Jesus!'

I could be grateful and say at least they're being honest now, about money being the real answer and Jesus being some kind of distraction for a good night out.

An inmate in a NSW jail was bailed to a Hillsong rehabilitation service. On the first day he was there, one of the young millionaire businessmen leaders took him out to show him his sportscar. The idea was to get the client to realise that with a bit of elbow grease and some commitment to the Jesus program, he too could have a car like that one day.

'He tried to impress me with money,' the young man told me from jail, where he chose to return rather than continue with the

Jesus program. 'We're drug dealers, criminals, working girls. We've seen more money than most people. We know what money can do to people. We don't want to learn how to make money. We need to know how to handle what we've got.'

New-monied people don't know any of this. They are willing to take trashy and kitsch to newer, higher levels than we ever dreamed possible, in the name of Jesus.

It started when they announced that God wants you rich. This was called prosperity theology. It was a case of 'don't ask why I am wearing a Rolex, ask why you're not'. Lots of people went to lots of prosperity conferences around the world. And got taught a version of the same thing.

Of course God wants you to be rich. He loves you, doesn't he? It didn't really matter in the nineties what version of this you heard. It was all about giving to the church in order to get back. And as all the evangelists will remind you constantly, the Lord loves a cheerful giver.

Dr John Avanzini, author of *Rich God, Poor God* and *It's Not Working, Brother John*, has his headquarters in Texas. He first started telling people in 1990, on Christian network TV, that whatever you give to the ministry/God would be returned 100-fold.

It was an offer that a lot of people couldn't refuse. And a lot of people lost a lot of money. Even worse, a lot of stupid people *made* a lot of money that they would never have and should never have made. And I saw a beast rise out of the water, and it was a multi-headed beast, with capped teeth and a glazed look in its eyes, and its skin was tanned and its clothes were Italian. It was the new-monied middle-class born-again Christians. And they were coming right for us.

Where previously the moral minority had been happy to stay at home and sew doilies, the new-monied Christians of the nineties became purpose-driven. Having wallowed in prosperity and power for more than enough time for it to become embarrassing, they had to find a way to justify the continual call for donations.

The church was so obsessed with cash not Christ that no one knew quite where to look.

Just in time, Rick Warren came along with his explosive best-seller *The Purpose Driven Life*. Promoted up by Oprah/Dr Phil, and every grotesquely rich evangelist, *The Purpose Driven Life* went on to become the book that 21 per cent of American pastors consider the most influential book on their ministry.

For now we have Prosperity with Purpose. Did you think we were wearing labels for our benefit? Don't be ridiculous. God wants us to be rich, of course he does. But not just to lie by the pool all day. We're blessed to be a blessing. When you have a life of purpose, money is just a tool. So are big fancy houses. Just a tool for sharing the love.

The real reason why the Christians need to get all the money they can is that it is their job to be the well-groomed evangelical Robin Hoods of this age. Blessed to be a blessing can mean whatever you like, as long as you give a little away. From dodgy development deals to cosmetic surgery, everything is permissible. As long as it's part of your vision, your dream, your God-ordained purpose, you can have all of the lovely money that you want, and bless other people at your discretion. Isn't God good?

It's sort of like a tax exemption. If my Mercedes means that you somehow get closer to God, then I am doing a good thing. And I will make sure it somehow gets you closer to God, so that I can buy another one.

The new-monied Christians have their eyes on anything by which more money can be made. They've been more than happy to bless by being a blessing to social services all over the country. And God wants their clients to be rich as well. And at Hillsong, they lead by example.

When the American-based Mercy Ministries was imported to Australia, a large house was bought in Glenhaven some miles from Hillsong HQ. Hillsong had a 'Mercy Registry' where people who didn't have a wedding to go to could still go the registry section at Grace Brothers and donate to the Mercy Girls. From dustpans to washing machines, Mercy Ministries got set up with the finest. The rules at Mercy are bizarre and stringent, anti-gay and pro-life. Still, compared to the shabbiness of many other rehabs, one virtual tour of the Mercy home online would win me over any time. Even stinky new money can be very inviting when you're needy.

It's cruel to lure desperate people in with shiny pretty things. Development estates sprung up all over the suburbs around the Hills Christian Life Centre, and many of Sydney's struggling families piled up their pennies, doubled their mortgages and left poorer suburbs to try to give their kids a classier upbringing. The concept of God's desire for them to be successful and rich must have been an oasis in Sydney's vicious financial desert. For many it was no more than a mirage.

For the message about money never stops. You can't outgive God. You have to keep giving if you want to keep receiving, and if it's not working, brother John, you better give some more. For many people who moved into the Hillsong Shire in Sydney, their hope turned to financial ruin.

Talking about money can go from lots of fun to lots of pain, and there were never any books called, 'I'm not kidding, Brother John. I'm sending my cousins around to your house to get my cash back'. No one likes to admit they've been had, especially if the con artist prayed in the name of Jesus.

Not content with the local victims, once called the Aussie battler, the new-monied folk want to run the entire country and possibly the world. They've got money, and the gospel to share. Who needs a law degree when you've been to bible college? Who needs bible college when you've got a Vision, and a Purpose-Driven Life, with a matching diary signed by Rick Warren himself?

And that quote echoes in my brain, like Brian's smile, strange and haunting. 'My personal vision is to fund and finance the salvation of the earth.'

Don't you miss the days when salvation was free? I wonder what Paris's salvation costs, or whether she's inheriting hers?

Maybe she can afford a different one every day. I wish I could. My original one ended up costing a bundle and I lost the receipt. Where can I get a refund now? Does anyone know who I can ask? I don't usually talk about such things. Real heiresses never do.

Chapter 20

I JUST CAN'T WAIT TO BE KING

> God loves you, and I love you. And you can count on both of us as a powerful message that people who wonder about their future can hear.
>
> —George W. Bush (3 March 2004)

It's intriguing to watch the press and the rest of the world try to work it out. Did the evangelicals win the US election for George W. Bush in 2000 and 2004? What's with the Family First Party? How do these people work? When did they all start voting together like that? How come they're all so shiny and happy? And why are they so committed to their cause?

Journalists can't understand a culture where people neither drink nor smoke. It is difficult for anyone literate to make sense of the illogical psychobabble that pours out of the pulpit. What is hurled as Truth has been refried so many times that logical thought is impossible to find. This makes journalists and politicians and educated people believe that rubbish like this will never have an impact on mainstream society. Not so fast. Indifferent to their own ignorance and inexperience, the Christian soldiers are marching onward.

The International Assemblies of God Conference 2005 was held at Sydney's Hillsong Church. Its theme was 'Take the Nation, Shake the World'. It got me thinking. If Sydney's Lakemba Mosque held a conference for all its international leaders and called it 'Take the Nation, Shake the World', there'd be more specially trained police doing overtime than in a month of Sundays. The city would be up in arms and old people would be digging out their gas-masks. When clean-shaven white men in suits do it, it's a cause for celebration, traffic jams in suburbia and overpriced t-shirts.

Fundamentalists of all persuasions believe that their god is the only true god and that their religion is the only true religion. It is their god's will for every person in the world to convert, and be willing to die for the religion. Separation of church and state is a left-wing detail. Everyone must think what they think or be punished for refusing to accept the truth.

This definition applies not only to the crazy terrorists that world leaders are doing chicken dances over, but to fundamentalist Christians who are as extreme as any other group. They've never hidden it. They're just wearing nicer clothes. Their women have blonde hair instead of veils. And they never film themselves threatening people. Apart from that, they're as crackerjack as the Other Side.

If mass evangelism comes across as an assault on the mind, the bodies and the rights of individuals and cultures, it is intended to. Christians have to get everybody saved or at least told about Jesus, so he can come back again. We were told throughout my youth that with technology going the way it was, it wouldn't be long before all the most hard-to-reach communities would hear the Good News. Everybody must get saved. Anyone who doesn't want to get saved, well, you can only pray for them. And be a good example to them. But their opinions are not of God. So legislate right over them, as soon as you can.

The senior pastor of Hillsong and the national president of the Assemblies of God, Brian Houston, has insisted that his church does not have a political agenda. Yet the prime minister and other senior politicians have made the effort to attend services. On Saturday, 12 October 2002, the Bali bombing killed eighty-eight Australians, forcing John Howard to cancel his appearance at the Hillsong opening the next day. With a nation in shock and grief, Mr Howard rescheduled his appearance for the following Saturday night.

Given the Liberal Party's slashing of community services, which has left church charities shouldering the care of people for whom the government was once responsible, one might think that a church would not seek alignment with our prime minister, a man who is seen by some as unforgiving, uncompassionate and ruthless. Instead, as John Howard broke the spiritual champagne bottle against the new SS *Hillsong*, the crowd went wild. The prime minister's glee was thinly veiled as Pastor Brian welcomed him and told him he was 'amongst friends'. Without an inkling how apt his analysis was, an envious John Howard beamed: 'You've gone from forty-five at your first service in 1983 to a congregation of over fourteen thousand. I've gotta tell you that I don't think there's any side of Australian politics that could do a branch stack as good as that.' (It's not called branch stacking in AoG, Mr Howard. It's called church planting.) Neither would Howard know that Brian had only recently come on board. Frank Houston's collar, after all, was as blue as it gets and Frank was a proud Labor man. It was Pastor Phil Baker, senior pastor at Western Australia's Riverview church and president of Australian Christian Churches, who had said, 'But, Brian, you believe in profit, don't you?'

'Yes,' said Brian.

'You believe in everyone being able to make money and reach their potential and not be reliant on the state, don't you?'

'Yes,' said Brian.

'Well,' said Phil, 'you're a Liberal voter then.'

Of course Hillsong does not have a political agenda. Getting as many people converted to fundamentalism as quickly as possible is as political as doing the dusting. What could possibly be wrong with telling everyone about the love of Jesus? Nothing, it's all for a good cause. Brian Houston wrote a book about it called *For This Cause*. The prefacing quotes for each chapter are, in the majority, from Jesus pop songs his son Joel penned. Intrafamily cross-royalties. Christmas has to be interesting at the Houston house.

Quoting Jesus's words from John 18, 'I am the Son and for this cause I have come into the world', Brian takes the word 'cause', puts a capital C on it and invents the Cause of Christ. He then outlines the differences between merely having a vision and being part of a cause:

- a vision can be personal but a cause is bigger than any one person
- a vision is something you possess, but a cause possesses you
- you wouldn't die for a vision, but you will die for a cause
- a vision has options, but a cause leaves you with no choice
- a vision can be ignored, but you cannot ignore a cause.

To conclude, Pastor Brian writes, 'No matter what you think about the IRA (Irish Republican Army) you cannot pretend they don't exist, especially if you live in Belfast. The fact is that they are motivated by a cause and cannot be ignored. If the Cause of Christ takes hold of your life or your church, those around you will not be able to ignore it either.'[1]

One of the most efficient ways to get people to work for you for free is to tell them it's for an external cause. As long as they believe in it strongly enough, no sacrifice is too great. And blind eyes will be turned. Scandals damage the Cause. No one wants that. That's how you filter out all the bad stuff, because it doesn't matter in the scheme of things. It's all for the Cause. And this Cause is decidedly political.

Back in South Australia, it happened that Stella Evans's boy, Andrew, Stella's Elijah, did not become the great prophet she had foreseen. Andrew Evans was not the Chosen One. He had pastored Adelaide's Paradise Assemblies of God Church for twenty years and still no revival. The Toronto Blessing had come close, and Dr Evans was a great supporter of Toronto. Once that died down, so did any attention given to Adelaide or Evans. Andrew and his wife Lorraine had two sons, Ashley and Russell, both in ministry. Andrew could have been content.

Still, it must have been hard for Andrew to watch Frank

Houston's boy come from out of nowhere and take Sydney to places Adelaide had never dreamed of. Not only did Brian have a bigger church than anyone had ever imagined, international TV distribution and a public profile, he had taken over from Andrew as the General Superintendent of the AoG. It was game, set, match Houston.

Ashley overthrew his father's leadership in the same style as Andrew had overthrown his father, Tommy, as soon as it was opportune. In AoG families this is called retirement. That left Andrew needing something to do. He knew there had to be higher places than even Brian had reached. There were dreams Hillsong hadn't dreamt and Andrew Evans turned his passion to something that would influence more people and change more lives than a church ever could.

Australian Idol. In 2002 Andrew Evans won a seat in the South Australian Legislative Council under the banner of the Family First Party. It showed him that there was support around. But could he make God famous? Was there Christian voting loyalty out there? There was one way of finding out, before he could feel confident of going federal with their politics.

Paradise Church knew that Hillsong advertised number-one CD sales. It also knew that all of those albums had been bought at Hillsong conferences, leaving the 'mainstream' claim an illusion. There was one way of checking faith and prosperity nationally and in 2003, Channel 10 showed Australia Paradise.

Guy Sebastian made no secret of his membership of Adelaide's Pentecostal headquarters. He is proudly born again, and has strong backing from the church and Pastor Ashley. He has a lovely voice and disposition, and there were no skeletons falling out of Guy's closet like they had with the contestants on *American Idol.* If Hillsong could make albums, Paradise could make an Idol.

Pentecostal thumbs text-messaged like there was no tomorrow, since many of them believe there isn't. Guy Sebastian was Australia's first Idol, and evidence that the Christian vote was strong nationally. Andrew Evans was now ready for the big time, ready to teach Australia about family.

There's usually no need to tell Chinese people about family. There are very few Greeks I know who aren't clear about family values. Most Australians know not to mix family and politics. But the Paradise boys decided to announce the wheel's reinvention. Let's put your Family First.

The idea is that the 1950s family unit is currently under attack. Satan hates families and the Australian dream of the house on a quarter-acre block. Family First is based on Christian values. Pray tell, what are Christian values? This must mean wearing one's Sunday best, being nice to old people and saying sorry when you have a fight with your friend. Somewhere in there is a hot lunch on Sundays, and a kind word for every tear.

Christian family values, however, have had an almighty turnaround. Jesus, allegedly, was not too interested in family and had a healthy mistrust of lawyers and politicians. Jesus never ran for office. Not even to see what the polls showed, or for the amazing opportunity of it all.

The Family First Party's explicitly homophobic agenda can't be based on the teachings of Christ because Jesus never mentioned homosexuality at all. Still, the party gave every Liberal member its preferences in the 2004 federal election, except for Ingrid Tall, an openly lesbian candidate. This was only because, as a volunteer accidentally slipped out, 'All lesbians are witches who should be burned at the stake.'

In 2004, thanks to the vagaries of preferencing, Family First's Steve Fielding was elected to the Senate. Another Tasmanian candidate came close to election too. This would all be another tale of politics if there weren't a bizarre twist. The members of the party are the staff and friends of Brian. The parents of the kids from youth group now include many would-be senators. Shouldn't they be going to retirement parties, not political fundraisers?

South African Archbishop Desmond Tutu required his ministers to sever all links with the African National Congress as soon as it won political standing. The church, he believed, must take an impartial stance and act as an observer, a critic and a respondent to the government, not intervene in its affairs.

Mainstream politics is about lots of compromise. Running a country is not as easy as running a church. Fundamentalists don't compromise, unless it's to do with tax law. Or remarriage. They believe they are enlightened, and have an imperative to share their truth with everyone. Any challenge is a direct threat, and an attack from the Enemy against God and his people. With the AoG holding the moral balance of power in parliament, Question Time may suddenly prove very interesting.

Chapter 21

WHEN THE GENERALS TALK

> If what a prophet proclaims in the name of the Lord does not take place or come true, that is a message that Lord has not spoken. That prophet has spoken presumptuously. Do not be afraid of him.
>
> —Deuteronomy 18:22

Brian and Bobbie Houston didn't make this stuff up. It would be called plagiarism if there were such a thing as an original. But as you wade through the murky swamps of TV evangelism, there's nothing even slightly unique about Hillsong. It's one imitation after another. And they have memories as short as goldfish. (An AoG youth group in Melbourne is named Heaven's Gate. In 1997, thirty-nine mainly middle-class forty-something Americans put on their Nikes, got ready to go with the aliens and committed suicide. Their group was called Heaven's Gate.)

In evangelical churches, an expert by definition is someone from out of town. The speaker from a faraway place necessarily has experienced God in an exotic, unknowable way that surpasses the home crowd's imagination. This mythology underpins the appeal of a mass rally. At Pentecostal conferences and churches, international speakers must know more than we do about God's word.

Brian and Bobbie are close friends with some of the grand poobahs of evangelism. Hillsong has Big Names speak at the church and at its conferences. Because the people they model themselves on have all copied each other, the same doctrine is regurgitated as breaking world news. Ideology is kept consistent, and confirmed by the spiritual expert from overseas. The Lord's words you hear from a pulpit in Sydney may well have been photocopied from last week's inspiring speech by someone else in Seattle. And vice versa.

All of the big names that appear at Hillsong, and most televangelists, will espouse the same beliefs: invest in me, and God will invest in you. Refuse, and you only have yourself to blame. Whoever draws the crowds is the most revered, and together they make up a small, opulent circle of friends from around the world.

After the infamy of the televangelists of the late eighties, many people went cold on religion on TV. Even so, audiences are booming. So who's watching? According to the non-profit religious watchdog the Trinity Foundation, 2500 radio and TV evangelists (including over 500 televangelists) are vying for a donor pool of about five million people. Fifty-five per cent of these are elderly women. Thirty-five per cent of donations come from a group Trinity call the desperation pool, made up of the poorest and neediest members of society, people who are poverty-stricken or have a terminally ill relative. The remaining ten per cent of viewers are from the upper middle class, a demographic that truly believes God wants it to be stinking rich.

The who's who of modern evangelism is a long, complicated, incestuous list and to draw a neat family tree is impossible. However, the one person all the wealthy DIY preachers have in common is Oral Roberts, the forefather of the Word of Faith movement and one of televangelist history's most prolific lunatics. The Word of Faith celebrities who visit Hillsong and then fly in their private jets back to the United States, stopping for a few days' rest in Hawaii, can all be traced back to a man who in 1980 had a vision of a 900-foot talking Jesus.

Without Billy Graham's public seal of approval, Oral Roberts, his Word of Faith university and all his prosperity protégés might never have come to be. Billy Graham, a Southern Baptist, arrived at a time when the liberal Christians and the fundamentalist Christians had reached a cultural impasse. While tensions were rising over theological difference, Billy Graham began his famous crusades, providing a united Christian front based on the message of salvation. He is universally regarded as a nice guy, the gentle evangelist, sincere, stable and kind.

Invited in 1950 by Graham to sit on the platform and pray at one of his meetings, the Pentecostal Roberts was given unexpected public acceptance. Fifteen years later, at the opening of Oral Roberts University (ORU), Graham invited Roberts to attend the World Congress on Evangelism in Berlin. There, in 1966, Graham introduced Roberts as 'a man that I have come to love and appreciate in the ministry of evangelism'. In 1967, Billy Graham appeared on campus to dedicate Oral Roberts University.

Billy Graham himself stayed away from flashy TV shows and excess. A long-time Democrat, though currently unregistered, he has been spiritual adviser to every US president since Dwight Eisenhower. He led the funeral for Lyndon Johnson in 1973, spoke at Richard Nixon's in 1994, and only missed Ronald Reagan's because Graham himself was in hospital. He is said to have close relationships with both the Clinton and the Bush families.

During the seventies, while Billy Graham was discussing Israel in the White House with Nixon, Oral Roberts' soon-to-be colleagues were getting on with the business of television. TV evangelists have been around about as long as television, yet there were only a handful in the fifties and sixties. Their numbers and influence grew in the seventies and have steadily increased ever since, as has their social and political clout. The seventies provided the current generation's forefathers and doctrinal bases. It was a time of solidifying the primitive foundations.

Oral Roberts first broadcast from a studio in Oklahoma to sixteen stations in January 1954, and over the next twelve years he also broadcast his TV show from a tent. After a two-year break, he returned to televangelism, based at the NBC studios in Burbank, California. By 1980, *Oral Roberts and You* was filmed at Oral Roberts University.

The now disgraced Jim and Tammy Faye Bakker had been working with Pat Robertson and his Christian Broadcasting Network (CBN) with their Christian variety show *Praise the Lord* (*PTL*) since 1961 and were instrumental in buoying Robertson's channel and his live television program, *The 700 Club*. In 1973 the Bakkers went to Tustin, California to set up the Trinity Broadcasting Network (TBN) with Paul and Jan Crouch. A year later, they moved on to Charlotte, North Carolina and started the PTL network.

Like the other political evangelists, Pat Robertson avoided the preaching limelight, although his fortunes were always large. In 1979, Jerry Falwell founded the Moral Majority, a lobby group credited with mobilising the religious Right in the United States. Falwell worked hard to influence elections and 'moral' legislation and to prevent an 'anti-family agenda'.

Right at the end of the seventies a little-known couple, Kenneth and Gloria Copeland, began *Believer's Voice of Victory*. Ken had worked as a pilot for Oral Roberts and had studied under Pastor Kenneth Hagin, founder of the RHEMA Bible College, sister college to Oral Roberts University. The Copelands were respectful admirers of Roberts and Hagin, and have been instrumental in getting the message of 'seed faith' out ever since. (Currently Nabi Saleh, Hillsong elder and bringer of Gloria Jean's Coffee to Australia, is a director of Kenneth Copeland Eagle Mountain International Church.)

There was no doubt among the leaders even then that most of what was being sold to the public as an individual interaction with God was leftovers warmed up from the generation before. Yet they continued to sell each revelation, no matter how clichéd or tired, as hot off the holy presses.

The man Kenneth Copeland calls Dad, Kenneth Hagin, was exposed in 1983 by two students at Oral Roberts University as having copied verbatim most of his teachings from a 1930s evangelist, E.W. Kenyon. Hagin also plagiarised the title and contents of a book by John A. MacMillan called *The Authority of the Believer*.

Yet no one took away the honorary doctorate Hagin had received from ORU in the seventies. Maybe that's because so many evangelists have dodgy PhDs. Dr Rodney Howard-Browne, who spread the Toronto Blessing, reported a Doctorate of Ministry degree from 'the school of bible theology' in San Jacinto California, which has no faculty and has been likened to a diploma mill. A college with similar allegations against it, Life Christian University in Tampa, Florida has provided many doctorates to evangelists, offering advanced standing for previously published works. Among its illustrious alumni are Dr Rodney Howard-Browne (Doctor of Divinity, Doctor of Theology), Dr Joyce Meyer, Dr Kenneth Copeland and Dr Benny Hinn, each of whom has a Doctorate of Philosophy in theology.

Putting your name to writing or ideas that aren't yours is much more common than believers realise. Christian ghostwriting is commonplace. Jerry Falwell's autobiography *Strength for the Journey*, Billy Graham's *Approaching Hoofbeats* and Pat Robertson's *America's Dates with Destiny* are only a few of the Christian bestsellers ghost-written by gay activist the Reverend Mel White. Which is why you won't find anti-gay stuff in so many of these books.

The Late, Great Planet Earth (1970) sold over 35 million copies and made little-known preacher Hal Lindsey a household evangelical and prophetic name. Lindsey later admitted the book had been written by an unknown woman, Carla Carlson.

The hedonistic eighties provided a cesspool of joy for the televangelists' fundamentalist beliefs. Everyday life was portrayed as an ongoing orgy of wilful rebellion against God. Before money became the overriding message, crimes of the body were the preachers' number one fixation. Anything to do with sex before, outside or after marriage, or for money, led to well-deserved punishment, beginning with the evils of divorce and illegitimate babies and abortion and going on from there.

Then the walls fell down. Jimmy Swaggart publicly criticised Jim Bakker for his financial and sexual scandals, only to have his own close relationship with the sex industry revealed months later. Jerry Falwell took over the PTL network when Jim and Tammy Faye left. His photographed involvement with prostitutes never stopped his campaigning against that sort of thing.

The ministries that were left, and the new graduates emerging, turned to Oral Roberts for advice. Oral Roberts' statements may strike a first-year psychology student as floridly psychotic, but he was prospering financially.

In 1980, God told Oral Roberts to open the City of Faith Health and Medical Center, a hospital that would have 777 beds. Later, Roberts announced a 900-foot Jesus had appeared to him and told him that City of Faith would be finished, and that God would use the research facilities to find a cure for cancer. (By late 1984, the hospital had only opened about 130 of its 294 beds.)

Although support was dwindling, Oral Roberts' advisers consulted with Gene Ewing, a successful tent evangelist. Ewing laid out the Word of Faith doctrine as it related to finances. It was called 'seed faith'. Audiences were told that if they planted a seed of faith with money, it would grow into a big ministry to save the world. And God would reward them by giving them the harvest of what they had sown.

In January 1987, Oral Roberts told his TV audience that God had instructed him to raise US$8 million (of which he claimed to have US$3.5 million already) by March or God would take him. How he would die, the Lord had not mentioned, just that God wanted scholarships for medical missionaries from the City of Faith to go overseas. Or else.

By 1 April 1987, Oral Roberts said that the ministry had received US$9.1 million, which was more than necessary. Reports say that his adviser, Gene Ewing, received a US$1 million commission from the project.

In November 1987 it was announced that the City of Faith was closing down, and the following January the medical scholarships were discontinued. By March the scholarship fund was bankrupt and students were required to repay their scholarships at 18 per cent interest. Oral Roberts told *Charisma* magazine:

It is clearly in my spirit, as I have ever heard Him, the Lord gave me an impression, 'You and your partners have merged prayer and medicine for the entire world, for the church world and for all generations.'

And then He said, 'It is done.'

And then I asked, 'Is that why after eight years you are having us close the hospital and after eleven years the medical school?'

And God said, 'Yes, the mission has been accomplished in the same way that after three years of public ministry, my Son said on the cross, "Father, it is finished!"'[1]

In 1989 the City of Faith hospital building was abandoned, having never been fully occupied or completed. All projects were suspended indefinitely. Nonetheless, after meeting with Ewing and outlining the principles of seed faith on national TV, Oral Roberts Ministries doubled its income from US$6 million to US$12 million in a year.

All the other evangelists consulted him and his adviser, Ewing, immediately.

Outdistanced in the seventies by Pat Robertson's CBN and Jim Bakker's PTL, it took the Bakkers' downfall amidst overwhelming moral and financial scandal to give the Trinity Broadcasting Network the market boost it needed to become a contender. With much the same folksy appeal as the Bakkers, Paul and Jan Crouch combined financial and media PR to build a formidable ministry media conglomerate, eventually eclipsing all comers. In 1989, just sixteen years after it was established, the net worth of TBN was estimated at US$500 million.[2]

So where are all these televangelists now? TBN hosts nearly every pastor worth knowing on its network: Oral Roberts, the Copelands and Benny Hinn.

Indeed, the sins of the father have been handed over to the sons. Billy Graham's Parkinson's disease was the catalyst to hand over to wildchild Franklin. Richard 'I'm so glad I got a normal name' Roberts took over from Oral. And so it goes.

They run ministries, some for the poor. Pat Robertson's Operation Blessing International, Franklin Graham's Operation Christmas Child, and the Trinity Broadcasting Network are all in the top ten highest-earning charities in the United States, with TBN at number nine, bringing in nearly US$200 million a year. On the record.

Gene Ewing used the nineties to expand his publishing house, St Matthew's, which, though tax exempt due to 'worship services', is contracted by other ministries for marketing of their seed faith campaigns. Currently, ministries are charged US$400,000 for the use of the services and promised US$600,000 profit.[3]

St Matthew's researches the poorest and neediest demographics in the United States, where one in four children under eighteen are deemed at risk of being hungry. Poverty-stricken neighbourhoods are inundated with prosperity progaganda and gimmicks. They are told that they are driving God away with their lack of faith. The publications they are sent guarantee miracles if only they give what little they have.

The business also operates a call centre which takes the prayer requests offered to viewers by the pastors on TV. The counsellors who take these calls are contracted to work under strict conditions. They must not spend more than two to three minutes with each caller, they must ask them to donate at least three times during the conversation, and they must get the caller's name and address. Their pay is docked if they talk over time, and there are bonuses for successfully getting credit-card details. The credit-card companies have deals with the St Matthew's company. St Matthew's Publishing Inc. reported US$15.6 million in revenue in 1997, US$26.8 million in 1999 and has refused to disclose finances since.[4] Gene Ewing is a very wealthy evangelist, who doesn't preach at all.

The 1990s set the stage for the present-day global enterprise of Pentecostalism, of which Hillsong is Australia's largest, proudest and most active member. Hillsong is now internationally acclaimed for its philosophies and music. It preaches a doctrine that is similar to all the preachers on TBN, and it holds TBN celebrities in high esteem. In fact, out of the ten visiting names advertised for the Hillsong annual conference in 2006, only three didn't have a regular show on TBN. Rick Warren, author of *The Purpose Driven Life*, doesn't and neither does Billy Hybels, ex-adviser to Bill Clinton and pastor of Vineyard's Willow Creek Community Church, because they don't need to. Frank Damazio is committed to prosperity evangelism but isn't on TV. Jentzen Franklin hosts *Kingdom Connection*, Matthew Barnett *The Dream Center*, Rick Godwin is on TBN's *PTL* and *The 700 Club*, and Rheinhard Bonnke appears regularly on others' TBN broadcasts. Gospel singer Alvin Slaughter, who toured with Benny Hinn for ten years, and in 2006 received an honorary doctorate from Canada Christian College, is one of TBN's music front men with his show *Highest Praise*. Israel Houghton and Cindy Cruse-Ratcliff appeared courtesy of Joel Osteen's 'biggest in America' Lakewood Church and appear regularly on TBN specials. Hillsong 2006 was one long TBN advertisement.

TBN has come under huge scrutiny in the past few years. An ex-employee sued founder Paul Crouch for sexual harassment, saying he was forced to engage in acts in order to keep his job. Crouch settled out of court, paying $425,000.

Ministrywatch.com has placed a donor alert on TBN, urging viewers not to send money. Ministrywatch lists that from 1999–2004 TBN received $643 million in donations and $341 million in cash and short-term investments, yet it continues to ask for more money. The Billy Graham Evangelistic Association is the only association given an A by Wallwatchers, a Christian group that monitors ministries and charities for their financial integrity. All the other major televangelists who have their own shows, who have been trained by Oral Roberts or at his university or by his teachers, got an F. Their books are closed. They don't have to tell. As is the case for Hillsong, in the United States a charitable institution or not-for-profit organisation is exempt from paying tax. Those who have sprung from Oral Roberts ministries, or who at least have close relationships with pastors who did, don't have to pay tax and don't have to tell anyone. In the States, the tax form for a not-for-profit is a 501c3. One website refers to all the prosperity pastors as '501c3 Chief Executive Officers'.

It's not clear where tax is paid when a visiting pastor speaks abroad. When it comes to an event the size of a Hillsong conference, however, someone must pay for the Americans to fly all the way to Australia. Even if your Gulfstream jet costs $3500 an hour to fly like Joyce Meyers's does.

If it all sounds like Amway, it's because it may as well be. It's not just because the wealthiest leaders live in Florida and Texas. There are about a hundred people in the world making an absolute killing out of millions of foot soldiers and thousands of captains. Pat Mesiti got a lot out of Amway. He rose high in the ranks, and learned the power of motivational speaking and of selling the tapes. Amway also teaches that God wants you to be rich. The punch-line with Amway is that no money is made selling cleaning products. It's only when you are important enough to teach other people how to be like you that you can make tapes and DVDs, merchandising and royalties.

The Double Diamonds in Amway and head honcho preachers are identical twins raised apart, only for their selling styles to be reunited once again in the early 1990s. Same mansions to prove success, same hopes and dreams for your kids to turn out okay, and same family-based solutions to your fears. The difference seems to be entry point. The evangelicals sell God first, money second. Amway at least offers you some floor cleaner to start with.

So never worry. It doesn't matter what happens. Brian and Bobbie will never be out of a job. Australia is too small right now for them to ever rise much above what would be in Amway a Pearl level, really only middle management. In Amway, those who are brought into the business are downline. Bobbie and Brian's downline are very loyal. Distributor-wise, they can't lose much. They are at the very top of Hillsong's corporate structure, with everyone below them. They are the tip of the iceberg, and are self-appointed presidents and leaders. In Australia, the buck stops there.

Brian and Bobbie also have very strong upline support. Upline are the people who bring you into Amway, benefit from your success, and teach you all you know. Brian and Bobbie are dear friends with their upline, Wendy and Casey, loving and defending them at all costs. If anything should go horribly wrong in Australia, I'm sure there's a top of the charts Emerald role just waiting somewhere on the US west coast for the Houstons. I could practically guarantee it.

Bobbie's own preaching reputation means she could actually have a show of her own. She's an internationally renowned speaker now. She could always copy her old friend Lyndie McCauley. When Lyndie ran away from her husband, Pastor Ray, in South Africa after thirty years, abandoning their 20,000 strong congregation at Rhema Church, everyone at Hillsong got a letter, and Brian went over to hold his mate's hand. Pray for Ray, the letter said, his wife ran away.

Lyndie McCauley tried to go back, but within three months Pastor Ray was engaged to a younger blonde. They decked out the church building like a fairytale for the wedding. Many of the white congregation left in disgust. The Africans poured in, curious about prosperity theology in a failing post-apartheid South Africa. Lyndie McCauley moved to Florida to start Lyndie McCauley Ministries. That marriage is something her website fleetingly refers to as 'a great challenge in her personal life in 2000'. Christian Life University recently presented Lyndie with an honorary doctorate of divinity.

Bobbie could do the same thing easy. Get used to the names, Brian and Bobbie Houston. They're not going anywhere.

Chapter 22

IF IT MAKES YOU HAPPY

Hope deferred makes the heart sick, but a longing fulfilled is a tree of life.

—Proverbs 13:12

Every nation in every region now has a decision to make. Either you are with us, or you are with the terrorists.

—George W. Bush (20 September 2001)

When Natascha Kampusch left her captor of eight years after being kidnapped at the age of ten, the Austrian teenager did not recall a world of pain. 'It is true that my youth was different to the youth of others, but in principle I don't feel I missed anything. I have been saved from some things, from starting to smoke and drink, or from having bad friends.'

The same could be said for me. I had one of the healthiest childhoods on record. However, should usual adolescent development be arrested due to the fear of God, the breaking out can be far worse. The bad friends I could have made as a teenager might have been more innocuous. By the time I found my bad friends, I was old enough to do what I wanted and drive there as well. And having a thorough idea of what good people think is righteous helps you get away with murder.

Some people claim that Hillsong is better than nothing; that it prevented them from ending up a juvenile delinquent, despite the embarrassing memories of playing guitar on Blacktown train station during outreach crusades.

The relief most people feel when they embrace Christianity can often be accompanied by health changes. Quitting smoking, drinking and drugs is common and usually expected. No pressure. Frank Houston used to say smoking won't keep you out of heaven, it'll just get you there sooner. Emotionally, being part of a world-wide crusade can be very comforting. In a church like Hillsong, being surrounded with so many good friends, a new sense of self-worth, and knowledge that any day now you're going to be rich, can certainly give rise to positive emotions.

The American market research group Barna randomly sampled 3000 adults throughout the United States. Its results showed that:

Evangelicals are almost universally 'happy' (99%) and were by far the segment that was most satisfied with their present life (91%). This upbeat frame of mind may be related to the fact that evangelicals are the least likely to say they are 'lonely' (8%), 'in serious debt' (9%) or 'stressed out' (16%). The percentage who admit to high levels of stress is less than half the level measured among adults connected with non-Christian faiths (33%) or those who say they are atheistic or agnostic (42%).[1]

So if Hillsong makes people happy, what could be wrong with that? There's just that one per cent problem.

Christianity made me deeply depressed for many years, before I left Hills and after. The concept of original sin meant I was born worthless, and was only saved by the bestowing of grace. Salvation is free, sure! It's a gift! But Jesus said if you love me you will keep my commandments. So getting in was simple. Staying in was excruciating. I hated carrying the burden of Eve. I hated knowing that I didn't believe and couldn't defend what I was being told, but that the alternative was a fiery pit. It kept me up at night, it terrified me in the day. It is literally a life lived damned if you do and damned if you don't.

Emotionally, for me it was a horrible way to live. All the blame and none of the credit. If anything goes well, it's because God did it or did it working through you. If things go badly, it's your fault. As evangelist Joyce Meyer says, if we all got what we deserved, we'd all be going to hell.

We were told not to trust our feelings. Feelings had nothing to do with the Facts. We were instructed not to see life as we see it but as God sees it. Thus the anxieties or sadnesses that might accompany a life event are to be repressed as an illusion. Instincts can't be trusted. According to fundamentalists, suspicion, doubt, worry must all line up with how the Word of God says your life should be. And if ninety-nine per cent of people around you are *happy*, then *happy* you should be.

Still, if Pentecostalism is engraved on my psyche forevermore, what effects might it have on other people? The system continues to reward those who comply with it and exile those who don't. While you are happy, you will stay happy. If you show resistance to your leader, by requesting to look at the books or asking questions about theology, your survival in that system is limited, and so is your happiness. Emotions, we know, have historically been the tool of the devil. What about the mind? I very nearly went crazy and that's one you don't want to tell at church.

Mental-health issues have traditionally been viewed as demonic by Pentecostals, and are largely ignored or countered with a bible verse from 2 Timothy, that covers anything remotely psychological. 'God has not given us the spirit of fear, but of love and of power and of a sound mind', it says. The inference, once again, is that if you're experiencing something that God didn't give you, then you had better take a closer look at yourself.

As Brian and Bobbie said, before removing the article 'You can be depression free' from the Hillsong website:

The bottom line is: depression is a supernatural spirit of destruction straight from the devil, and as such, needs to be treated like an enemy. We must take a strong stand against it and deny it any power in our lives. Depression stems from an underlying root of unbelief in God's care, His goodness, His faithfulness, or even His ability to get you out of seemingly 'impossible' situations.[2]

Kind of makes Tom Cruise's Scientology look passé.

One 1994 study looked at the mental health of Pentecostal baby boomers in North Carolina. Investigators found that compared to Protestants, the Pentecostal group had up to three times higher rates of short-term and life-time depression, anxiety disorders and life-time risk for any DSM-III disorder (the manual used by psychiatry professionals to diagnose mental health). Frequent church attendance did not seem to be hazardous to one's health, but low-attending Pentecostals had the highest rates of life-time psychiatric disorder of any subgroup. Yet not one Pentecostal baby boomer in the study had consulted a mental-health professional in the previous six months.[3]

Some people hear audible spiritual voices, some see visions of people who talk to them. Other people just espouse beliefs that make no sense in any arena other than their own religious rationale. So what's the difference between Moses talking to a burning bush, Frank Houston's visions for Australia, and the homeless guy in the park talking to himself? There seems to be two ways we treat these people. As fifty per cent of people with 'mental illnesses' have religious ideations, we either schedule them involuntarily to a psych hospital when they see God, or we give them a church, a bunch of people to look after and a car. It's all about what's socially acceptable.

Back in reality, people who leave Hillsong and Assemblies of God churches often suffer responses common to individuals who leave thought-reform groups. Dr Margaret Singer, a long-time researcher into cult theory, described the psychiatric casualties of these groups as exhibiting standard behaviours. She said that the most common reaction regardless of length of membership is:

a varying degree of anomie—a sense of alienation and confusion resulting from the loss or weakening of previously valued norms, ideals, or goals. When the person leaves the group and returns to broader society, culture shock and anxiety usually result from the theories learned in the group and the need to reconcile situational demands, values, and memories in three eras—the past prior to the group, the time in the group, and the present situation.[4]

Yep, that was me.

The person feels like an immigrant or refugee who enters a new culture. However, the person is re-entering his or her former culture, bringing along a series of experiences and beliefs from the group with which he or she had affiliated that conflict with norms and expectations. Unlike the immigrant confronting merely novel situations, the returnee is confronting a rejected society. Thus, most people leaving a thought-reform program have a period in which they need to put together the split or doubled self they maintained while they were in the group and come to terms with their pre-group sense of self.[5]

No wonder I feel like I've had multiple personality disorder all my life.

Dr Singer also talks about more extreme responses such as post-traumatic stress disorders, and atypical dissociative disorders which involve memory loss. It was only when I had met several ex-AoG members who could not remember the name of their senior pastor that I began to give credence to this. Dr Singer also lists other reactions such as relaxation-induced anxiety and:

miscellaneous reactions including anxiety combined with cognitive inefficiencies, such as difficulty in concentration, inability to focus and maintain attention, and impaired memory (especially short-term) … and psychological factors affecting physical conditions …[6]

These reactions occur equally in those with no family history of mental-health problems and those with such a history.

Fundamentalism can make you crazy. That's because its logic is impossible. It is impossible to say that every word of the New Testament is truth when four different gospels give a Picasso effect to the basic story. For some people, that's okay; for me it didn't work. Taking the bible in its entirety literally, it is logically impossible to know or please the God it outlines.

Still, as the world's most famous born-again Christian, *The Simpsons*' Ned Flanders, says, 'We believe all the bible, even the bits that contradict the other bits.'

All of this might otherwise be kooky and funny if the crazy people kept their truth to themselves. But they can't and they don't. When the AoG men of God tell the world that their fundamentalism—prosperity theology—is truth, it is cruelty to a hungry world.

TV evangelists and prosperity proponents are targeting the weakest groups, not just in the West but internationally in developing countries. 'It is probably the single most dangerous religious trend because it is causing further impoverishment of the poor in the Third World,' said Hector Avalos, an associate professor of Religious Studies at Iowa State University. 'It is a religious version of Wall Street,' he added. 'It focuses on people's need and greed. You give money to the church, and you are supposed to get multiple returns on your investment.'[7]

But it offers people hope. Hope, even if it is temporary, or disappointed, is a good thing, isn't it? In some countries, hope is all there is to work with, hope is all they have. Better than nothing, right? It's just the premise their hope is based on is all askew. No, God is not Santa Claus. Santa Claus isn't even Santa Claus. The rich kids always get the best presents. Even if you are good all year, not everyone can be a millionaire.

The American social critic H.L. Mencken said that fundamentalism was by definition 'a terrible, pervasive fear that someone, somewhere, is having fun'. Fundamentalism of any kind is far-reaching. And they're all the same, according to The Fundamentalism Project, sponsored by the American Academy of Arts and Sciences. From 1988 until 1993, over 100 scholars from a range of disciplines were briefed to report on every fundamentalism in existence. Their conclusion: all fundamentalisms share five 'family resemblances', regardless of the belief system they put forward for emulation.

1. Each fundamentalist group believes in its truth as the only truth. This truth must be applied to all areas of life, and to all people. Ideally, there should be no separation of church and state.

2. Men have the power, through physical strength and through making the rules. Women are defined by men, generally by their biological capabilities—that is, they should be submissive wives

and mothers, kept in the home. Independent women are hated and sexual freedom is highly restricted.

3. Control of the children is essential. In order to reproduce a fundamentalist culture, children must be educated exclusively and with much censorship.

4. All fundamentalists espouse a demand for a return to an ideal age that never existed. Change and modernity are seen as enemies to this process, and so technology, science and social progress are often strongly resisted.

5. While fundamentalists remain obsessed with modern society's failure to uphold their utopian system of morality, they fail to see how their own doctrine is clouded with all kinds of historical and cultural themes. Fundamentalists insist their scriptures or dogma be taken literally; it is unchanging.[8]

Fundamentalists like their world view. I can't. Seeing the world in black and white misses out all the colours of the rainbow. And being human is an incredible concept, one that entails all sorts of failure, disappointment and mistakes, some for no reason at all. It is also strung together with irrational hope, unmanageable love and beauty that surprises us and humbles us when we least expect it.

Culturally and politically, fundamentalism has devastating effects. Because of its refusal to acknowledge anything besides black and white, many subtleties as well as the inexplicable do not exist in this world. The essence of fundamentalism is found in its opposition to difference and diversity in every sphere of life. Humour and art shrink to live within narrow borders in fundamentalist societies. They are unnecessary, and way too open to interpretation. They challenge the absolutes that are vital for fundamentalist thinking's survival. Fundamentalism is a state of mind that takes life very, very seriously.

Chapter 23

CONSIDER ME GONE

> But I cannot leave it at that; there is more to it than that. In spite of everything, there was in the life I fled a zest and a joy and a capacity for facing and surviving disaster that are very moving and very rare. Perhaps we were, all of us—pimps, whores, racketeers, church members, and children—bound together by the nature of our oppression, the specific and peculiar complex of risks we had to run; if so, within these limits we sometimes achieved with each other a freedom that was close to love.
>
> —James Baldwin, *The Fire Next Time* (1963)

> Where were you when I laid the earth's foundation? Tell me, if you understand. Who marked off its dimensions? Surely you know! Who stretched a measuring line across it? Have you ever given orders to the morning or shown the dawn its place? Do you send the lightning bolts on their way? Do they report to you, 'Here we are!'?
>
> —Job 38:4, 5, 12, 35

May you get what you wish for. I have been writing stories since I could use a pencil; self-published at the age of seven, I wrote all my life.

They say you should write about what you know, and this topic was all I knew. Sad, but true. Christianity is what had consumed my thoughts for most of my life.

When the possibility of a book arose, I attended Hillsong

every now and then from late November 2004, a few Sunday mornings over a few months. They have friendly, spacious child-care facilities, and for a (single) parent an hour off is an hour off. Nothing could go wrong in an hour.

Sam liked the biscuits and the juice. Sam would attend a neo-Nazi rally if there were biscuits and juice. God help us if they served Tim Tams and strawberry milk. Apart from that, he reported that the music went on for too long and that there were too many people, so he didn't get a turn at anything. This is a standard complaint among Pentecostal adults, so I thought nothing of it.

I began this project still feeling guilty and unsure. I ended with the rock-solid confidence that I had been searching for all those years. It was not a happy ending. The jigsaw complete, it was a picture of a train wreck.

No spirit appeared on the end of my bed with a revelation. Rather, it was a year full of meeting an as-yet-undiscovered tribe of the walking wounded, isolated from each other and themselves, ashamed, angry and hurt, their families in tatters, their careers wasted and their self-respect annihilated. I had had no idea. When I started I'd known I was on to something, but I had also wondered if I was being the troublemaker again.

I was still afraid of hell when I started going to Hillsong for research purposes in early 2005. I believed that somehow, somewhere, God had his reasons, and he would allow justice to prevail.

Within weeks of my return, the house of cards fell down flat. In Hemingway's *The Sun Also Rises*, the protagonist describes the process of going bankrupt as happening 'gradually, and then suddenly'. This was what Hillsong was like for me. Five years of attendance, twelve years of hell, three years of daring to suspect, and six weeks of watching it disintegrate. And once it's gone, it's gone. Once you know the magician's tricks, the show's over.

Initially, I was amazed by the nonsense that poured out of their mouths: illogical, irrational arguments, sourceless claims, biblical malapropisms, dreary personal anecdotes, all coated with some maple syrup Jesus songs. There was nothing 'spiritual' going on. Still, oddly, it was now my employment, my most important library. I started meeting with people who wanted to talk and I put myself on the mailing list.

Midway through February, I was standing with a friend outside a restaurant in Parramatta, evaluating the menu, when I looked up to see Geoff Bullock. I hadn't seen him in sixteen years and, in shock, I pointed at him. He remembered my name, shook my hand, and I told him about my project. He agreed to meet me for coffee another time and we went inside to our tables. My companion is a devout Christian.

'So that's Geoff Bullock,' she said admiringly.

'Yeah,' I said, grabbing status where I could, 'I've known him since I was a kid.' Celebrity is in the eye of the beholder.

Geoff left Hillsong in late 1995. I knew that his marriage had broken down and he had remarried but, not having stayed in touch with the Christian music scene, not much else. The Geoff I shared cappuccinos with was the same man as always. Same piercing blue eyes, soft mannerisms and a voice born for the BBC. Geoff is not, by nature, an AoG salesman. Rather he represents a large group of artists who are attracted to the Pentecostal church by the opportunity for creative expression for Jesus.

What I didn't expect was the brokenness. Although I had worked with people from a diversity of backgrounds for years, I assumed all the old wise men of God were naturally of stronger character than me. Over the time we spoke I found it not to be so. It was Geoff's openness and willingness to talk that prepared me for a world of people damaged for the long-term by the work of Hillsong and the AoG.

Geoff says he remembers having episodes of mania when he was a child, although he wasn't diagnosed with symptoms of any kind until after he had left Hillsong. He sees a therapist to work on his long periods of depression, which are often followed by episodes of intense creativity. The other obstacle in his life is the nightmares he suffers dating from his time with Hillsong, an offshoot of his post-traumatic stress diagnosis.

As the Hillsong conference expanded in the late eighties, so did Geoff's responsibilities and pressures. He and his wife, Janine, were expected to spend infinite hours away from their children to run the music department. International interest in the music grew and so did Geoff's profile. The couple travelled extensively with the Praise and Worship team, and personally with their old friends Brian and Bobbie. Despite the bright lights and the glory, his music career at its peak, Geoff was finding less satisfaction and spirituality in what he was doing.

After the most successful conference yet, Hillsong '95, Geoff went to Brian and told him he was leaving. It was time, he felt, spiritually, to pursue other interests. Nothing personal.

Geoff Bullock had left a career with ABC-TV as a production manager to become a pastor with the Hills Christian Life Centre in 1978. For nearly twenty years he was able to use those skills to produce Hillsong music, and the show that accompanied it. During that time he wrote, produced and performed countless songs, and released seven albums. Because Hillsong still uses those songs, has remixed them and re-released them, Geoff's royalties are growing at the same rate as Hillsong.

Which is lucky for Geoff. Hillsong did everything in its power to prevent his future success. Due to speak at a bible college occasion soon after leaving, he received a phone call with a sudden apology. Hillsong had informed the bible college that any association with Geoff Bullock meant no further association with Hillsong. Christian magazines were told the same thing. Piles of the CD Geoff was about to release were found dumped at a tip in Blacktown, not far from Hillsong headquarters.

In Bobbie's *I'll Have What She's Having*, this period is clearly referred to (the emphases are hers):

*In July 1995, we witnessed a wonderful HILLSONG Leadership Conference. It was our 9th conference and in our nation and in our context of influence, to put it delicately—'**we put the wind up the***

devil!!' *Stories would flood into our offices of churches and towns being turned upside down with a revival spirit. God is good (all the time). Brian and I took a week to tie up loose ends and then together with our friends Pat and Liz Mesiti we took a little holiday. (I think God was just being terribly kind to give us a rest, because he knew what lay around the next bend.)*

We came home a week later, stepped off the plane ('hello, hello … lovely to see you … we missed you all … had a lovely time!') and literally all hell broke out with one of our key people. ***It was the first and only time*** *that something like this had happened to us. (I must admit prior to that conference I sensed something brewing, and had called all our pastor's wives to prayer.)*

… For the ***next several months*** *it was as though demons came out of the woodwork on every front. When attacks come from every side it is a sure sign that you are doing something* ***right*** *(which is contrary to some people's belief). We experienced a barrage of attack—cancer, accidents, stinking thinking, people throwing in the towel, disloyalty in our team that disappointed our heart, devil induced confusion, opposition and a fine thread of 'cancerous attitude' bent on contaminating and taking out* ***this particular Body of Christ.***[1]

Eventually, a Hillsong board member had lunch with Geoff. 'We tried to destroy you,' he told him, 'until we realised you weren't a threat.' Geoff continues to work and write music, though he gave up performing years ago.

The nightmares remain one of the most intrusive spillovers from the old days. Three or four times a week he dreams about Hillsong events, being humiliated by Brian's demands, being screamed at, berated and bullied along the way. His psyche is deeply affected. He is very aware that he, too, became a bully. Years later, Geoff has tried to make amends to many people he treated ruthlessly in order to avoid punishment from above.

At the end of our first meeting at a café, Geoff is exhausted. He tells me he feels drained by the remembering. I realise I have stumbled into a much more serious affliction in people's lives than I had anticipated.

Feeling a bit more informed, I confidently booked myself in to the Hillsong Colour Your World international women's conference in March. Being an old-school feminazi, I have been to many a women's conference. Jewels said this one was very good. I bought myself a new pink Barbie notebook.

One doesn't look out of place taking notes at Hillsong. Highlighting your bible with different coloured pens to show your studiousness is out of fashion since bibles cost more now, but catching Houston pearls is important. If you don't take notes, people may question your commitment.

I'm not sure what everybody else was noting, but I couldn't write fast enough. From time to time I would look up, look around and try to catch another face, stunned by what I heard being preached. It didn't happen. Women were too busy nodding and noting.

'Who here believes that women have value?' Pastor Bobbie shouts the first night. 'Yay!' shouts the audience. To enter the building, attendees walked up a red carpet to the doors, while lines of men applauded. I wasn't sure whether it was a wedding aisle simulation and, somewhat confused, slipped in sideways. Bobbie was the opening speaker that night and gave one of her breathtaking performances on the theme of Beloved Daughter (the words on the pink entrance wristband), Let's Get Better. We can always get better, she taught, and we have to get better at: one, loving God, and two, wisdom.

It was also on this first night that Bobbie spoke about the media. She made precisely the same comments the following week too. They weren't one of Bobbie's famous slips.

'Let me tell you about the media,' she said. 'There is that which is positive, that which is neutral and that which is the Antichrist, a dark spirit.'

I slid a little bit back in my chair. If a few journalists asking obvious questions were the Antichrist, then I was in trouble. I still had many more questions to go.

'We at Hillsong,' Bobbie reminded us throughout the conference, 'created Colour Your World because we believe that women have a special contribution to make. We place value on womanhood.' Feeling an enormous sense of relief, I tried to discover what that contribution was over the three nights and two days. It wasn't too long before I found out it was the usual, money and self. Except at 'Colour', as it is affectionately known in-house, women are also special because they can give endlessly of themselves.

Excusing that message as just Bobbie, I started again the next day at 9 am. Now bear in mind, gentle reader, that by March of 2005 I considered myself a soldier. Scales off my eyes, I was cynical and ready to critique objectively, I thought. I was not in any way prepared to be emotionally devastated, which is how I left Colour, wounded and limping. Later, watching the DVD of the conference eventually got me sobbing, and it was months before I could go back to view the material again.

American Marilyn Skinner from a church in Uganda spoke first that morning. She started with the standard stories of healings and miracles, always unverified but great for cred. Then she described how her husband and she had suddenly decided to start ministering to Uganda's AIDS orphans. She told us that some of the orphans work as prostitutes from the age of ten. The entire room of women gasped in unison, having never been to Sydney's Kings Cross. You see, she explained, 'Jesus doesn't see those children with the flies on their faces and their snotty noses and their bloated bellies. He sees what they will be one day.'

Marilyn and her husband opened an orphanage called Watoto and we heard that the children were getting care. And that they got to go to church and learn about Jesus. Marilyn ended many sentences with, 'That's my Jesus.' Then the children went to bible college. The Skinners were hoping to raise up great leaders in Uganda one day.

Better than that, they had trained the little things to sing gospel, and were traipsing them around the world like the von Trapp family to perform songs of gratitude to the white man. In fact, Marilyn shared, they had only recently performed in front of

George W. Bush. Jesus doesn't care about Iraqi children, but he sure loves hearing those Ugandan kids sing.

Marilyn reminded us that the CDs of the choir, t-shirts and other merchandise were available outside, which all goes to help the orphans.

Then Bobbie got up onstage. 'Women can stretch themselves beyond what's natural and normal,' she said. 'This is a godly alliance with Marilyn. Everyone can adopt an orphan. We have orphans waiting upstairs to be adopted at the expo. Please keep your hearts open.'

It was break time. Holding up a sample lunchbox, Bobbie said, 'Lunch is weighty—does this mean we're going to weigh this much after we eat?'

Women left the auditorium inspired and flushed. I was bored and noticing we didn't hear about the bible.

Time to have some fun with the volunteers. What's missing on the pamphlet for Hillsong's bible college is that part of the privilege of paying $3000 to $5000 tuition per course is compulsory volunteering. If you don't volunteer, you fail bible college. Colour Your World 2005 was staffed by 1000 unpaid workers, the majority of whom were bible college students.

There were ten food stalls at Colour; five were for Gloria Jean's Coffee. Curiously, they were all run by the volunteers, who secretly complained to me that they didn't even get a free cappucino.

All the volunteers were wearing a special t-shirt emblazoned with 'Hey princess. Heaven believes in you and so do we'. Bobbie had used the slogan in a billboard ad on Sydney's northwest M2 tollway, next to a big picture of herself, to advertise the conference. I felt this should be justified. And who better than those closest to the Lord himself, the bible college students. They should know what their own t-shirts mean.

'Who is this heaven that believes in me?' I asked a few. 'And who are "we"? And how do I become a part of we?' They couldn't help.

I asked the male volunteers what they were doing at a women's conference. I told them I had attended women's conferences at uni where they would have been beaten to death for being on the premises. They said they didn't know what they were doing there either.

They were all very nice people, if not that quick on their feet. About eighty per cent of them had accents from the south of the United States. They came to Hillsong's bible college because, as one Texan girl told me, 'it is the finest theology being taught in the world today'. Another told me she had worked three jobs for two years to get to Australia. She was hoping her parents might help with her second-year expenses.

Going back in after lunch, a string of paper dolls representing pledges for child sponsorship was lined up along the stage. Each time someone signed up with Hillsong's Compassion charity and 'adopted' an orphan in Uganda, a doll was pinned up. There was one actual Ugandan orphan available on the spot. Bobbie held her arm straight in the air, bracelets jangling, as she challenged, 'Who wants to adopt Agnes from Rwanda? Agnes is a cute name. That's how I chose my orphan, because she had a cute name.'

Someone bid for Agnes, and she was adopted. The spotlight and cameras homed in for fifteen seconds of fame, and Bobbie handed her biographical rundown over to its new owner, now that Agnes had been auctioned like a cow at market.

Bobbie spoke with fondness about her own orphan, adopted in Uganda. After she came back to Australia, Bobbie thought it strange how human she'd found the child to be. 'I miss her,' she shrieked. For me the room started spinning.

Then Bobbie introduced her 'gift from heaven, most loyal beautiful friend' Holly Wagner. The so-sassy, blonde American Holly (she used to be a model, you know) wasted no time in recommending her line of resources. She then spoke about the broad and narrow path in life and the shoes the people are wearing on those roads. That was the title of her message that night.

(The shoe fetish at this conference was unspeakable. There were paintings of shoes for sale, a boot in a glass container for sale, and each person was given a miniature ornament shoe. Mine was a red stiletto called Red Devil, an apparent mistake in a big order. In all, 10,000 souvenir shoes because Isaiah 52:7 says: 'How beautiful are the feet of those who bring good news!')

Holly's talk was all about being happy for other women in ministry, supporting them and not complaining about what you've got. Then, breaking off from her impassioned speech, she told her audience, 'Turn to the person next to you and say, "You're looking skinnier by the minute."' The women obeyed. The room started spinning in the other direction.

The rest of Holly's message was about how to be a good wife. Tell your husband he's sexy, respect him, watch how you talk to him. Our job is to demonstrate respect.

'If I'm not careful, my mind will dwell on his weaknesses, not his strengths. Genesis says I was created to be a helper for him.'

I wondered what you would do if you didn't have a husband. No one seemed to be considering this. Everyone thinks Holly's cool.

That night Pastor Phil Dooley, a lifelong participant and Hillsong board member, appeared on stage to host a domestic goddess competition. Two women were involved in a race to see who could change the baby doll's nappy and then fold the washing and run the basket to the top of the stadium and back the quickest. The crowd went wild.

The room kept spinning. Then the music started. Brian and Bobbie's eldest child, Joel Houston, led the singing, and more and more men were appearing on stage as musicians.

When they finished, Pastor Christine Caine grabbed the spiritual baton. 'We've already had Praise Reports,' she announced, 'miracles are happening, awesome things are happening.' What? Where? Her job was to speak before the offering. 'Jesus just wants the little you've got and then God will put his lot on our little and do something awesome.'

It was Bobbie's turn again. 'One day your Compassion child will just thank you that you cared enough.' Then time to watch the movie of Brian and Bobbie and their dear eighteen-year-old daughter Laura in Uganda meeting their souvenir orphans. You can't help but feel the awkwardness as African children dance around them dressed in Jesus shirts. Brian smiles, inconvenienced by all this humanity rubbing on his sleeves. Bobbie can't believe how easily children can sing without a band.

There was some kind of intermission. As people were returning to their seats, they were greeted by The Picture on all the big screens. The room stopped moving and went smack on my head. An African boy of about eight stood, pleadingly looking up, his hands resting behind his head. The title read: 'Will you be my sponsor?' The pamphlet with the same photo said: 'Adopt: to take and make one's own.'

Somebody had to say something, and at times like this it's usually me. I stood up, looked around and said, 'They're for life you know, not just for Christmas.' I wondered if anyone would object if the African kids wore bikinis and lip gloss. I was so sad. Holly Wagner prepared to speak. She said that it doesn't matter if you're not married. 'If you're single, the husband you marry will be grateful,' she said, that you have been to conferences like these.

I left the auditorium, knowing I couldn't take the heartache any more. I figured I may as well make my way downstairs to the Christian expo to find out what such a thing was and to see if I could find Shazza or one of the other girls. I was not alone. Behind me was Judith. I'd met Judith in the turn-around-and-greet-someone bit before I left. She had followed me out.

'I want to talk to you outside,' she said.

'Why?' I asked.

'You're not happy with something. I'm concerned that you're not happy.'

I stopped. 'Talking to you, Judith, is not going to make it better.'

She followed me to the stairs.

'Judith, you're following me,' I said. 'Please stop.'

'But you're not happy. We have to talk.'

'Judith,' I said, in my best refuge worker put-the-knife-*down*-Sheree voice, 'I am asking you to stop following me.' I looked at the people nearby in the lobby. 'Can anyone see that I am asking Judith to stop following me?' I said in a regular voice. No one cared. I had no idea who Judith was.

I went downstairs and Judith followed. At the entrance was the Compassion table full of photos of children, someone for everyone. Judith tried to stop me from talking to the nice ladies behind the counter.

I saw Shazza and the girls on the other side of the room. Surely they could make sense out of this. Judith followed.

'Shazza, why is Judith here following me?' She didn't know. Eventually I left.

It wasn't until the next day that I found out Judith was Brian's little sister.

The second and final day of conference was almost too much to bear. I felt completely pointless without a husband to apply my knowledge to, so I hung with the volunteers. They were finding it hard to bear as well. I suggested to the boys that they be put to better use. What about the single girls? I asked them. Did they need trainee husbands? The boys were surprisingly keen on this idea. I wandered in to see Darlene Zschech speak.

Now, Darlene is not a preacher, she is a singer. But she spoke clearly, and gently. Her theme was choice: how our lives are about choice and how hard choices are. Then she had her wedding dress brought on stage with her daughter's baby dedication dress. These were to represent the two stages of a woman's life, childhood marked by dedication at church, and a wedding dress to symbolise adulthood.

Choose to love, said Darlene, choose to forgive. Life is richer with forgiveness. Darlene seems to love and forgive like a pig in mud. One cannot imagine her otherwise. She appealed to the women on choosing to stay.

'Some people think it's a choice between good and evil,' she said. 'I find it's between good and greater. Not all choices,' she continued, 'require you to leave your post. Like Holly said last night, you can outlast a problem.'

Then the smiling stopped. 'Some of you are not excited to go home to your husbands tonight, and I'm serious. If you are getting hurt, you need to put your hand up, but if there are emotional things the Holy Spirit could resolve, you need to choose to stay. Try to stay.'

Think about your children, she said, and their children.

I couldn't. All I could hear was, 'You slut, these kids don't even look like me'—smash! And then, 'Choose to stay, it's just emotional stuff.' I wanted to hand out the domestic violence hotline number to the girls as they streamed out of the auditorium. Put your hand up? What does that mean? What about, 'If you're getting hurt, pack up and go'?

My shoulders weighed right down. My heart fractured. It hit me then. Darlene thinks it's okay to stay for emotional stuff, but the state might disagree. I figured she was putting an entire community of children at risk. Emotional abuse is domestic violence, and by the time the black eye materialises the damage is already done.

As the conference was nearing an end, I was determined to find Donna, my old youth pastor. I tried to track her down in the old building where the offices are, but all I could find were the gold doors to Brian's room. I wanted to know about the sexual abuse course she was running. S.A.F.E., Sexual Abuse Finally Ends. After what happened with Frank, they had to know what they were doing. Twice during Colour I had asked her personal assistant where I could find the theoretical base and the model they were using in practice with clients. Twice she referred me to a useless website. I finally spotted Donna in the front section where pastors and their personal assistants sit. As I walked up to try to tap her on the shoulder and noticed security getting itchy, I heard, 'Tanya, Tanya.'

I looked up and there was Christine Caine sitting in the pastors' section. 'Come sit here,' she called to me. I smiled at security and happily obliged.

Christine Caine is Australia's leading female evangelist. She impressed Joyce Meyer so much that Joyce wrote out a cheque for a year's salary for a nanny so that Chris would be free to travel the world. Now she and and her husband spend just three days a month in Australia.

Chris Caine arrived as Christine Cariofylus at Youth around the time I was leaving. She stood at the side and was the most unremarkable person in the group. A Greek girl from Blacktown. Short and plain, she tied her hair back and looked disinterested in the hype going on around her. I remembered the night Donna first mentioned her.

'Christine,' Donna almost whispered, 'has led two people to the Lord this week while visiting someone in hospital.' Chris looked uncomfortable at the attention.

Jewels spent some time with Chris at bible college. She remembered her giving up smoking the day class started. Chris just quit. She was determined. She could do anything.

Chris was always busy. My memory is that she started her church work at the Hills District Youth Service. She was an ex-law student who'd graduated from Arts with distinctions. After university she ran away to Greece, got convicted by the Spirit, and came back home to start again.

Chris moved on to work with Pat Mesiti and Youth Alive. They were two Mediterranean powerballs of energy together. Then she got her own ministry. She married, had a baby she named Catherine Bobbie, and life took off.

Grateful to Chris for saving me from security, I nestled into my seat next to royalty. I hadn't seen her since a Hillsong women's Thursday morning some years ago. By then, she had become very blonde, very toned and very expensively dressed. We had chatted while American ladies lined up to be photographed next to her, on their way upstairs to sit for a moment in Darlene's chair.

I had always liked Chris, but I noticed her eyes had become glazed. New Chris was here.

I couldn't help myself. 'Chris,' I whispered. 'I know you're in there. You're still in there, aren't you?' She smiled and stared ahead. Donna was about to speak. 'Chris, you're the smartest person in this room. How do you do this, day after month? How?'

'Shh,' she smiled, and stared ahead.

'Chris, you'd be missing Pat,' I sympathised. 'Now you have only Aussies to work with.' She smiled again. 'Come on,' I pushed. 'You're the smartest person in this movement, how do you do this?'

She scribbled me a note: 'I'm not being rude but there are about 700 pairs of eyes on me at the moment. I can't talk.' Fair enough. I forgot she was at work.

Her gesture was the most kindness I got from an AoG pastor all year. I won't forget her for it. She wanted a Barbie notebook like mine. She gave me her email. Her assistant, Annie Dollarhide, made arrangements for us to have coffee, but right at the last minute she cancelled. After that, Annie said Chris was too busy with her travelling and pregnancy to make it after all.

I stayed to see Donna talk for an hour about how your emotional baggage will ruin your marriage. Everyone had a good time; I went home devastated. Don't call me daughter. I'd just paid a hundred dollars to watch 4000 women be demeaned and degraded. I'd been at a marketing expo for Compassion.

I was talking to Shazza not long after. She was getting nosy about the book, maybe a little defensive, and told me it was time I spoke to Brian. She said that it was just like Pastor Ray MacCauley had said, people never confront the source of their problems. People like me just like to complain for the sake of it. If I had genuine issues, the best way to address them would be to ask Brian himself.

It was still early days. I told her I hadn't contacted Brian and Bobbie because I didn't know what exactly I wanted to talk to them about. At that point it seemed a waste of everybody's time.

Still, if the 'bitter and wounded' label was starting to circulate, I decided I might as well clear the air. I wasn't lashing out. I was just wondering what was going on.

So I emailed Brian and Bobbie.

From: Tanya Levin
Sent: Friday, 8 April 2005 12:26 PM
To: Brian Houston
Subject: Greetings
Dear Brian and Bobbie,
I hope this finds you well.

As you may be aware, I have recently been given the opportunity to write a book. My publishers, Allen & Unwin, have asked me to write a book on my experience growing up in Australia as the daughter of a Jewish mother and an English father, who both became born-again Christians, and then Pentecostals.

The story is very much about what it is like to grow up in a small church, leave, only to come back and find that the church is anything but small and is now influencing governments and communities in a way that I believe is uniquely Australian.

The rumour mill, reliable as it may or may not be, has questioned me as to why I have not contacted you for an interview. My immediate response was that I had not wanted to waste your time—I am still trying to get my head around everything that's going on. However, I think it would be appropriate for us to meet, so that my attending Hillsong does not become an issue for anyone, particularly for you. Meeting with you would be an opportunity for me to extend a formal courtesy and to minimise unnecessary sparks from the rumour mill. To me it seems simplest for Hillsong members to know that the leadership are working with me directly, and thus they have nothing to fear.

Ideally, I would like to meet with you every month or two if your schedules allow over the next few months. This is a big work for me, and I have by no means begun to write. A one-off interview would not serve the personal purpose I am trying to achieve, any more than a one-off visit to Hillsong would depict the big picture.

Perhaps a cup of coffee in the next couple of weeks would be a good start. Look forward to hearing from you.

Best wishes,

Tanya Levin

Two days later the general manager of Hillsong, George Aghajanian, wrote to me. He thanked me for my email, and he informed me that 'We are aware that during your attendance at our recent Colour Your World Women's Conference you caused significant disruption to the meetings you attended.'

What I had done was not described, but it was enough for Hillsong to 'ask you to refrain from attending any future Hillsong church services or events; including accessing Hillsong's land and premises at any time'. Also, leadership and staff were 'unable to provide assistance for your proposed book'.

They appeared paranoid. Being brought up a nice Jewish Christian girl, however, I wanted to give them one 'it is written' and one 'brother, let us work this out'. So I wrote back.

From: Tanya Levin

Sent: Friday, 22 April 2005 11:18 AM

To: Brian Houston; Bobbie Houston

Subject: FW: Hillsong Church

Dear Brian and Bobbie,

On the 8th of April, I sent you an email through Brian's address. This, for some reason, has been passed on to the General Manager, a George Aghajanian, someone whose name rings a bell but whom I have never met. You can imagine my distress when I received his response (see below).

This has left me baffled. After some consideration, I have decided that this must be an administrative error because it would be impossible for the Brian and Bobbie that I know to endorse this type of treatment of anyone in their name. After twenty years, to be turned away by email by a stranger like a rabid dog or typhoid Mary just couldn't happen.

Surely the church that you see is not a church without ME?

No, indeed, the Brian and Bobbie that I know taught us to be mindful of entertaining angels (Heb 13:2) and to treat the alien living in your camp as one of your native born (Lev 19:33, 4). Just like Bobbie says in *I'll Have What She's Having*, Ch 6 (iv):

When it comes to STRANGERS AND FOREIGNERS conviction rises above any shyness or insecurity, because often such people help stretch our world. The planet is such a big, bright, fabulous place and meeting such people enlarges our small world view.

(The bible also says 'you just better be nice too, because you never know when you might be entertaining angels unknown', which is food for thought. Wouldn't it be a major shame to discover you'd just been rude to an angel!)

Mr Aghajanian is, after all, a general manager, which strangely suggests a corporate response to my request to you in your pastoral role. I had previously understood that you were a Christian church that professed a commitment to biblical principles.

As Bobbie says in *I'll Have What She's Having*, chapter 5, in section 1, 'Guard the Specifics':

EVERY CHURCH HAS A SPIRITUAL HEAD. If you understand God's delegated authority and how the body of Christ works in our individual churches, then you will understand that the spiritual head is the Senior Pastor and his partner.

Thus when seeking an opportunity to be transparent about my attendance at Hillsong, I presumed you were the people to speak to.

I have searched my bible and those of others, and have found no instruction on the General Manager. I had thought you were the shepherds of the sheep and not in the wool industry. Still, if biblical principles no longer apply, and it is now a corporate structure I must negotiate, please may I be directed to the Chief Executive Officer. I would also appreciate a copy of the new mission statement without the 'bible-based' bit.

What seems even stranger is that Mr Aghajanian does not appear on any of the advertisements welcoming everyone to Hillsong. Nor does he sign his letters with 'love you forever', forever being the operative word. But you do.

With all due respect, if you're going to advertise yourself as so approachable, beware. People might start approaching you.

And on a personal level, Mr Aghajanian wasn't my senior pastor throughout my teenage years. He didn't shepherd me through the eighties and oversee my youth group. He didn't dedicate my baby to God nearly six years ago. It was you. That's the part that seems to hurt.

It can't be a case of mistaken identity. Despite the tens of thousands of people you must have met, Bobbie remembered my full name clearly when we caught up at a funeral last year. Amazing, and quite flattering, I might add. But I guess we have always greeted each other over the years, as you have known my family and so many of the friends I still have in Hillsong all this time. In any case, the phone calls made to people close to me following my email eliminate any possibility of your uncertainty as to who I am.

You can now understand my bewilderment at Mr Aghajanian's email. *I must ask you, therefore, to verify Mr Aghajanian's statements as your own, as I wrote to the two of you, not him.*

From all the people that have read his thoughtful paragraph, in Hillsong and out of it, locally, and overseas, the same question is being asked of me over and over:

'*Why didn't they answer you themselves?*'

One proposal was that, given the sheer volume of the mail you receive, mine could have been overlooked or delegated incorrectly. This is the only explanation that makes sense.

For this reason, I am sending you the GM's response and my original mail, flagged and to both of your addresses.

Looking forward to hearing from you.

Warmest regards,

Tanya Levin

I never heard from Brian, Bobbie or George again.

You can't just go banning people from AoG churches. You have to *do* something to be excommunicated as a Catholic, and they can't ban you from every church in the world. I hadn't *done* anything. It's impossible to be disruptive in a Pentecostal meeting, or it ain't the real McCoy. In any case, my mother brought me up never to be rude in church. I find it hard to sit still through some parts, but I didn't disrupt their meeting.

No one has been able to answer my questions about the ban. Is it for life? Am I offered no opportunity for atonement or forgiveness? Is it international? Am I able to worship at any of the other locations, London, Paris, Kiev? Is it multi-generational?

My son got saved at Hillsong. That's the ironic best. During the couple of times I left him at Kids Church, they got him. He told me months later when we were talking about prayer. He said they had all prayed at Hillsong for Jesus to come into their hearts. Is Sam banned by proxy?

I am no longer allowed to visit the characters from my youth. I am not permitted to see the faithful in the congregation, the kind faces that smile at me; even the ones who ignore me provide sentimental comfort to me in my own private way. They were always friendly to me, and any time I wanted to I could go in and see the girls and their husbands and children, and glean a little Christian gentleness from the people still there all these years later. Like going back to one's hometown for a wedding or just to shoot the breeze. No more of that for me. I'm uninvited.

I am a single mother. I haven't really been anywhere except Hillsong since 1999. I don't mind that. I'm tired these days. I rely on my best friend Ilona to introduce me to interesting people. Around this time, she told me of a lawyer friend who knew all about the church. Emails were exchanged and Michael and I met for coffee.

Michael is an environmental lawyer of much success. He is also a devoted athlete. His time is precious. Coffee started at 7 pm, although Michael doesn't really drink coffee. He left at midnight because his morning started at 6. He never invoiced me. I couldn't have afforded him. But the sun rose differently the next day.

Michael was openly agonised by dredging up the pain of the Pentecostal problem. At university, his older brother became a strict fundamentalist Pentecostal and changed completely. Determined to understand what his brother was going through, Michael spent five years researching, studying and attending the Pentecostal churches. He emerged with answers.

Michael defines himself as a 'weak atheist'. In other words, he cannot see any evidence for God, but says it is logically impossible to prove a negative, that something *doesn't* exist. He admits the possibility that he may be wrong.

For five hours, I asked him questions. And for five hours he was willing and able to answer them. A strong believer in science, he countered everything I queried with what he called 'knowledge-gathering techniques', the ones he said that we relied on.

Why, I asked, why? And patiently he sat, and he never said, why are you doubting, or why can't you just catch on?

The next day I accosted various acquaintances and neighbours. Are you atheists? I asked them. You haven't believed in all this stuff for a long time, have you? They smiled. It was like finally being let in on the big secret. And the truth will set you free.

Then I read about agnostics and how being an atheist involves too much fundamentalist faith in science. For agnostics, it was explained, can't say they don't know because we'll never know, how could we know? Who the hell do we think we are to know? I liked that. Atheism, while intellectually perfect to me, denies me the opportunity to play with two-dollar emotion-based decisions that have no rationale but make my life beautiful. For if religion is nothing but people's futile fears, insecurities, hatreds, hopes and dreams put together, then I better find a place for all of those in my own life if there's no God or Satan to throw it off on to. Albert Einstein said: 'I believe in mystery and, frankly, I sometimes face this mystery with great fear. In other words, I think that there are many things in the universe that we cannot perceive or penetrate and that also we experience some of the most beautiful things in life in only a very primitive form. Only in relation to these mysteries do I consider myself to be a religious man.'

The freedom to say 'I don't know' is magnificent, since there no longer needs to be an answer. Why are there still starving nations? I don't know, but the answers no longer lie with an inconsistent God. Why is the world the way it is? Not because God has allowed it to be, because his special plan must prevail. That lets too many villains off the hook. Armageddon's only coming if we make it a self-fulfilling prophecy.

As for people, they still fascinate me. Some of the kindest, most peaceful, non-judgemental heroes in my life are ardent atheists. Some are Christians. Some are Jews. A few Buddhists, and some passionate tree-huggers. Go figure.

And thus, it seemed the book was closed. After all these years of tossing and turning and playing attention-seeker to God, I had the answers I'd been looking for. Liberating and depressing. And awfully sophisticated. It has taken me years to untangle fundamentalism from my life. And it's still not gone. Michael also said that he kept trying to get away from the topic. Every time he tried to get the Penetecostal debate out of his life, something would drag him back in. He found it fascinating but distressing each and every time.

I had decided that as neither of the actual addressees had answered, George Aghajanian's email was null and void. I had plenty of work to do. I had neither the time nor the resources to pursue my sudden excommunication.

I attended another three or four times over the next couple of months. Now thoroughly bored by Praise and Worship, I would sneak in at halftime and sit in the back row at the edge, in case my phone rang. I didn't want to be noticed. I had been banned, but no one was doing anything about it. If I wanted to stay, I knew there was no more fun to be had with the volunteers.

By July, my best friend Ilona had become curious enough to take a trip out from the city. We chose to see the American preacher Joyce Meyer, since the men can all sound the same. Ilona called Hillsong and was told that Meyer would be there that Saturday at 5.30 pm. We each brought a friend and figured we'd all be out by dinner. I was usually by myself on previous visits and was pleased to have company that night.

We arrived at the beginning of the service, and Ilona and her friend chose the upper seating of the auditorium while my girlfriend and I sat in the back row of the floor section. We sat through the fast songs and read through the brochures. At the start of the slow songs, I noticed Grant Thomson sitting in the same row as us, alone. Strange. Grant is a golden boy who looks like a Grant. Blond, sporty type, big sweet smile. Sincere. Quiet. Hard-working. From the old days, younger than me, though. He married the little sister of a friend from Youth and they had three kids. She was all of the above too. I ran into her a few times at the supermarket near my mother's.

Before the next song started, he moved over to me and said, in a polite, low voice, 'Hi, I'm Grant. I'm one of the pastors here at Hillsong.'

'Grant, it's me,' I said to him.

He smiled. 'Hey, how are you, Tanya?'

'Good,' I said.

'Hey, can you come outside and have a chat with me, please?' he asked.

I knew this routine from working with the homeless. Come outside, have a chat with me while my offsider calls the cops. Sure. I left my bag on my seat and followed him.

Just outside, Grant was waiting with a friend, a big bearded fellow, who also wanted to talk. I made the fatal mistake of stepping outside the building onto the path. I looked at Grant.

'Tanya, you know you're not allowed to come here,' he started.

'Can you tell me why?' I said. 'No one can tell me why.'

'That's not up to us,' he said. 'That's something you'll have to take up with the church.'

'You know they won't take my calls,' I told him.

His friend tried to help. 'We need you to leave,' he said.

'I have to go back and get my bag,' I announced. Clever me.

'You're not allowed back in the building,' the bearded one said. 'We'll go back and get your bag.'

'Not allowed back in the building?' I felt like Guy Fawkes. 'What happens if I do?'

'Then we call the cops.' I don't like the bearded one.

'Grant,' I stall. I have to check if he's still alive. I smile at him and his face lights up. He's a nice guy. 'You're a Christian, right?'

'Yes.' He's happy. Can't get that one wrong.

'I've known you forever. You married Heidi, you've got little children, can you honestly tell me that you can go home tonight before God'—always a good one to throw in—'and sleep next to Heidi and the children, and think you've done the right thing?'

'We're just doing what we have to do,' he said.

'So you're just following orders.' I was sad.

They were getting antsy. Well, I told them, I'm getting my bag. If you throw me out, you throw me out in front of everyone, I said. They yelled to someone, 'Close the doors,' and indeed the doors were closed, but a little too late. I managed to shoulder my way back into the building and went towards the entrance to the auditorium. More human bodies blocked my entrance.

Two security guards appeared and came towards me. They picked me up by my elbows and carried me out of the building, with about thirty people in the lobby still craning to see the preaching on big TVs. They plonked me down and moved away. They hurt my back and broke my heart. For the last time—had I said that before?—for the last time, Hillsong broke my heart.

Strange things hit you sometimes from out of the blue. I wasn't surprised by Hillsong's removal of me, or even their short-sightedness given the publicity it could ultimately give me. The kick in the guts was that they did this to my father's daughter, and nobody disrespects my father. He had at that time been a faithful attendee for nearly twenty years. Among the good guys, my dad's the best. I'm one of the lucky ones. And his integrity throughout my life is how come the bad guys' stench is so strong to me. Nobody treats my dad like that. He pays these zombies' salaries, for crying out loud.

My eyes squealed up with tears. I put my jacket on and started walking. 'Fuck,' I called out to the dark winter sky.

'Oh,' said the rodent behind me. 'Nice language. Obviously not a child of God.'

'Because he tells *you*, doesn't he?' I turned and glared at him. Security guard for a mega-church. I didn't want him at my dinner party either.

Almost all of the not-very-bad-looking-at-all guards who work for Hillsong's private security company happen to be Hillsong members. Nobody better even think about touching their Boss.

Then suddenly, there was Dion, a very tall, handsome Maori man of about twenty-four. He was dressed in black suit pants and a long black jacket. He oozed Secret Service, which made security look like car-park attendants. He had been told there was someone upset, and had come down to check it out. The security boys scurried away back down their drainpipes.

Through the whole walk across the car park, Dion denied knowing anything about me or what had happened that night. I cried at Dion. I told him about my dad, and faithfulness and loyalty. I asked him if he played football. As a matter of fact, he said, he did. Brian likes football players, I told him. The insanity of the night made me want to grab Dion as the last survivor and run him right out of the stadium. Whatever kind of Hollywood Angel he was dressed as that night, there would come a time when he would outlive his usefulness to the Firm. And then he would lose that simple genuine look he stared at me with. I told him to go home and read his bible, and go and ask the preachers why it doesn't match what they say. He listened like one does to the ravings of a lunatic, and I made him listen because that's his job.

He made sure I got in my car and left. Apart from a quick trip to the resource shop, and a photo shoot with the *Australian* a month later, I have never been back to Hillsong.

Three weeks later I got an email from Donna.

From: Donna Crouch
Sent: Tuesday, 26 July 2005 7:42 PM
To: Tanya Levin
Subject: Hi Tanya
Hi Tanya
Thought I would send you an email—just to say this—

I know you from Powerhouse [youth group at Hills] days—a long time ago now—and have not been in your world for many years—I know there has been a bit going on from what I've seen in the paper—to be honest I am not really interested in that—but I think it could be good if we got in contact.

What do you think?
Donna Crouch

From: Tanya Levin
Sent: Tuesday, 26 July 2005 7:45 PM
To: Donna Crouch
Subject: RE: Hi Tanya
Donna!!!

I thought you were the one who gave the directive for me to be thrown out that night. Nothing would make me happier right now than to get together with you.

Lovely. Call me on ... when you're free.
Cheers,
Tanya

In August it was my birthday. Hillsong sent me a card that said 'Happy birthday princess'. It was one of only two cards I got in the mail.

In September I wrote to Pat Mesiti. He had been moved to Phil Pringle's church, and I found him one Sunday night. He said, 'Hi, Tanya, how's your dad?' I showed him the letter that banned me from Hillsong. I asked him if we could have coffee. He told me he couldn't help me. 'Brian and Bobbie are not the people that you think they are,' he said, and made his way back into church.

From: Tanya Levin
To: Pat Mesiti
Sent: Tuesday, 27 September 2005 11:10 AM
Hi Pat,

As we spoke about earlier this year, I am writing about my life growing up Pentecostal. One of the things I am looking at was the original pastors at Hillsong. All I have to go on when I get to the part on Pat Mesiti is my own adolescent memory and the *Sydney Morning Herald* articles, as well as various rumours that paint a varied picture of the way you've been treated over the past few years.

I am not looking to drag you into any controversy or quote you unless you wish to be quoted. I simply wish to offer you a genuine opportunity to help me with the accuracy of my story as I was only young when most of my attendance at Hills took place. I say genuine because I do have personal heartfelt memories of the place and it is my aim to present the story as accurately as possible.

Please let me know if we can have a cup of coffee and a chat, as off the record as you like.

Thanks Pat,
Tanya Levin

Pat responded promptly by email. He told me in a few short sentences that he would not like to meet with me, and that his 'life at Hillsong was nothing but a pleasurable experience'. Pat then went on to say that if his name appeared in the book at all that the 'next communication will be from his solicitors', and that this wasn't a threat, but 'it will be definitely followed through'. He concluded by writing that 'Hillsong is the most integrous church in the country, and its leadership is above reproach'.

One less Christmas card that year.

Meeting with Donna was wonderful but strange. I can't help but feel attached to her in a big sister sort of way. She has a kind and open freckled face and an ability to maintain sincerity beyond the call of duty. We talked for two hours over coffee. She denied being thrust out by the Boys to do their dirty work by checking up on me. She insisted that she wanted to get to know me again, coincidence as it was.

We talked about the old times. We talked about children. She told me some things that had happened to people. Every now and then I would throw her a question. Donna, you know I've been banned. Can you find out what's going on? The first time she grew serious and said, 'We don't sit in the office and gossip. I don't know about all that.'

She remembered my teenage years. She told me her memories of my mother and me clashing. Yes, I agreed. We had. I suspect she was hoping I would realise that my parents had tainted my views of God. That I was trapped in my adolescent rebellion still. 'Tanya,' she told me, as she had always done whenever I had questioned the status quo, 'you have a great brain. Why don't you use it for something constructive, something good, something positive?'

I was determined. 'Donna,' I threw in, when I got brave. 'Donna, on the night I got carried out of Hillsong –' I started. 'Tanya,' she interrupted. 'I don't want to talk about all that. I want to talk about *you*.'

She talked about her work as the co-ordinator of the S.A.F.E. program, which advertises pathways in, out and through sexual abuse. She told me how humbled she was by the experience, how much she'd learned, how far people had come in their journeys. She was the Donna I remembered, passionate and serious about causes. She told me they were in the early stages of the course for male survivors of sexual assault. And she was just wondering if they should work with perpetrators in the future. Nobody wants to work with perpetrators and, well, with Jesus all things are possible. Oh, dear God, Donna. I didn't know what to say.

Right as her nanny was calling, I tried one last time. 'Donna, you were one of only three leaders that night. Who decided to have me removed?' She shooshed me sweetly and took the phone call. I don't know what she gained from me, or why she was there. And vice versa, I suppose.

A week after we met I sent her an email to ask her the same old question. I never heard anything back.

In December I got an invitation to Colour Your World 2006. Actually, 'the Levin Family' got it, which is curious since it doesn't exist. Levin is a name I made up years after my divorce, after my maternal grandmother who was a Levy.

The third and final week was already sold out.

Feeling all concluded, and having read an avalanche of scandal in mass-evangelism around the world, I knew I had achieved what the Americans love to call closure. I understood the workings of the machine and having dismantled it, I found it strangely repetitive, almost textbook. Same same. I knew I was not to be the rescuer of the spiritually abused en masse or individually. Therapy has never been my strong point—giving or receiving. It had worked out best that I transcribe my personal experiences and investigations and leave it at that, my own message in a bottle. I was emerging enlightened, confident that while I don't know what is, I sure as hell knew what isn't, which is a much better place all in all. As for the treachery of the men of God, I was certain there wasn't a hair left to stand up on my neck.

It was a matter of formality and some curiosity that I downloaded Christian City Church's re-inauguration ceremony for Pastor Pat Mesiti. Dr Phil Pringle officiated over the proceedings on 19 February 2006. Pat, his new wife and baby were prayed over before Pat began to explain himself. And I find my pile of socks going unsorted as Pat introduces a whole new genre in motivation, and describes the same old textbook story, only this time it's reconfigured to celebrate the AoG, and the power of God's forgiveness.

In standard fashion, Mr Motivation, as he calls himself on his website, does not specify the situation that lead to his depastorisation in 2002. Instead his past is a springboard for a new flavour of snake oil. 'I was a bad bad person, but I'm great now, thanks to God.'

Pat reminds people early to tithe and keep going to church. He found he always had money in the bank.

Frighteningly Pat describes at lengths the various forms of psychological distress his situation caused him. He describes acute and chronic memory loss, hearing voices, suicidal thoughts and sleep problems. His marriage ended in divorce, his daughters were devastated and he was publicly shamed. His career didn't suffer too badly. His motivational website describes all his achievements minus the details about their being Pentecostal-related.

Pat is back. He did four years of restoration; whatever that entails we are not specifically told. He has a new young wife, a new baby, a new congregation, and new ways to serve the kingdom. Same same.

My breathing increased, and my heart started pounding. 'C'mon church,' says Pat, 'I'm preaching better than you're responding.' The show must go on.

Fundamentalism won't leave me alone. It continues to upset me despite my best efforts to exit, stage right. It is arrogantly dominating the world's resources, and exploiting humans in innumerable splintering ways.

Apparently lots of people already knew this and tell me that all churches are corrupt and my work here was obsolete before it began. I consider correcting them and saying, 'But we were the puritans, the simple bible-believing Christians with no stained glass or statues. It was supposed to be different for us.' These days, however, I try to be more dispassionate and wonder why, if that's the general consensus, is the whole charade of church allowed to go on? But, goodness, this is crazy talk. We couldn't possibly live without organised religion, and all the benefits that are added unto us.

The residue of religion remains with me in some undeniable ways. Like my inability to fathom why there's enough food and we still have starving people in the world. All I'm wondering is if we Feed the World, is it really so important to let them know it's Christmas time?

Jewels tells me there's an Emerging Church, a new Christian movement who are very cross with the prosperity family and while not yet gaining the airtime, want to take Christianity's future back to where it was supposed to be, saving the world. She said they estimate that if the tithes the US gave went to world aid, they could feed the world in a year. I'm a Jewish mother now, and I want everyone to eat, eat. And the die-hard Pentecostal in me knows that would be a miracle worth paying for. Amen?

NOTES

TWO TRIBES

1. Hazel Houston, *Being Frank: The Frank Houston Story*, Marshall Pickering, London, 1989, p. 19.
2. ibid., p. 13.

WALK THIS WAY

1. <http://www.parliament.nsw.gov.au/Prod/Parlment/HansArt.nsf/5f584b237987507aca256d09008051f3/e6cbb80ee0b7f185ca2570bc001fc50f!OpenDocument>.

WILL YOU MISS ME WHEN YOU'RE SOBER?

1. Robert Jay Lifton, *Thought Reform and the Psychology of Totalism*, University of North Carolina Press, Chapel Hill and London, 1989.
2. Dick Sutphen, 'The battle for your mind', 1984 talk, <http://www.dicksutphen.com/html/battlemind.html>.
3. Diana Doucet, *Charisma Magazine*, 2/96, pp. 20–21.
4. Julia Duin, 'An evening with Rodney Howard-Browne', Christian Research Institute, Rancho Santa Margarita CA, 1994.
5. Bobbie Houston, *She Loves and Values Her Sexuality*, CD, Maximised Leadership Incorporated, Castle Hill, NSW, 2004.

SAVING ALL MY LOVE FOR YOU

1. REALMEN e-newsletter, Christian City Church, May 2005.
2. Bobbie Houston, *I'll Have What She's Having*, Hillsong Australia, Castle Hill, NSW, 1998, p. 56.

KIDS

1. *The Animated Kid's Bible*, episode 1 'Creation', Pips Premiere, 2005.
2. Marilyn Manson, *The Long Hard Road Out of Hell*, Regan Books, New York, 1998, p. 22.
3. <www.hillsong.com/emerge/default.asp?pid=786>.

THERE'S NO BUSINESS LIKE SHOW BUSINESS

1. Warren Snowdon, Member's Statement, 'Misuse of Indigenous business grants', <http://www.warrensnowdon.com/speeches/060216.htm>.

IF I WAS A RICH GIRL

1. Brian Houston, *You need more money*, Brian Houston Ministries, Castle Hill, NSW, 1999, p. 2.

I JUST CAN'T WAIT TO BE KING

1. Brian Houston, *For this Cause*, Maximised Leadership Incorporated, Castle Hill, NSW, 2001, p. 25.

WHEN THE GENERALS TALK

1. Oral Roberts, 'Victory out of defeat', *Charisma*, Dec. 1989, p. 88.
2. Ziva Branstetter, 'Reaping from Faith', *Tulsa World*, 24 April 2003.
3. ibid.
4. <http://www.wallwatchers.org>, 18 March 2005.

IF IT MAKES YOU HAPPY

1. Barna.org, People's Faith Flavor Influences How They See Themselves, 26 August 2002, <www.barna.org/FlexPage.aspx?Page=BarnaUpdate&BarnaUpdateID=119>.
2. 'You can live free of depression', <www.andrewbartlett.com/blog/?p=208>.
3. HG Koenig, LK George, KG Meador, BG Blazer & P Dyke, 'Religious affiliation and psychiatric disorder in Protestant baby boomers', *Hospital and Community Psychiatry*, 45, pp. 586–96, 1994.
4. Margaret Singer and Richard Ofshe, 'Thought Reform Programs and the Production of Psychiatric Casualties', *Psychiatric Annals*, 20:4/April 1990.
5. ibid.
6. ibid.
7. *Chicago Tribune*, 17 May 2001.
8. For the Fundamentalism Project, see especially Martin E. Marty and R. Scott Appleby, eds, Vol. 5, *Fundamentalisms Comprehended*, University of Chicago Press, Chicago, 1995.

CONSIDER ME GONE

1. Bobbie Houston, *I'll Have What She's Having*, Hillsong Australia, Castle Hill, NSW, 1998, pp. 127–8.

ACKNOWLEDGEMENTS

There are many people without whom this book would not have been possible for too many reasons to list. There were many people who were supportive of this project and of me, and their confidence has made this idea become a reality. So many gave of themselves freely—their intimate experiences, their time, their patience and their honest humanity—as this work unfolded. I was and am humbled and very grateful. Some people are not listed here because they can't be. They know how much they are appreciated. Also there are some on this list whom I haven't actually met. That's neither here nor there. Their help meant a lot too.

My family was my biggest concern when I started work on this manuscript. My parents' unqualified support of me and my endeavours has been invaluable all my life. Their willingness to believe in me when I was challenging our entire foundations was incredible. I'm a lucky kid.

And a lucky mother. Thanks to Sam for putting up with a book that took so much time away from us. I hope it's worth it to you in the end. You are an extraordinary person.

A massive thank you to the people who are Black Inc., particularly Chris Feik for his unwavering belief in this project and his editorial genius.

The following list is in no particular order. It's just a thank-you note for the generosity I encountered in this quest.

The makers of Up & Go, Lyn Tranter, Kathryn Harries, Grant, Deirdre O'Shea, Peter Damir, Ilona Tar, Richirich, John and Louise Borg, Sam Tree, Rebecca Kaiser, Jenny Sipkema, Rebecca Huntley, Bruno, Janis Schindler, Sarah Silverman, Naomi Wolf, Fiona Collins, Bruce Springsteen, Philip Powell, Henry Sheppard, Geoff Bullock, Noah Fischel, Angela Clarke, Michelle Dyball, Bevan's Thirroul, Clare Henderson, Christine Borg, Jim Cummings, Bek and Ali, Michael Jose, Alicia T., Sam Wegner, Dean de Haas, Melissa Scott, Stephen Grant, Suzie Matthews, A.A.

Milne, Pete Evans and the Trinity Foundation, David Gaudiosi, Kathy Boon, Meg Simons, Cherry Hardaker, Shatter, Paul and Kyle Kohn, Matthew Oborn, Penny and Natasha, Jane Kennedy, Anthony Venn-Brown, Bessie Bardot, Peter Dwyer, Geoff Barker, Nic Coloquhoun, Matt Legge, Lichelle Mangakahia, Tyla Kenzie, Holly Klein, Peter and Delores Theodore, St Vincent de Paul Wollongong, Dr Carmen Lawrence, Bono Vox, Stephen King, the boys from the Chaser, Dr Louise Newman, Vilma Ryan, Dr Jason Pireh, and my current Christ, smile ... we will be Friends For Life.